Tribalism and Society in Islamic Iran 1500–1629

JAMES J. REID

Tribalism and Society in Islamic Iran, 1500-1629

Iranian society came under the domination of tribal elites during the first part of the Safavid era. While other elites also played a role in controlling the Iranian empire, the tribal ruling clans were the most important at first. In order to analyze this period, materials concerning the socioeconomic organization of tribalism in the Iranian plateau are presented, and a prototypical model of tribal state structure is constructed based entirely on contemporary accounts. Three tribal organizations, each representing a separate tradition, are then examined in detail; the lives and careers of their chieftains are traced in a biographical dictionary containing nearly 240 entries. The theory that initial support for the Safavid movement came from Anatolian or North Syrian tribes is demonstrated to be false, and to be either the product of nationalist historiography or due to the misunderstanding of certain tribal names. The book seeks to show how Iranian elites differed from other contemporary elites, to assess the place of the Iranian system in the world pattern of the sixteenth and seventeenth centuries, and to contribute toward the understanding of a non-European society on its own terms and according to its own realities.

Studies in Near Eastern Culture and Society

Issued under the auspices of the
G. E. von Grunebaum Center for Near Eastern Studies
University of California, Los Angeles

1.
Ismail K. Poonawala
Biobibliography of Ismā'īlī Literature
(1977)

2.
Emilie Savage-Smith and Marion B. Smith
Islamic Geomancy and a Thirteenth-Century Divinatory Device
(1980)

3.
Richard G. Hovannisian, editor
The Armenian Image in History and Literature
(1981)

4.
James J. Reid
Tribalism and Society in Islamic Iran, 1500-1629
(1983)

5.
George Bournoutian
Eastern Armenia in the Last Decades of Persian Rule, 1807-1828: A Political and Socioeconomic Study of the Khanate of Erevan on the Eve of the Russian Conquest
(1982)

Tribalism and Society in Islamic Iran 1500–1629

JAMES J. REID

Undena Publications Malibu, California

Undena Publications

Malibu, California

ISBN: 0-89003-125-8 (cloth)
0-89003-124-x (paper)

Library of Congress Catalog Card Number: 82-50984

Printed in the United States of America

To Mehri

Acknowledgments

This book would not have been possible without the perceptive and thought-provoking insights of my advisor, Professor Amin Banani. No teacher of mine ever devoted so much time to helping me develop as a scholar. He also made many sacrifices for me. I am eternally indebted. I also wish to thank Professor Stanford Shaw who has helped me in many ways, particularly in making my book more concise. I owe a debt of gratitude to Professor Andras Bodrogligeti for inspiring me to focus my attention on Central Asia and for helping me to perceive the influences of Eurasia on the societies living in the Iranian plateau. It was he who first brought the cultural influences of Central Asia to my attention. None of the people mentioned above, however, are responsible for any errors that may be found in this study.

I wish to express gratitude to the following people for taking time from their busy schedules to discuss ideas and problems with me: Professor Speros Vryonis, Jr., whose works I admire greatly, and who, despite a heavy burden of responsibilities, nonetheless found time to discuss things with me; Sherri Smith, whose comments I found highly challenging and illuminating; Professors Nikki Keddie, R. I. Burns, S. J., and David Farquhar. I wish especially to express my appreciation to Professor Afaf Lutfi al-Sayyid-Marsot for helping me solve a crucial, last-moment problem that was holding up completion of the book. Special thanks are extended to Professor Jean Aubin of the Sorbonne who read the book critically and made several valuable suggestions. Any errors found here, however, are solely my own responsibility.

I wish to thank Teresa Joseph and Ralph Jaeckel for their invaluable and highly skilled editorial assistance in preparing this book for publication. Their services and their many hours of work on my book are deeply appreciated by me.

I am deeply grateful to Mehri for the patience, endurance, and insight she has shown me in this project. My parents, too, deserve a debt of gratitude for their unflagging moral support in a difficult task.

Thanks must also be given to the staff of the Gustave I. Von Grunebaum Center for Near Eastern Studies and the History Department: Nina Bertelsen, whose great capabilities made life much, much easier; Mollie

Copeland; Evelyn Oder, who always kept my best interest at heart; Helga Morpurgo, who always gave help when it was needed; Barbara Kelley, whose advice always proved to be a decisive factor; and Stephanie Slosser. Thanks are also extended to the staff of the Department of Near Eastern Languages and Cultures.

Contents

Illustrations

Abbreviations

See Bibliography for complete references

AAS	*'Ālam Ārā-yi Ṣafavī*
'Abbās-Nāma	Muḥammad Ṭāhir Vahīd Qazvīnī, *'Abbās-Nāma*
Amīnī	Faḍlullāh b. Rūzbihān Khūnjī, *Tārīkh-i 'Ālam Ārā-yi Amīnī*
AQ	J. E. Woods, *The AqQuyunlu*
ASh	Anthony Welch, *Artists for the Shah*
AT	Ḥasan-i Rūmlū, *Aḥsan al-Tavārikh*
Āyanda	Sayyid Aḥmad Āqā Tabrīzī, "Īl-i Afshār"
BK	G. R. Garthwaite, "The Bakhtīyārī Khāns: Tribal Disunity in Iran, 1880-1915"
BOD	J. K. Birge, *The Bektashi Order of Dervishes*
Busse, *Untersuchungen*	H. Busse, *Untersuchungen zum Islamischen Kanzleiwesen*
CA	Lawrence Stone, *The Crisis of the Aristocracy, 1558-1641*
CHI	*The Cambridge History of Iran*
Dhail-i TAAA	Iskandar Beg-i Munshī, *Dhail-i Tārīkh-i 'Ālam Ārā-yi 'Abbāsī*
DJ	Don Juan of Persia (Ūrūch Beg Bayāt), *Don Juan of Persia: A Shi'ah Catholic, 1560-1604*
DK	Dede Korkut Kitabı, *The Book of Dede Korkut*
DLT	Maḥmūd al-Kāshghārī, *Dīvān ül-Lüghāt it-Türk*
EI[2]	*Encyclopedia of Islam*, 2nd ed.
Fasā'i	Ḥasan-i Fasā'ī, *History of Qajar Rule in Persia*
FS	Marc Bloch, *Feudal Society*
HA	*Ḥudūd al-'Ālam*
HS	Ghiyāth al-Dīn Khāndamīr, *Ḥabīb al-Siyār*

Ismā'īl	*'Ālam Ārā-yi Shāh Ismā'īl*
"ISP"	A. K. S. Lambton, "Islamic Society in Persia"
JA	*Journal Asiatique*
JAOS	*Journal of the American Oriental Society*
JT	Rashīd al-Dīn Faḍlullāh, *Jama' al-Tavārīkh*
Kasravī	Aḥmad Kasravī, *Tārīkh-i Pānsad Sālah-i Khūzistān*
KhT	Qāḍī Aḥmad Qumī, *Khulāsat al-Tavārīkh*
"KSOTM"	Jean Cuisenier, "Kinship and Social Organization in the Turco-Mongolian Cultural Area"
LHP	E. G. Browne, *A Literary History of Persia*
LP	A. K. S. Lambton, *Landlord and Peasant in Persia*
Martin, "Seven Safawid Documents"	B. G. Martin, "Seven Safawid Documents from Azarbayjan"
MD	Martin B. Dickson, "Shāh Ṭahmāsp and the Üzbeks"
MK	Ṣādiqī Beg Afshār, *Majma' al-Khavāṣṣ*
Nikitine	B. Nikitine, "Les Afshars d'Urummiyah"
"NRPMI"	Farhad Kazemi and Ervand Abrahamian, "The Non-Revolutionary Peasantry of Modern Iran"
OECA	Nora Chadwick and Victor Zhirmunsky, *The Oral Epics of Central Asia*
Perry	John Perry, "Forced Migration in Iran in the Seventeenth and Eighteenth Centuries"
"PO" [1]	R. M. Savory, "The Principle Offices of the Safavid State during the Reign of Ismā'īl I"
"PO" [2]	R. M. Savory, "The Principal Offices of the Safavid State during the Reign of Ṭahmāsp I"
PR	E. J. Hobsbawm, *Primitive Rebels*
"PSI"	V. Minorsky, "The Poetry of Shāh Ismā'īl I"
PZP	Klaus M. Röhrborn, *Provinzen und Zentralgewalt Persiens im 16. und 17. Jahrhundert*
RC	Chalmers Johnson, *Revolutionary Change*
RR	P. Avrich, *Russian Rebels: 1600-1800*
SAAI	Anthony Welch, *Shah 'Abbas and the Arts of Isfahan*

Sarwar	Ghulām Sarwar, *History of Shah Ismā'īl Ṣafawī*
SAWB	South African Wool Board, *An Illustrated World History of the Sheep and Wool Industry*
"SECII"	I. P. Petrushevsky, "The Socio-economic Condition of Iran under the Ilkhāns"
SīNā	Nizam al-Mulk, *Sīyāsat-Nāma*
SN	Sharaf Khan Bidlīsī, *Sharaf-Nāma*
SS	E. Bergel, *Social Stratification*
"SSE"	Richard Tapper, "The Shahsevan in the Safavid Era"
T	Shah Tahmāsp, *Tezkire*
TA	Mīrza Rashīd Adīb al-Shu'ara, *Tārīkh-i Afshār*
TAAA	Iskandar Beg-i Munshī, *Tārīkh-i 'Ālam Ārā-yi 'Abbāsī*
TG	'Abdullāh Fūmenī, *Tārīkh-i Gīlān*
THA	Bāyazid Bayāt, *Tadhkira-yi Humāyūn va Akbar*
TJA	Qāḍī Aḥmad Ghaffārī-yi Qazvīnī, *Tārīkh-i Jahān Arā*
TJG	'Atā-Malik Juvainī, *The History of the World Conqueror*
TK	Aḥmad 'Alī Khān Vazīrī-Kermānī, *Tārīkh-i Kermān*
TM	*Tadhkirat al-Mulūk*
TMG	Rashīd al-Dīn Faḍlullāh, *Tārīkh-i Mubārak-i Ghāzānī*
"Une liste"	J. Bacque-Grammont, "Une liste d'émirs ostağlus révoltés en 1526"
VP[2]	Jean, Chevalier de Chardin, *Voyages en Perse*, vol. 2
ZDMG	*Zeitschrift der deutschen morgenländischen Gesellschaft*

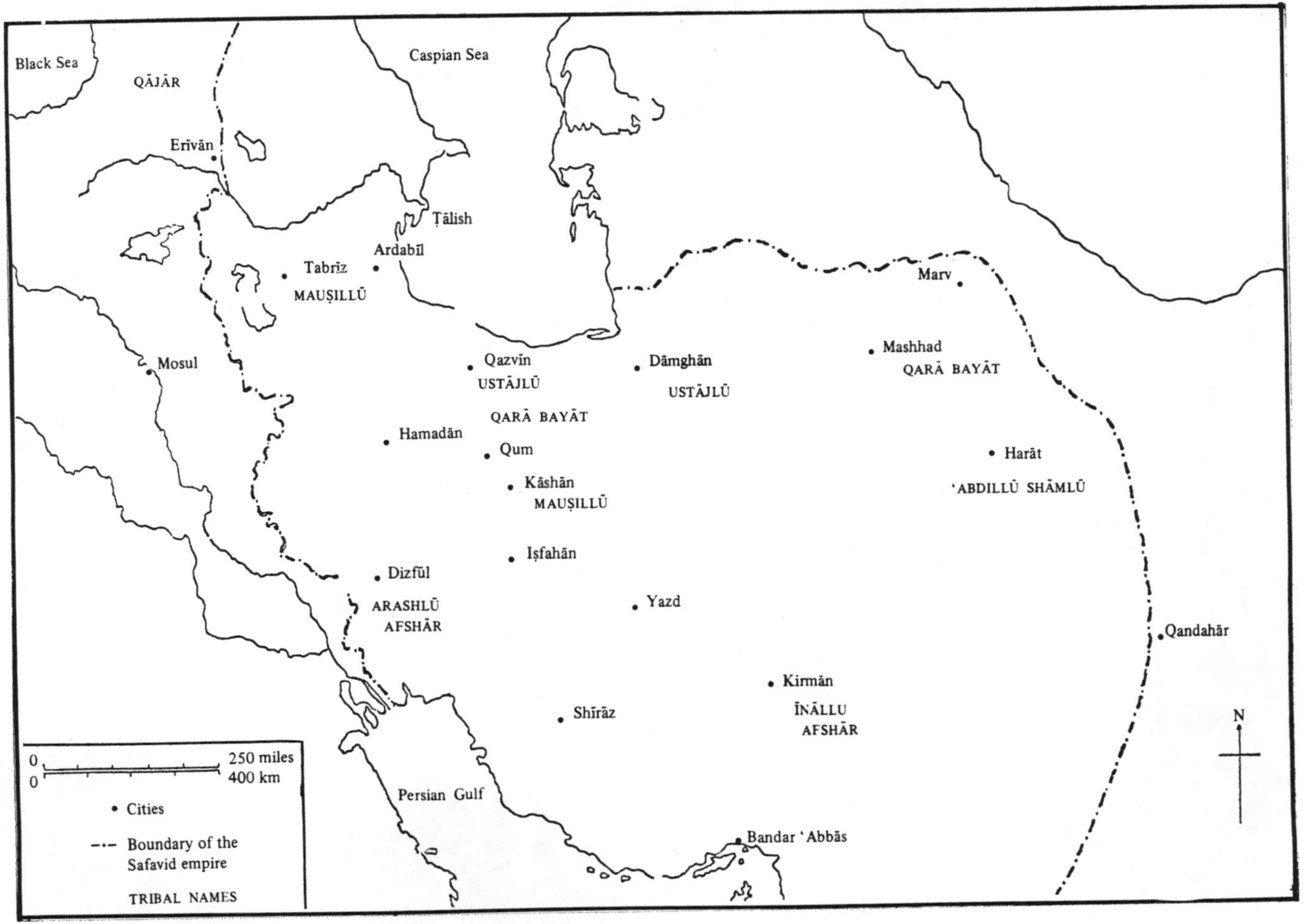

Map of Safavid Iran.

Introduction
Development of the Steppe Tradition and Its Influence upon Iran

The steppe exerted an intense pressure upon Iran during the whole course of its history down to recent times. Ancient Iran was itself the outgrowth of the steppe and was periodically subject to waves of conquerors from Central Asia.[1] From the tenth century on, new waves of invaders entered Iran from the steppe, but this time they were partly Iranized Turks, unassimilated Turks, and Mongols.

Before these last invasions, Iranians had established a village economy in which pastoralism served only as an adjunct to the main economic task of cultivation. Even such tribal groups as the Bakhtīyārī had their origins in an agricultural economy.[2] The Turco-Mongol invaders brought a new concept of property organization and a new system of organizing production that differed fundamentally from the Persian method. They thus created a dualistic system of land utilization and altered the concept of the state as well as the principles of economic organization.

The prime unit of wealth in the steppe economy had been anything that was movable: sheep, cattle, horses, camels, and other animals; agricultural produce; light tools and implements; and precious items such as jewelry, precious stones, and coins. All were prized as primary wealth and marked with special tribal brands (*tamgas*). Possession of the land was determined according to the location of the movable wealth and in particular to the needs of the animals. The basic pattern of settlement upon the land was the establishment of permanent campsites on either end of a longer or shorter migration route. Dwellings were movable just like any other form of prime property. Land was not owned within legally established, limited boundaries, but campsites were assigned by tribal rulers, who might give the same campsite to different families each year. Tribal units migrated from winter quarters to summer quarters and back again once a year. Grazing lands belonged to the tribe as a whole and were allotted to units within the tribe at general tribal congregations convened at some central point on the edge of the pasture lands. The chieftain would establish his quarters and parcel out the land to the leaders of the units accepting his authority. This prototype tradition had innumerable variations, of course. There were also various degrees of combination with other economic units that shared the steppe with the pastoralists.

The prototype formula, or something very close to it, was transplanted to Iran during the course of several centuries. The Iranian concept of property was evidently based more upon the ownership of legally defined and bounded lands than was the case among steppe peoples. Each social unit settled upon the land in one stationary position, and, though needs for pasture may have required flocks or herds to move to distant places, the basic mode of settlement remained singular. Iranian peoples had once been pastoralists of the steppe prototype, but they had gradually lost their traditions as their contacts with the steppe economies decreased. The steppe economy reemerged in Iran four or five centuries after the Arab conquest, with the continued influx of Turkic and Mongol pastoralists. Iranian land systems were subverted, sometimes harshly, to the concepts of property current in the steppe. The conquerors did not regard grain production as the major function of the economy, and, in any event, did not establish a proprietary system of control over the land. Lands were allotted according to the needs and functions of the movable units. The agricultural sectors were permitted to survive only in so far as they produced taxable wealth that their imperious overlords could consume on the spot or carry off easily.

The steppe system was first noticeable under the Saljūqs, but it was implemented most harshly by the Mongol *Īl-khāns*, who regarded Iran as their personal *yurt* (camp, pasture site). This is not to say that agricultural wealth was not valued, but, rather, that it was forced into second place until the reforms of the Īl-khān ruler Ghāzān, under whom Turkmen and Turkified tribes began to develop a more symbiotic relationship with the village agriculturalists. The dualistic system of property organization reached its zenith with the appearance of the *qizilbāsh uymāq* system, in which the power of tribal chieftains over village and pastoral systems was formalized and integrated more fully with the urban sector.

The term "qizilbāsh" did not initially refer to a certain grouping of tribes but to a distinct class of initiates belonging to the mystical order headed by the Safavid family. At formal gatherings this class of initiates wore a red crown (hence, *kızıl* "red" and *bash* "head") as a mark of their position in the order. In the late fifteenth century, as the Safavid Order became more involved in politics, many tribal chieftains were attracted into Safavid service and there rose to the position of qizilbāsh. After 1500, conquests brought many other great tribal chiefs into the Safavid fold and these chiefs brought entire tribal systems with them. In order to maintain his authority, the Safavid ruler Ismā'īl I Safavī (1501-1524), as well as his successor, Ṭahmāsp I (1524-1576), developed a regularized tribal system. Most tribal chieftains of high status were designated as qizilbāsh, and, like the older qizilbāsh, they were more involved in secular than in religious affairs. In the qizilbāsh organization, steppe practices were adapted to the agricultural systems of the

Safavid Empire. The formation of the qizilbāsh system represented the high-water mark of the steppe pastoral communities within Iran. Even the reforms of ʻAbbās I Ṣafavī (1587–1629) could not eliminate the functions performed by the qizilbāsh tribes, though they did alter the political and social roles of the Turkish tribes and rearranged them in a way that ʻAbbās hoped would be less of a threat to royal power in Iran. The story of these changes in sixteenth-century Iran has been neglected or distorted. It is the purpose of this book to give Iranian social and economic history of the Safavid period the attention it deserves and to correct the misunderstandings of tribal history in Iran.

NOTES

[1] The early Iranians or Aryans, including the Saka tribes, were pastoralists: R. N. Frye, *The Heritage of Persia*, (New York: The New American Library, 1963), p. 65; T. Sulimirski, *The Sarmatians*, (London: Thames and Hudson, 1970), passim, esp. pp. 25-26; Otto Maenchen-Helfen, *The World of the Huns*, (Berkeley and Los Angeles: University of California Press, 1970), pp. 75 ff. The Parthian tribes were also originally pastoralist: B. P. Lozinski, *The Original Homeland of the Parthians*, (ʻS-Gravenhage: Mouton and Co., 1959), pp. 12-21; Malcolm A. R. Colledge, *The Parthians*, (London: Thames and Hudson, 1967), pp. 25 ff.

[2] *BK*, pp. 59-60.

Timūr Khān Shaikhlū Ustājlū.

1

Merging of Central Asian and Persian Traditions

Hierarchy and Power in Iran from the Eleventh to the Eighteenth Century

Now that the basic development of the "steppe" tradition has been clarified, it is helpful to retrace briefly the derivation of the concepts of social order in Iran from the eleventh to the eighteenth centuries. The Turkish tribes which began to enter Iran in the eleventh century imposed some of their own social and economic practices, chief of which was the method of distributing wealth among servants of the state and the army. Implicit in this method of distribution was their idea of state. The Turkic tribes merged into a system that was organized in a specifically Iranian manner or at least according to Iranian tradition. While Turkish methods of organization eventually influenced this Iranian administrative system, the inspiration was and always remained Iranian in character and tradition.[1] The fusion of Turkish and Iranian administrative concepts was caused by the victories of Ismā'īl I. The uncertainties and competitiveness of the steppe tradition were balanced off in the Iranian tradition by the propensity to rank things and arrange them in a precise order. This resulted in a struggle between the Tājīk and Turkish elements early in the reign of Ismā'īl I, a struggle that seems to have been immortalized within the Safavid system by the balanced arrangement which resulted.[2]

From early times the Iranian perception of hierarchical order was idealized in a number of formulas. One of the most common was the ranking of society into four stations that symbolized Zoroastrian and Muslim concepts of universal order.[3] The ideal was stated on less ideological planes as well. Nizām al-Mulk, grand *vazīr* (minister—cf. definition p. 76, table) of the Great Saljūq sultan Malikshāh, regarded hierarchy and status as the more important elements in the maintenance of an orderly and secure life for all:

One among the other servants [of God] will obtain fortune and felicity with the help of God. God will bestow upon him prestige according to his own merits and He will give him wisdom and knowledge with which he would treat his subordinates according to what they deserve and he would rank them according to their status and he would choose servants for them [his servants] from among people. Again he would appoint each of them [these servants] to a position. He [the ruler] would have confidence in them. In the priorities of religious and worldly affairs, he would have confidence in them.[4]

It is significant that Nizām al-Mulk is setting the stage for presenting innumerable, vertical orders of Iranian society—"each [person] having his own position and dimension of control." It is indicated here that each individual has his or her own "dimension" (*andāza*) or "measure." This hierarchical structure coupled with the words for status—*martabatī* (rank of honor, dignity, stage), *manzilī* (stage in time, rank), *maḥalī* (also stage in time or rank), and *pāygāh* (place of standing, rank)—provide the framework for an entire social organization. Society is seen in relative, vertical terms rather than in dialectically horizontal ones. The emphasis is on hierarchic orientation of roles and functions rather than upon class.

The survival of the Iranian or Irano-Turkish bureaucratic tradition during the Īl-khān era is well documented by Rashīd al-Dīn in *Jāma' al-Tavārīkh*, a work not only of an historian but of a practical bureaucrat interested in classifying and knowing as much as possible of the ethnologies, genealogies, histories, and social backgrounds of the tribes and peoples he was administering. No detail or tidbit of information escaped him. We find not only the accounts of the herds and flocks of the qa'an (Īl-khān), but also the record of the assignment to an *amīr* (military chieftain) of the smallest piece of ploughland or pastureland. His history is a monument to the methodical and patient administration of its author. The section of this work devoted to Ghāzān Khān[5] may be regarded as the public testament of Rashīd al-Dīn and his master Ghāzān, both of whom set about to restore order to their society.

A similar view of the world order was expressed in Safavid times by Iskandar Beg Munshī (or Iskandar Beg-i Munshī or Iskandar Beg Turkamān). In his opening statement about 'Abbās I, he takes up two topics: (*a*) the place of the shāh in society, and (*b*) the organization of society itself. He states:

He (Shāh 'Abbās) is the beginning of all matters in the secular state, being the world-ordering, wish-fulfilling ruler. He is also the initiator of all affairs concerning the religious government, being the domain-governing ruler with the power of controlling the revolutions of the world. In relation to the twins of state and religion, he is the overseer of the organization of religion and government, being highest among those who are high-ranking over the people.[6]

The intent of this passage is clear. Iskandar Beg[7] shows a society arrayed in stages and degrees from a central point. While the terminology is taken from epic poetry and philosophy, his statement reflects the underlying reality of 'Abbās's reign and an understanding of the traditional organization of Iranian society.[8] A few lines later, he begins a much fuller exposé of the hierarchical arrangement of affairs emanating from the position of the shāh and moving down. The term Iskandar Beg uses to indicate the degree of importance of anything is *pāya*, "place of standing, rank, degree," a shortened form of one of the terms used by Niẓām al-Mulk. The passage also reveals a sound understanding of the hierarchical arrangements of the religious and secular world order.[9]

These hierarchical, social relationships were recorded early in the eighteenth century *Tadhkirat al-Mulūk* by an unknown Safavid scribe. The governors of each *ūlkā* (district) received varying incomes and could engage in variable sets of extracurricular economic activities. In addition, there were governors who possessed special rank or status as opposed to other amīrs, who, though equal, perhaps, received other distinctions.[10] The different functions of state and society (organization and defense of the religion, military preparedness, administration of revenues) received similar treatment in the *Tadhkirat al-Mulūk*. A definitely descending order of rank and hierarchy is the pervasive message that V. Minorsky fathoms only in a vague way.

Within the Safavid society the qizilbāsh formed an order in the narrow sense of the word.[11] In the best Iranian bureaucratic tradition, Iskandar Beg has shown the ranking of certain qizilbāsh tribes. Of the Shāmlū, he states: "They are the greatest of the qizilbāsh tribes and in priority of service and rights and sacrifice, they are first among the uymāqs."[12] None of the qizilbāsh tribes appear to be ranked in such a precise way as the Shāmlū, but, as other narratives show,[13] there were elaborate systems for ranking the different tribes. Obviously such rankings cannot be regarded as permanent since the qizilbāsh system was a dynamic, ever changing complex. The principles of social organization that the ranking of the tribes represented was derived from an Iranian bureaucratic tradition.

The arrangement of social categories into an hieratic order was also evident among the Turkic tribes. Hierarchical order was less elaborate and less graded than in the Iranian system. When too many individuals of the same or similar status existed within a given political structure, a situation common enough in Safavid Iran, the only means of determining the relative status of each was to fight with the rivals until one forced the other to accept his superior status.

The Turco-Mongol institution that led to the fratricidal wars plaguing most Turkish states or communities was ruled by the family rather than by a single individual. Where no authority structure existed within the ruling family, or where the structure had broken down, only armed confrontations could restore order.[14]

In order to reveal the qizilbāsh system as a derivative of this Turco-Mongol prototype, it is necessary to show an example of the internal authority structure of the Turco-Mongol ruling families and then the internal structure of the tribe.

'Atā Malik-i Juvainī's story of how Changīz Khān divided his realm among his relatives is an excellent case in point. The authority structure of the Changīzid ruling family (like that of other ruling families among the Turks and Mongols of Central Asia) was determined through the familial structure. Juvainī writes: "Now according to the custom of the Mongols the rank of the children of one father is in proportion to that of their mothers, so that the child of an elder wife is accorded greater preference and precedence."[15] The very elaborate kinship terminology of the Mongols supports Juvainī's generalization.[16] Ranking by age appeared important not only for the wives of the patriarch but also for all relatives living in the household, since property was distributed according to age, as many stories from Juvainī illustrate.[17]

A neatly ordered kinship system was an ideal that could be as false as it was true. The elaboration of kinship relationships such as the Mongol prototype is an anthropologist's dream, but does not portray anything more than a cultural ideal.[18] In reality, authority relationships within Turco-Mongol tribes were determined by power relationships, not by kinship structure. Between the eleventh and the eighteenth centuries Turkic tribes in Iran were based less on kinship relationships than upon power relationships. Power within the group "was exercised by a war chief whose titles are inherited through the paternal line but whose real authority is based on talent and success."[19] The *oba* (camp group), far from being a tightly knit kinship society, was a cluster of families and smaller camp units "around an already existing entity that is identified by a name, various emblematic marks, and a legendary genealogy."[20] The qizilbāsh of sixteenth- and seventeenth-century Iran organized themselves in this fashion as well. Over time, original oba units often broke down into a number of splinter obas, and these often made alliances with other outside groups.[21] Obas or groupings of obas could have "a warlike purpose" such as raiding for booty and conquest of territory.[22] After the Mongol period, the tribal obas located throughout the formal structure of Turkish tribal societies is summarized by Jean Cuisenier in four points:[23] (1) Power was exercised in Turkish tribal societies by a war chief (not necessarily by the head of a family or families); (2) obas were not kinship societies but groups arrayed around an existing entity to which they had no blood relationship; (3) as the obas grew in size, they broke into splinter obas that formed alliances with groups they were not related to by blood; and (4) the obas, or the larger tribal units to which they belonged, also had a military purpose. After the Mongol period, tribal obas located throughout Iran did not have a military purpose in the sense Cuisenier intended. The chieftains of the tribes often formed the army, but oba groups and the migrational communities to which they belonged (*tīra*s or *ok*s) were almost totally economic units subordinate to the khans of their tribe which organized for war only as (*a*) a member of the khan's army or bodyguard and (*b*) for self-defense.

Cuisenier's prototype bears its greatest resemblance to the situation of the qizilbāsh in points 1, 2, and 3. Most qizilbāsh units were aggregations of families, camp groups, or even groups of unrelated individuals formed around an already existing power entity. Most of the tīra groups that belonged to the Īnāllū Afshār of 'Urūmīya, for instance, bore the name of a distant, usually forgotten, founder.[24] Each of these groups claimed descent from their founder as well as genealogical links with the other Afshār groups in the area, particularly with the most powerful one, the descendants of the Īnāllū chieftain Qāsim. From the beginning of the seventeenth century the position of *beglārbegī* (provincial governor) of 'Urūmīya and/or governor of the town and environs of 'Urūmīya was traditionally given to a descendant of Qāsim. The Īnāllū or Qāsimlū chieftains bore all the qualifications Cuisenier enumerated in point 1 with the exception that their genealogical links to Qāsim were not legendary. The other Afshār (and Kurdish) obas and tīras settled all around the main unit in a network that protected and isolated the place held by the family of the chief.[25] The different tribal units were not joined by actual genealogical links (except through exogamous marriage), but rather by links between a patron group with a clearly defined genealogy and status and a large number of client groups, the combined sum of which formed an *intisāb* (protégé) unit.

Among the qizilbāsh groups the office of khan was given to military leaders, as in Cuisenier's prototype for the Oghuz (point 2). Inheritance of the chief's office through the paternal line was also a factor that the qizilbāsh had in common with the Oghuz. The resemblance between the Oghuz and the qizilbāsh is somewhat superficial at this point, however. The qizilbāsh were members of a significantly different political and cultural system. Most qizilbāsh chieftains were part of the Safavid government and in this capacity performed more than military service within their own tribe or subtribe. It was their duty to administer the wealth and tax revenues of the region they governed in the name of the Safavid shah and to recruit troops both inside and outside their tribe for service as *qūrchīs* (government troops maintained by tribal leaders) or as garrison troops.[26] Even during the reign of 'Abbas I, the qizilbash chieftains held posts in the Safavid government that required them to perform duties the Oghuz would have considered outside the responsibility of a tribal khan. What Cuisenier regarded as the essential characteristic of an Oghuz war leader—that he maintained his authority solely through success in competition with other khans—was also true of a qizilbash chieftain.[27]

The element of competition in the qizilbāsh intisāb system continued to be significant in the Safavid political organization, even though the promise of high office was in most instances eventually taken away from the qizilbāsh sector. Competition within a qizilbāsh group was always keen, especially when the domain of a chieftain was divided among his heirs. The most talented or politically astute heir would normally eliminate his rivals and reunify the office of chieftain.[28] When ‘Abbās I eliminated the qizilbāsh khans from all but a few of the major offices of state, the qizilbāsh intisāb system broke down partially so that the power struggles for position or wealth were increasingly centered within the groups themselves. This led to the evolution of a few, distinct power groups such as the Shāmlū, Qājār, and Afshār and to the gradual eclipse of weaker entities such as the Ustājlū, Takalū, and Dhu'l-Qadr.

A similar evolutionary trend can be traced among the qizilbāsh for the third point, that is, they, like the Oghuz, tended to form into "larger aggregations made up of splinter groups belonging to different *oba*. When it was formed, the Qājār tribe consisted of a mixture of Bāyandur, Bayāt, and other subgroups.[29] The Kūh-Gīlū Afshār was composed of Gündüzlü, Īnāllū, and perhaps some Arashlū Afshār groups, plus a mixture of groups that had at one time been Lurs, Kurds, or Musha‘sha‘ Arabs.[30] The intermingling of different subgroups around a power center for economic or military purposes was not the sole means by which different entities formed associations in Safavid Iran. The qizilbāsh chieftains formed power coalitions among themselves, both inside and outside their own uymāqs. The tendency to go outside the group was strongest during the first century of Safavid rule. Younger sons with little hope of gaining part of their patrimony could move more freely outside their group and find employment in the military or at the Safavid court. Others, who already possessed their domainal rights, were encouraged to go outside the family alliance to form new associations with powerful officeholders at the court. As opportunities for court service decreased, however, so did the potential for making outside contacts. Those who had formerly obtained employment at court were restricted to less permanent and/or less political positions. As a result, the qizilbāsh intisāb units vied with one another for different economic goals. Affiliation in an intisāb confederation was confined in some cases to competing segments in particular tribes or in rival, regional communities composed of parts of several tribes.

As for Cuisenier's fourth point there is no significant similarity between the Oghuz and the qizilbāsh. Warfare certainly held an important place in the qizilbāsh economy. Most booty, however, was kept by the chieftains, their retainers, or their clients.[31] The obas and the families pursued an economic way of life significantly different from that of the Oghuz. The Oghuz were more self-sufficient and totally mobile units. They had more than one breeding animal from among such animals as camels, sheep, goats, horses, and cows and did not practice agriculture or generally migrate annually. Their contact with the populations in the path of the migrations tended to be violent, causing them to maintain: (*a*) a multiple herd economy, and (*b*) a society organized on the basis of warfare. At least one segment of the Afshār, the Īnāllū, originated in the time of the eleventh-century migrations. They may have been the followers of a military leader (*īnāl* or *yīnāl*), and the central pole of their organization was based upon military expediency and maintenance of a self-sufficient mobile economy.[32]

The qizilbāsh, on the other hand, were not breeders of multiple herds. The main breeding animals were the sheep and the goat, and, because most sixteenth century qizilbāsh uymāqs possessed distinct migration patterns, they also had more or less friendly relations with the other groups they encountered along the route of their semiannual migrations. As a result their subtribes were not geared for war, and whatever disputes occurred between groups could not be classified as organized war efforts.[33]

Qizilbāsh military organization was not, therefore, the function of, but the leading element in the oba (or group of obas). The qizilbāsh chieftain considered pastoralists who sought his alliance to be his subjects rather than his equals. If the Oghuz īnāl (war chief) did not consider himself the equal of the pastoralists in his following, he did not have the power that the qizilbāsh chieftain had to raise himself to a position of exclusive authority. A qizilbāsh *beg* (chief) who held an official, military position in the Safavid government received subsidies, allotments of Pāzūki (Kurdish) foot soldiers, the right to exploit specified tax revenues due the shah in a particular district, and the right to maintain a permanent military establishment (a fortress, an arsenal, and troops), something that normally had little or no relationship to the uymāq of the chieftain. The chieftain considered the nonpastoralists in his area to be his subjects also, though such relationships beyond the economic necessities of maintaining the military were often more than clandestine. The central unit of a qizilbāsh tribe was an exclusive, ruling entity that was difficult for the average tribesman to penetrate.

NOTES

[1] I do not mean to imply that this was a "nationalistic" tradition, but that it was a system Iranian rulers established in the past which they and their successors used to rule over a multinational society.

[2] "PO" (1) and "PO" (2).

[3] This idealization seems to be almost as old as Iranian society itself. A summary is available in "ISP", pp. 74-76.

[4] *SīNā*, p. 10.

[5] *TMG*.

[6] *TAAA*, p. 377.

[7] Himself a qizilbāsh.

[8] This statement indicates that Iskandar Beg himself was not 100 percent "Turkamān" and also reflects the basic difference between Ismā'īl I and 'Abbās I. The former did not understand Iranian society well and tried to impose his will by force. 'Abbās and his slave subordinates belonged exclusively to neither Turkish nor Iranian social backgrounds, but to both cultural entities as the chief element of order.

[9] The terms such as *nāzim* (overseer) or *masnad-ārayān* (high ranking officials, literally, those who adorn official places) show awareness of a well-ordered organization.

[10] *TM*, pp. 43-44, 100-105.

[11] M. I. Finley, *The Ancient Economy* (Berkeley and Los Angeles: University of California Press, 1968), p. 46 gives a good definition of order, which does not apply on every count to the qizilbāsh, however.

[12] *TAAA*, p. 138.

[13] *SN*, passim, treats the Kurdish tribes of the seventeenth century in such a fashion.

[14] The following sources illustrate apsects of the Turco-Mongol system of hierarchical organization: "The Revolt of the Outer Oghūz" in *DK*, pp. 182 ff. and an account of how Chaṅgīz Khān divided his realm among the members of his family, *TJG*, I, pp. 40-41.

[15] *TJG*, I, 40. This practice was ultimately derived from Chinese precedents.

[16] E. Bacon, *Obok: A Study of Social Structure in Eurasia* (New York: Wenner-Gren, 1958), pp. 61-64 and passim. (Note particularly comparisons with other Mongol groups, which show that the system was not universal.) Bacọn takes her kinship terms from the *Secret History of the Mongols.*

[17] Ibid., p. 63; *TJG*, pp. 41-42.

[18] This statement is not meant to deny the obvious value of a useful guide to kinship relationships such as Bacon's. It must be realized that the elaborate kinship terminology betokens a formal and impersonal system, not a personal relationship as can be found in most modern families.

[19] "KSOTM", p. 215.

[20] Ibid., p. 215.

[21] Ibid.

[22] Ibid.

[23] In the subsequent discussion these points are referred to by the numbers used here.

[24] Nikitine, p. 75. Qarā Ḥasanlū, Kūsa Aḥmadlū, Gündüzlü, Qāsimlū, and the like.

[25] For a similar organization see: R. Tapper, "Black Sheep, White Sheep and Red-Heads, A Historical Sketch of the Shāhsavan of Āzarbāijān," *Iran*, 4 (1966), 61-84.

[26] Martin, "Seven Safavid Documents," pp. 196-197.

[27] It must be noted that the reasons behind the competitive system employed by the Safavid rulers inspired a quite different environment than for the Oghuz, who quite frequently had no administrative superstructure to guide the competitors in their ambitions.

[28] There were two fratricidal disputes among the Afshār in the reign of ʻAbbās I.

[29] *AT*, p. 215, note 2; *Amīnī*, p. 26, note 3.

[30] F. Sümer, *Oğuzlar: Türkmenler* (Ankara: Ankara Üniversitesi Basimevi, 1967), p. 267 citing Aşıḳpāşāzāde, *Tārīhī*. The Khudābandilū Afshār in the Kūh-Gīlūya controlled a heterogeneous following of Arab, Lur, and Kurdish groups.

[31] In most cases the retainers and the clients of a chief did not belong to the same tribe, so that income in the form of pillage did not always find its way to the tribesmen.

[32] Claude Cahen, "Le Malik-Nameh et l'histoire des origines seljukides," *Oriens*, 2 (1949), 57-58. The name "Īnāllū" remained often in distorted forms (Īmānlū, Aināllū, Īnānlū), as the Īnāllū adapted to their environs, but the social organization and economy changed.

[33] The Afshār of Khūzistān were the first Turkish tribe to possess such migrational organizations (from the eleventh or early twelfth century). Other Turkish and Mongol tribes established themselves in Iran later.

2

Iranian Social Order and the Qizilbāsh

Qizibāsh chieftains were more than the heads of pastoral tribes, they were the representatives of the locality or localities they ruled, and they acted as small-scale sovereigns. For themselves, they reserved all the good qualities: prowess, bravery, courage, and manliness. They also possessed the right to intercede in behalf of their dependents with the central government, if not to control the daily lives of their followers entirely. But, beyond the mere delineation of the social status of the qizilbāsh amir, it is evident that he was the last remnant of a tradition injected into Iranian social organization by the Saljūqs and brought to fruition by the Mongols.

SALJŪQ AND MONGOL TRADITIONS

The most distinctive legacy the Saljūqs and Īl-khans passed on to the qizilbāsh was that of rulership. If the qizilbāsh were not de jure rulers in their corners of Iran, they were de facto controllers of the land and the revenues attached to it. The manner in which they utilized the land was also reminiscent of their predecessors, though in a transformed system.

Saljūq administration represented the fusion of pastoral customs developed in the Central Asian steppe and Iranian/Islamic bureaucratic traditions. "In the steppe, each tribe had its own grazing ground or *yurt*, over which the leader of the group, as the representative of the tribe, exercised dominion, probably allotting, in the case of large tribes, specific pastures in it to the various subgroups, though guided in this by tribal custom and limited by tribal tradition."[1] The various tribes or subtribes tended to hold certain areas for some time and were allowed to return to the same yurts year after year. When the Oghuz conquered Iran, they considered it the personal estate of the Saljūq khan, who allotted land, property, and wealth to the individuals in his service.[2] Land, in many cases pastureland as well as prime agricultural land, was parcelled out to the khans who had served the Saljuqs. In both Azerbaijan and Khorāsān, Türkmen pastoralists had been granted collective grazing rights instead of *iqṭā'* (revenue assignments by a higher authority) that included agricultural parcels.[3] Central Asian practices survived in certain areas of Iran, notably Khorāsān, but were superseded by a combined form of land tenure in other areas, in which plowlands and yurts together were granted to the tribal chieftains as iqṭā‘ assignments.[4] The symbiotic relationship between pastoral and village communities in Iran was the product of the stabilization of Saljūq rule in Iran.[5]

The Mongol leaders were less assimilated to Iranian culture than the Oghuz and the Saljūq and Qarā-Khān leaders had been. Their conquest of Iran greatly reinforced steppe traditions for they regarded Iran not only as the land of the Īl-khān, but as the yurt of the ruler and his family.[6] The Īl-khān regarded their conquest as yurt in theory as well as in practice. Rashīd al-Dīn records that the herds of the Īl-khāns were huge and that the Mongol khāns headed a special economic structure for the supervision of the herding during migration season and the pasturing of sheep, cattle, camels, and the like. The chief supervisor of Īl-khān herds or flocks in a particular region was known as a *qā‘ānchī*. Serving under him were many shepherds (*chūbāns*) who were responsible for taking the animals to pasture and protecting them.[7] Rashīd al-Dīn, Ghāzān's vazīr, also possessed large herds and flocks of animals, supervision of which was farmed out to different Türkmen and Arab tribes.[8] The old system of land tenure was in abeyance under the early Īl-khāns, but as time passed, they and other Mongol leaders began to acquire land.[9] The Īl-khān rulers were able to assimilate pastoralists and villagers very poorly, however, and their poor abilities as administrators led them to severely exploit Iran's rural economy. Officials of all types lived off the countryside so that until the reforms of Ghāzān Khān the village population was taxed two or even three times the amount actually due in any given year.[10] As a result of this burdensome taxation, village cultivators either vanished from villages and began to keep movable property (livestock) in place of immovble grain crops or, as Rashīd al-Dīn records, fled their villages upon the approach of Īl-khān troops or officials.[11]

The reforms of Ghāzān Khān were an attempt to remedy the problems created by direct supervision of the land. They produced a new and more final assimilation of the pastoral and the agricultural communities of Iran.[12] The difficult times that preceded these reforms left an indelible mark upon the economic system of Iran. Not only were the pastoral communities networks of migrant camps, but the villages were also forced into a movable economy upon the model of Kurdish villages that had always been partly pastoral. The economy of Iran was reorganized to bring it into accord with the hierarchical and demanding order of the state and the army/bureaucracy imposed upon it. The iqṭā‘ system formulated by Ghāzān Khān was designed to organize agricultural and pastoral production around the needs of the army. This system of assignments was well regulated in the reign of Ghāzān Khān, but subsequent rulers and dynasties, including the Safavids, were never fully able to integrate these "military patronage" estates into their domains.

In accordance with the Mongol iqṭā‘ system, yurt was distributed to pastoralists, usually for pastoral exploitation to which agriculture was subsidiary or peripheral. The Īl-khān gave a great bloc of land to tribal khans known as *mīng-bāshīs* (commanders of a thousand). This land was then subdivided into lots of 100 units and redistributed to chiefs known as *yüz-bāshīs* (commanders of a hundred), who in turn distributed the land to their subordinates.[13] This system of descending allotments was a reflection of steppe practices. Through it land found its way into the possession of particular tribes or families, where it remained for generations.[14] The combination of pastureland with plowland was a pragmatic reality in the Īl-khān and subsequent systems of iqṭā‘ organization. E. Quatremère cites numerous instances where pasture (*‘alaf-khār*) was associated either with an allotment or an iqṭā‘.[15] On one occasion a "Sultan gave assignments (iqṭā‘) and pasture (*‘alaf-khār*) to each tribe."[16] On another occasion some princes received "great cities and fertile pastures."[17]

The revenue system associated with this iqṭā‘ organization remained basically the same wherever it was applied. Amounts of revenue taken, however, varied in each district. In many cases the taxes represented little more than the regularization or legitimation of the extortion of money, wealth, or services on the spot by armed bands of troops. These taxes included levies of fodder (*‘ulūfa*), food (*‘alāfa*), forced labor (*bīgār*), forced guide service (*alām*), "presents" (*pīshkish*), and various dues in kind for the entertainment of traveling envoys, couriers, heralds (*īlchīs*), and squadrons of troopers. Extraordinary levies (*ikhrājāt va khārijīyāt*) were the most notorious of these taxes and were implemented by local amirs on the slightest pretext.[18] The same names for taxes used in the Īl-khān era are found in documents of subsequent periods, though after the Safavid period they are often applied to different exactions.[19]

Throughout the early development of this system of military assignments, it is evident that the agricultural economy of Iran became more and more adapted to the pastoral economy brought from the steppes. This shift was most evident in the change in the names given to the military appanage system. The term "iqṭā‘" was in general use throughout the period until the seventeenth century but had its most restricted meaning before and during the early Saljūq period. The terms "yurt" and "‘alaf-khār" were often used in place of iqṭā‘ throughout the Saljūq period, but generally when the area so designated was mostly pastureland. The Mongol Īl-khāns also used the term "iqṭā‘," but designated certain iqṭā‘ holdings as *tuyūl* or *soyūrghāl*, according to the purpose of each. The tuyūl was a temporary assignment to an amīr of the right to collect,for his own benefit, government taxes in a certain district. This type of holding, says Lambton, is traceable to Saljūq personal iqṭā‘. The soyūrghāl was a grant that was generally immune from the extortions and extraordinary levies listed in various documents mentioned above.

The tuyūl represented the fusion of pastoral practices and the agricultural economy of Iran. The term "tuyūl" initially meant "the searching after something" or "the following of a path (as if in search of something, such as fodder)."[20] It could also mean "the assignment of that property or wealth."[21] The idea behind tuyūl must originally have been related to the search for pastureland in unexplored areas, wasteland, or conquered territory. The term eventually came to designate the division or allotment of booty, conquered land, and/or pasture land.[22] That the successors of the Īl-khāns (also others including both the Ottomans and the Safavids) used the assignment of territory to exploit not only the produce of the land but also the movable chattels upon it is indicative of the continuing influence of pastoral activities. In the Safavid period the Mongol term *ölgä* (*ūlkā*) was applied to territories which had been assigned as tuyūl under Safavid predecessors. The right to assess all or part of the extraordinary taxes and levies was given the holder. The ūlkā was to some extent a merging of tuyūl and soyūrghāl.

The Emergent Social Order

The steppe exerted a continuous influence in Safavid Iran. Not only had Iran itself become part of the steppe, but the culture of Turkish Central Asia continued to be imported into Iran. Each of the qizilbāsh tribes continued to use its own Turkic language, often descended from an Oghuz dialect (Afshār, Bayāt, and perhaps Qājār), but in the early sixteenth century, Chaghatāī Turkic became the *lingua franca* of the qizilbāsh aristocracy.[23] After the Mongol invasion, however, the steppes of Central Asia never again exerted such a direct influence upon Iran, and the borrowings of the qizilbāsh from the Üzbeks were restricted to what Üzbek prisoners taught the Safavids. For all intents and purposes, then, the qizilbāsh system represented an outgrowth of earlier steppe traditions imposed upon an Iranian society.

The leaders of the qizilbāsh system belonged to Türkmen tribes, many of which had memories of their Oghuz or Mongol antecedents. The internal organization of the qizilbāsh tribes was dualistic, a factor which distinguished them from the Türkmen tribes that entered Khorāsān in the reign of Ṭahmāsp I (1524–1576) and which differentiated their practices from those in use in the Central Asian steppe.[24] The military leader and landowning chieftain of the qizilbāsh tribe was the Īl-khān who could possess any of a number of different titles (khan, *sulṭān*, or *beg*). The leaders of the economic unit(s) were the *āḳ saḳāl*s or *rīsh sifīd*s ("elders").

The difference between the chieftain and the rank and file pastoralist was determined by economic status. The chieftains mentioned in the sixteenth- and seventeenth-century Safavid histories have at least the title of beg, which indicated a certain military status in the Safavid administration. The rank of beg was the lowest in the qūrchī military establishment of the Safavids. The administrative title represented the narrowing down of the meaning of the term beg. The beg was wealthy enough to support his own contingent of troops and could support a life-style profoundly different from that of rank and file pastoralists. Economic and military status were therefore intertwined in the meaning given to the administrative title. "Beg" was also used to designate an individual without official status. The chieftain of any tribal group was frequently referred to as *īl-begī* regardless of his military or official status. He might even be an independent functionary without official government position. In this context "beg" meant the chieftain who was the wealthiest, most powerful individual, or one of a number of such, in the group to which he belonged.[25] Thus the beg had a unique position, and his wealth provided him with an unmatchable position as the patron of his group.

The beg secured his wealth and safeguarded the investments of money or tools in the economic ventures of those he ruled by forming a military institution composed of his personal retainers. Permanent retainers were ideally not members of the groups or families who recognized the suzerainty of the beg. In the era of 'Abbas I the permanent armies in the service of the begs were recruited from different sources. A specified number of service troops was provided to each chieftain who had official status. These service men were normally from the Kurdish Pāzūkī tribe, but the beg could raise additional troops from the domain that he ruled. Extraordinary levies of troops were sometimes also given to the chieftains as was the case in 1609 when a large number of Jalālī refugees were provided.[26]

Economic and social distinction is accorded to the chieftain in literary, documentary, and historical writings. The evidence clearly indicates that the beg and his family held privileges and duties given to no one else as long as they were successful in war and maintained their wealth. The dualistic distinction between the tribal military unit and the tribal economic unit was reflected in the literature of the tribes, particularly of those in Azerbaijan. One of the most important monuments of Turkish oral literature in the period from the fifteenth to the seventeenth centuries was *The Book of Dede Korkut*. The distinction between master and servant, experienced and inexperienced is a variant of the theme of aristocratic predominance which weaves its way through all the *Dede Korkut* stories.

The relationship between the shepherd Karajuk and his master Salur Kazan in the story "How Salur Kazan's House was Pillaged," is a direct conceptualization of the distinction between shepherd and chieftain. Salur Kazan was clearly amazed by the presumptuousness of the shepherd in this story. In the opening sequences of the story some Georgian infidels have pillaged Kazan's house and abducted his family and the families of his retainers. Kazan and his retainers were hunting. Kazan, who had been told of this occurrence in a dream, commanded his retainers to continue the hunt. He commanded further, that if they did not hear from him by the end of the day, "to look for yourselves, I shall have gone too."[27] Then he set off for home. His intention was to combat single-handedly, in the manner of a champion (*mubāriz*), the evil that had befallen his family. This sequence in the story is the first sign of Salur Kazan's high status and military prowess. Kazan considered himself the champion of his people, and no one of similar or lower military status had the right to meddle in his affairs.

When Kazan arrived where his home had been, he saw that everything had been plundered and taken away: his family, livestock, and chattels. He set out immediately to find his family. After traveling a short distance, he came upon the dog of his shepherd, Karajuk. In this passage the dog symbolizes the lower class of people who served the chieftain. Karajuk's sheep dog represents a particular facet of the economic organization of a conglomerate pastoral domain. The labors of the common pastoralist and the shepherd—the protection of the flocks, the herding of the sheep, and the exploitation of the usufruct of the sheep—were functions reserved to the station of the common pastoralist. The dog serves as the prototype of this station or class. Its loutish presumptuousness in attacking Kazan's horse, an act which symbolized the station or class of warriors, is a parallel to the impudence of Karajuk, who tried to interfere in the affairs of his master, Kazan. Seeing the dog, Kazan asked:

> Have you news of my encampment? Tell me,
> And so long as my dark head is in life and health I shall
> treat you kindly, dog.
>
> But how should a dog give news? The dog snapped at the legs of
> Kazan's horse and whined. Kazan hit the dog with a stick,
> and the dog slunk off by the way he had come.[28]

The contempt of the martial Kazan for the dog clearly indicates that the dog, and by extension the dog's master, were symbols of a lower station. The qualities that belong to the low station do not bear the finer mien that Kazan associated in his own mind with the higher station, that is to say, valor, prowess, courage, and the other values belonging to a champion who is the guardian of his people. The patron-client relationship is explicit in this passage when Kazan tells the dog he will "treat him kindly" as long as the dog performs in the desired way. Kazan expects the dog to perform contrary to his wishes, however. The dog, having the attributes of the lower class, reinforces Kazan's bias by attacking Kazan's horse. The exchange between horse and dog accentuates the relationship that develops between Kazan and Karajuk in the following sequence. There Kazan is portrayed as having the same prejudice against Karajuk that he had against the dog. The open violence between the dog and Kazan's horse is transformed into a latent hostility based upon the class distinction between Kazan and Karajuk.

The dispute between Kazan and Karajuk reveals the class distinction between the warrior Kazan and the shepherd Karajuk. Each is assigned the prerogatives and duties of his station. Any attempt to cross the class line by performing or assuming the duties of the other class would be the grossest presumption. In this case, Karajuk offers his aid to Kazan, and, indeed, refuses to leave Kazan until he has helped him. Karajuk's persistence represents rebellion against authority, though it does not take the form of a violent attack. After relating the story of the attack by the Georgians, Karajuk says to Kazan:

> Give me your chestnut horse,
> Give me your sixty-span lance,
> Give me your shield of many colours,
> Give me your pure sword of black steel,
> Give me your eighty arrows in your quiver,
> Give me your strong bow with its white grip,
> I shall go to the unbeliever,
> I shall rise again and kill,
> I shall wipe the blood off my forehead with my sleeve,
> If I die I shall die for your sake;
> If God Most High allows, I shall deliver your family.

The prose narrative resumes with the comment: "These words offended Kazan and he abruptly moved on."[29] Even though Karajuk shows loyalty to his master, Salur Kazan is offended because Karajuk, a lowly shepherd, has presumed to place himself in a status equal to or better than that of his master.

When the shepherd persisted in following along, "Kazan thought to himself, 'If I go with the shepherd, the nobles of the teeming Oghuz will put shame on me and say, 'Kazan could never have overcome the unbelievers if the shepherd had not been with him'.' Jealous for his honour, he tied the shepherd tightly to a tree, mounted his horse and rode away."[30]

Kazan's justification for refusing Karajuk's help illustrates the tension between classes that existed in the conglomerate pastoral community governed by the chieftain and his retainers. Such a relationship between master and servant did not begin to grow until the thirteenth and fourteenth centuries. Beginning about this time, and continuing on into the seventeenth century, there was a growing tendency to exclude the regular pastoralist from military service. If regular pastoralists were included in an army, they performed the less glorious military tasks. The rulers of Karaman, for instance, who were originally Afshār chieftains, began to employ slave troops as early as the mid-fourteenth century. The qizilbāsh revolution of the fifteenth and early sixteenth centuries was a brief respite in the growing trend to exclude pastoralists from independent participation in their own communities. Only one of the qizilbāsh leaders following Ismā'īl I had any relationship to the old aristocracy. The reign of Shāh Ṭahmāsp marked a return to the previous trend, and the newly established qizilbāsh leadership became the new aristocracy. Kazan's justification for excluding Kārajuk from his venture is an excellent illustration of the trend toward greater aristocratization of the pastoral societies on the western border of Iran. Within the framework of this trend, it is evident that the regular pastoralist or the shepherd could not presume an equal status with his chieftain. To assume equality was cause for chastisement and even punishment, both in this story and in the actual relationships between chieftains and the pastoralists who recognized their authority.

The dualism evident in *Dede Korkut* is a manifest declaration of Turkic tribal adaption to an Iranian social environment. Türkmen qizilbāsh society was continually affected by the tensions caused by this dualistic system. There was always a struggle between rival military cliques for the control of the means of production within their particular areas. The complexity and intensity of local struggles was unbearable, and in such instances, the economic units and their indigenous leaders, the āḳ saḳāls, rīsh sifīds, *kalāntar*s (town provosts), and *kadkhudā*s (village heads) emerged as a new military class which defended itself and their villages against the exploitation of their competing masters. The Safavid movement and the qizilbāsh chieftains emerged from such a situation at the end of the fifteenth century and triumphed over all the other competing units.

THE GROWTH OF THE QIZILBĀSH SYSTEM

The Book of Dede Korkut represents a transitory stage in the history of at least one of the qizilbāsh tribes, the Bayāt, but the other Türkmen of the period could also identify with the content of the stories. The reader is at once struck by the Middle Eastern features in the stories,[31] but many Turco-Mongol traditions survived in the stories as well. The distinctive features of the Turkic tribes that are found in *Dede Korkut* and continued to influence Iranian and Middle Eastern society include: (*a*) their economic organization; and (*b*) their social habits and frame of mind (though not their social structure). By far the most important element of the narrative is its insight into the development of a dualistic social organization.

The qizilbāsh system was an outgrowth of the social order portrayed in *Dede Korkut*. The original qizilbāsh cannot be associated in character with Karajuk the shepherd, but they definitely did not belong to the social order of Salur Kazan. Before 1502-1503 none of the qizilbāsh were members of the Āq Quyūnlū or Qarā Quyūnlū ruling classes.[32] The only complete tribal units under Safavid control seem to have been the Ṭālish, Shāmlū, Rūmlū, and Ustājlū tribes, all of which seem to have been composed of varied social and tribal elements. Not one of these tribes had a distinct social memory that went back as far as the early fifteenth century[33] except for the Ṭālish, the earliest supporters of Shaikh Ṣafī al-Dīn.[34] Aside from these tribes, members of innumerable trades, occupations, and social units belonged to the qizilbāsh order in places as far away as the Balkans, then under Ottoman dominion, and northern Syria.

The qizilbāsh were members of particular Sufi or Darvīsh orders, notably of the Bektashiye in Anatolia and of the Ṣafavīyya in Iran. They were not members of pastoralist groups or of tribal organizations nor in their initial groupings were they villagers or urban dwellers. Affiliation was based largely upon a relationship with a religious leader. The qizilbāsh may, in fact, have been bands of heterodox or non-Muslim qalandars (heterodox mystics), who filtered into the part of Anatolia least controlled by the Saljūqs.[35] They do not appear to have possessed one particular economic organization, at first, but, in the spirit of the times, they engaged in multiple economic activities. The leaders of these groups may have been little more than *qam*s (shamans), and the disreputable character later attributed to most qizilbāsh may partially have been due to the origins of many of the qizilbāsh groups.[36]

The multiple social and economic organization of the Oghuz and Mongol-Tātār invaders of Iran was supplanted by sets of more specific, even hierarchical, social-economic bands. Early in the fourteenth century the *ḳızılbāsh* (Anatolian qizilbāsh) were relegated to a lower position in Anatolia once the entire peninsula had been conquered. This decline in status was noted by later Ottoman historians, who indicated that the early Ottoman begs gave white headgear to their *Yengī Çerī* (Janissaries [lit. new soldiers]) to distinguish them from "all the rest of the soldiers" who "wear red head-pieces."[37] The ḳızılbāsh were *alevi* (village and mystical associations which revered the Prophet's family) groups according to J. K. Birge. The Bektashis regarded the ḳızılbāsh as a related but inferior branch of their order. Though there were many points of resemblance between the two groups, there were two major differences: the Bektashi order consisted of whole villages and the villagers were initiated at the proper age.[38]

The ḳızılbāsh were more than villagers in the fourteenth to the sixteenth centuries. They were pastoralists, farmers, or both and members of hierarchical societies often separate from and opposed to the Ottomans.[39] The hierarchical order of the ḳızılbāsh groups of Anatolia comprised substrata of Ottoman society not easily controlled, economically or religiously. The events of the late fifteenth and early sixteenth centuries demonstrated how easily the ḳızılbāsh could detach themselves from allegiance to the Ottomans. Many ḳızılbāsh began to accept the message preached by the Ṣafavīyya *dädä*s (or *dede* "preacher") sent out into Anatolia, Syria, and Iran from Ardabīl. The Ṣafavīyya do not appear to have preached open revolt against the Ottomans or any other political group but to have foretold the coming of a *Mahdī* (a final imām who would destroy the worldly order and bring humanity to salvation). The rebellion stirred up by generations of activity among the ḳızılbāsh erupted in the early sixteenth century, when Ismā'īl I, the descendant of Shaikh Ṣafī al-Dīn, came out of hiding in Lāhijān. A young boy who had just reached the age of puberty and who misunderstood the fine points of religious doctrine or reasoning, he proclaimed himself the Mahdī.[40] He had been given religious training by an 'ālim (religious scholar) who knew the Qurān, but after the death of his father and eldest brother, his chief companions and tutors were ḳızılbāsh/qizilbāsh tribal warrior/chieftains who had a poor understanding of religious matters. Ismā'īl's emergence from hiding in Lāhījān provoked a reaction throughout the network of the Ṣafavīyya order and the ḳızılbāsh affiliate branches. The ḳızılbāsh substratum of Ottoman society was prōvoked into rebellion. The Ottomans were now confronted by highly dangerous, internal and external attacks in Anatolia. Selim I Yavuz (1512–1520) crushed the internal revolts in 1511–1512, notably in the province of Teke.[41] Those ḳızılbāsh who escaped his wrath went over to the Ṣafavīyya, though the leaders of the Takalū (or Tekelü) were executed by Ismā'īl for attacking Persian merchants.[42] The external attacks, led by Iranian qizilbāsh chieftains such as Muḥammad Khān Chāūshlū and Dīv Sultān Rūmlū, were quite successful. Between 1502 and 1511/1512 they defeated several Ottoman armies, composed of the same type of mounted troops. Selim I put an end to this external threat by disarming or destroying the ḳızılbāsh in Anatolia and defeating the Safavids.[43] The ḳızılbāsh, however, remained in Anatolia and during the sixteenth century their number even increased, but they were subordinate mainly to the Bektashi and only rarely had contact with the Ṣafavīyya.

The Iranian qizilbāsh had similar origins. Many, but not all, were Turkish speaking. By the mid-sixteenth century Chaghatāī had not yet become the lingua franca of the qizilbāsh ruling elite, so most of the qizilbāsh continued to speak various Turkic, Kurdish, and perhaps Lurī dialects. This linguistic compartmentalization was merely a physical manifestation of the composition of the Ṣafavīyya order itself. There was a hierarchical relationship between the *murshid-i kāmil* (perfect spiritual guide or master) and various groups of his *murīd*s (followers or initiates into the order). The sinews of the hierarchy stretched from Ardabīl to the Ṭālish tribesmen in the Mughān steppe and the Caspian seaboard, to the highlanders of Gīlān, to the Qarā Dāgh Sufis, and to the Ustājlū, Shāmlū, Rūmlū, Varsāq, Dhu'l-Qadr, and Takalū tribes. The internal mechanisms of this hierarchy will be discussed more fully later.

The qizilbāsh of Iran, like the ḳızılbāsh of Anatolia, originated in the Turkic and Mongol groups that entered Iran between the eleventh and the fourteenth centuries. The Turkmen of the two regions were one and the same people and possessed similar traits. Like the Turkmen who were moving into Anatolia, the Turkmen of Iran eventually developed social and economic ties with the peoples who lived in the areas they entered. The result was the development of a more distinctive socioeconomic organization. The use of multiple economic activities was narrowed down considerably. Among pastoralists the multiple herd economics of the invasion period were supplanted by single-herd sheep breeding. Economic variability remained an important aspect of both pastoralism and the village economy of Iran. The ideal was to maintain a socially and economically self-sufficient community. While self-sufficiency was difficult to achieve, economic variability was easy to maintain, especially under difficult circumstances.

The significance of the social attitudes developed by adaptation to the new social and economic environment was that the Safavid Sufi organization molded itself into an hierarchical organization in order to deal with the widely dispersed and isolated communities that came increasingly into the Safavid camp. This tendency, noted for the Anatolian ḳızılbāsh, was less evident in Iran. The mūrīds of the Ṣafavīyya in Iran were more widely dispersed and more evidently in the minority. Although population estimates and statistics on the affiliation of individuals and groups to various causes are not available for Iran or even Anatolia, the sources clearly show that the Afshār, Qājār, Bāyandur, Bayāt, and other leading groups did not support the Safavids.[44] The majority of the manpower and economic resources supporting the Ṣafavīyya were located in northwest Iran between the Qarā Dāgh/Mughān steppe area and Gīlān. The leading members of the qizilbāsh who owed allegiance to the Ṣafavīyya did not belong to the most pretigious or powerful tribes nor did they possess extensive wealth. The majority appear to have been urban artisans in Ardabīl, pastoralists, and village agriculturalists.

The hierarchical order established under Safavid dominion during the fifteenth century was severely disrupted by the assimilation into or the development of an intermediate strata of petty rulers throughout Iran, that is, the qizilbāsh amīr system. The dualisms apparent in the tribe of *Dede Korkut*'s Salur Kazan, discussed above, now became a part of the Safavid system as well. The intense devotion that had previously been directed to the murshid-i kāmil was now dissipated in the developing tribal systems. There were two sources of stratification that led to the weakening of loyalty ties with the Safavid shah.

The primary source of disequilibrium in the Safavid system was the internal growth of high-status individuals possessing wealth and armed forces to back them. The process was already noticeable at the time of the marriage of Shaikh Junaid's son to the daughter of Ūzūn Haṣan. Everyone in the Safavid order, from the murshid-i kāmil down to his immediate subordinates, was seeking a higher status and thereby coming into competition with individuals who would normally be considered their masters (the Āq Quyūnlū and their chieftains). The narrowing of the gap led the members of the Safavid order to rush to secure more property for themselves at the expense of the Āq Quyūnlū and others. The tendency to seek out more wealth was evident among the followers of Ismā'īl I.[45] The Ṭālish khans were rulers in the Mughān steppe and possessed extensive economic ties with the artisans of Ardabīl.[46] Malik Muzaffar Khulafā Beg, probably of the Ṭālish tribe or a Tātī affiliate of the Ṭālish, owned a house in the village of Khalkhāl, where he possessed land as well as animals.[47] Ḥamza Beg Ṭālish possessed an extensive network of armed retainers each with his own military forces and fortresses.[48] Qiriq Sidī 'Alī Purnāk, though not a highly placed amīr, was the *ḥākim* (castellan, governor) of the fortress of Alānchiq.[49] Ḥusain Beg Lala Shāmlū apparently owned, or held in common with other Shāmlū, some "fields," that is, land used perennially for agricultural production, specifically for growing melons.[50] The rulers of Gīlān, who were not qizilbāsh but who nonetheless from an early period followed the Safavids, also possessed extensive wealth in the fertile pastures and farmlands of Gīlān.[51] The Takalū chiefs of Teke also appear to have had property rights to the production of the Tegirmishlū pastoralists and of the fishing villages of the Anatolian province.[52] The increase of status and wealth in many of the instances cited above brought with it (*a*) changes in the value structures of the socially mobile Safavid elite: the previous emphasis upon piety through abstention changed drastically to an emphasis upon obtaining material goods;[53] and (*b*) the growth of an inappropriate ensemble of political, military, economic, and religious roles.[54] The result was that late Āq Quyūnlū/early Safavid Iran was in the throes of a multiple conflict involving established political authority (represented by the Āq Quyūnlū), established or semi-established religious authority (partially represented by the Safavids themselves), and the substrata that underlay these two institutions. Revolts against Safavid authority by military chieftains were as commonplace as revolts against Āq Quyūnlū chieftains, and the rebels were members of groups such as the Ṭālish, who for generations had recognized Safavid leadership. Mīrzā Muḥammad Ṭālish, a retainer of Ḥamza Beg and the ḥakīm of the fort of Marbī, revolted against Ismā'īl I as early as in the late fifteenth century.[55] Takalū leaders, survivors of the revolt of 1511, did not appear to recognize Ismā'īl I's authority in 1512 when they plundered a caravan heading into Anatolia, thereby threatening to cut off Ismā'īl's valuable silk revenues.[56] The same problems that had caused the severe dysfunction of the Āq Quyūnlū state were tearing away at a less aggravating pace at the Safavid establishment as well. As long as the Safavids remained strong or continued to appear so, revolts from within did not disturb the equilibrium of the state, but as soon as the ruler showed signs of weakness (such as the defeat at Chaldiran, or the inexperience of Ṭahmāsp I), the chieftains scrambled among themselves for power and supreme economic position. The second source of disruption in the early Safavid system was the entrance of former enemies into the service of Ismā'īl I. In 1502 the bulk of Ismā'īl's forces was composed of lower level chieftains and a large assemblage of ill equipped, poorly trained pastoralists, and of cultivators led by the lineage chieftains (kadkhudās, kalāntars, āḳ saḳāls, rīsh sifīds). As Ismā'īl I became more and more successful and more tribal leaders began to enter his service (mostly through coercion),[57] the deterioration of such qizilbāsh values as loyalty, belief in the doctrines of Ismā'īl and his ancestors, and religious sincerity was greatly accelerated. The dissatisfactions that had caused these chieftains to revolt against the various Āq Quyūnlū sulṭāns was transferred onto the Safavid family. The structural disabilities that had plagued the Āq Quyūnlū also placed stress on the Safavid system. One factor that saved Safavid dynastic organization is that, at the top at least, the practice of the steppe tradition was not used to determine succession to the throne. The Shī'a religious doctrine of imamate fused with the concept of political dynasty to form a new concept which replaced the Turco-Mongol tradition of rule by the family, thereby providing the Safavid dynasty with a strong principle of succession, something even the Ottomans did not possess. Discontent and rivalry for power and wealth remained and increased on the lower levels of Safavid society.[58]

Qizilbāsh Tribalism and Intisāb

The intisāb (protégé) system was as important a factor in the organization of Safavid state and society as it was in the Ottoman state. In the sixteenth century status in Safavid society was determined not only by merit but by one's patron and/or friends. The intisāb system worked along two basic political lines. An intisāb relationship could be formed on the basis of genealogical links or it could be established as a power arrangement around the households of the most powerful individuals regardless of genealogical associations.[59] The intisāb method of political organization predominated in the Safavid government at the center as well as in cities, villages, and pastoral groups away from it.

When the political structure and the economy of Iran were stable, especially when the shah was experienced and capable of handling disputes, the intisāb groups were kept in their places, but, when Iran was racked by political dislocation, the power groups struggled with one another to control the most important source of wealth. Particularly devastating social and political dysfunction usually occurred at the accession of a new shah, notably Ṭahmāsp I and 'Abbās I. The losers in the struggle were exterminated en masse or deserted to the enemy.

The reign of Ṭahmāsp I witnessed a number of vicious examples of the intisāb system at work. Ṭahmāsp had been a young, inexperienced boy at his accession to the throne. Early in his reign he displayed his inability to manage the state by assigning various high offices to two individuals instead of one. In 930/1524, for example, he granted the office of *amīr al-umarā* (chief commander) to Kūpūk (or Köpek) Sulṭān Ustājlū and Dīv Sulṭān Rūmlū. The two intisāb groups they represented, the Ustājlū and Rūmlū qizilbāsh, became involved in a struggle to control the offices of state. By placing the leaders of the intisāb groups in a position to grant offices to their followers and control the organization of the state, Ṭahmāsp had set the stage for a large-scale conflict. For two years, the Ustājlū and Rūmlū chieftains vied for the favor of other qizilbāsh and non-qizilbāsh leaders. Dīv Sulṭān eventually won out over the Ustājlū and gained the adherence of a broad sector of Iranian society.[60] The Ustājlū chieftain, Kūpūk, and other Ustājlū begs retaliated, but since they had few followers outside the Ustājlū establishment, their act of hostility toward Dīv Sulṭān was considered a rebellion. For two years a large Ustājlū army barricaded itself in northwestern Iran and Gīlān, suffering defeat after defeat at the hands of combined qizilbāsh forces. By 936/1529-1530, out of a dozen Ustājlū chieftains, only three remained, and they made their peace with Ṭahmāsp I.[61]

The conflicts did not end at this point, however. In 933/1526-1527, Dīv Sulṭān, who had just defeated the Ustājlū, was himself assassinated by Chuha Sulṭān Takalū, the *muhr-dār* (keeper of the seal), who became grand vazīr in his place.[62] Chuha Sulṭān remained in his position for three years until his influence with the shah and the other qizilbāsh groups was undercut by Ḥusain Khān Shāmlū, who had been responsible for defeating the Üzbeks. When Chuha attempted to have Ḥusain Khān murdered, a great battle occurred between the Shāmlū and Takalū. Since the Takalū had been in the wrong, the other qizilbāsh groups gave their support to the Shāmlū and war ensued. Revenge (*intiqām*) for the attempt on Ḥusain Khān's life was exacted not only upon the immediate following of Chuha Sulṭān but upon all Takalū affiliates. Open warfare between the Takalū and the Shāmlū-led qizilbāsh followed, and a large force of Takalū, led by Ulma (or Alma) Sulṭān Takalū, the governor of Azerbaijan, deserted to the Ottomans.[63]

In at least two cases, the Ustājlū and the Takalū, the deposition of the grand vazīr meant armed reprisal against his entire following. The mechanism of intiqām was justifiably utilized to the full by everyone who had been wronged by a Takalū or an Ustājlū. This time of troubles affected the whole of Iranian society. The fury of partisan strife worked its way into local politics. The dysfunction of the state at the top had caused numerous problems on the lower levels of society. Troops and government officials went without pay, officers began to make illegal exactions from pastoralists, villagers, and townsmen in order to pay their men, and sometimes violent competition for local offices arose. In 932/1526-1527, a Safavid official, his entire family, his servants, and his friends were killed by disgruntled Shāmlū troops seeking their pay.[64] Ḥasan-i Rūmlū (or Ḥasan Beg Rumlu) was himself a victim of these intisāb disputes. Although only a child, he felt that Qazvīn, formerly his grandfather's domain, should have remained in his family. Instead it was given to Pīr Sulṭān Rūmlū. In his history Ḥasan on several occasions addresses this individual with bitter invective.[65] By the time this incident was recorded, however, Ṭahmāsp I had gained control of the state and little came of the dispute. In 953/1546-1547, the great Afshār chieftains had a dispute with the Dhul'l-Qadr chiefs, but Ṭahmasp did not allow the factional break to develop and forced the two groups to negotiate their grievances.[66]

The Principle of Intisāb in the Reign of 'Abbās I

The conceptualization of intisāb appeared in a formalistic application in the reign of 'Abbās I. The shah was a private administrator as well as the leading figure in the government. The royal palace was a private living area, for instance, where certain areas were set aside for the shah's public functions. The throne room and the portico of Chihil Sutūn were such public areas. The private quarters of the palace included the harem, where the family of the shah resided and where private store rooms, a treasury, and sitting rooms were located. Semiprivate regions in the palace included the library, where the shah worked closely with his highest public officials.[67] As a public figure, the Safavid ruler often had a bedazzling array of unlimited worldly and supernatural powers.[68] Official powers far outstripped the real power possessed by the shah, who was forced into a series of political alliances by those of his amīrs in favor of his rule.[69] The regularization of such alliances came to be known as *intisāb-i shāhī* (the royal protégé arrangement). Some of these alliances were public power arrangements between one office or segment of government and the royal office. When Iskandar Beg used the term, he employed it in this sense. Qūrchīs and other servants of the state were considered to be a part of the intisāb-i shāhī. As the administrator of the greatest private estate in Iran, the shah also possessed private alliances with the qizilbāsh chieftains. The entire uymāq system was nothing more than the relationship of the different tribes and power groups with the shah.[70] The result of these distinct sets of relationships was the means by which the two systems received support. The qūrchīs and other public protégés of the shah were supported out of funds raised from dīvān (state) lands.[71] Other chieftains who were the heads of private households or who belonged to such private households, needed good personal relations with the shah or his high officers before they could receive grants of wealth or of gubernatorial positions. Such grants were frequent as posts were vacated.[72] The distinction was blurred nonetheless because high state officials received the governorship and revenues of certain areas normally specified by tradition. Since qūrchīs were also qizilbāsh, they often obtained provincial posts, which, like other qizilbāsh chieftains, they held for long periods.

The ambivalence characteristic of the intisāb relationships of earlier generations was also evident in the intisāb-i shāhī system. This institution probably had its origins in the religious doctrines of the Ṣafavīyya order, in which hierarchies of protégés were presented as serving God, the Prophet, and the imams.[73] The term, almost totally religious at first, became increasingly secularized after Ismā'īl I assumed power. New heights of secularism were attained by 'Abbās I, who continued to use the system only as a political institution, though there were distinct evidences of the coterminous nature of both the religious and the political institutions of the Safavid state even in his reign. The system of intisāb-i shāhī became devoid of all meaning once it became a political system and a more integral part of the Safavid state. Even in the reign of 'Abbās I, the theory or doctrine behind intisāb-i shāhī was referred to in correspondence between qizilbāsh chieftains.

A letter remarkable in this respect was written by 'Alī Qulī Sulṭān Qich-oğlū (Fatḥ-oğlu) Ustājlū in 995/1587 to 'Alī Qulī Sulṭān Dhu'l-Qadr.[74] It is a masterly effort to manipulate the Safavid system for personal advantage. In it 'Alī Qulī Sulṭān Qich-oğlū, for his part in opposing the new ruler's assumption of the throne, reveals his fear of reprisals from 'Abbās I and explores every conceivable possibility for playing on the sympathies of his antagonist, 'Alī Qulī Sulṭān Dhu'l-Qadr. The letter opens with an appeal on two counts: (*a*) one based upon the common membership of the sender and receiver of the letter in the Ṣafavīyya Order, (*b*) the other based upon the common brotherhood of the two in the political or military service of the shah. In order to emphasize the first point, 'Alī Qulī Sultān Qich-oğlū dispatched the letter with a small group of Sufis in his following, but the second part of his appeal, inspired by fear for his life, was merely lip service to a dead religious institution. The frequency of 'Alī Qulī Sulṭān's reference to the tribal-political institutions serving the Safavid state shows that the political side of the qizilbāsh system had gained the upper hand over the religious. The letter gives a fine account of the organization of the uymāqs and also highlights the link (or rather the lack of such) in the uymāq system.

'Alī Qulī Sulṭān's letter points to two major elements of organization in the qizilbāsh system: the *īl* (sub-tribe, tribe) and the uymāq. The īl was a conceptualization of the union of all the different qizilbāsh tribes. It was similar to the concept of *ūlūs* then current in Central Asia among the Üzbeks, and the remnants of the ūlūs Chaghatāī. Such a concept of unified tribes, though artificial to an extreme, was not entirely an ideal. Most qizilbāsh chieftains and their retainers spoke Chaghatāī Turkish, the lingua franca of the qizilbāsh from as early as the reign of Ismā'īl I and a literary language in which great literature, both prose and poetry, was produced.[75] That this literature reflected a common cultural life among the qizilbāsh is clear from the writings of Ṣādiqī Beg Afshār, the chief librarian of 'Abbās I early in his reign. The work which best reflects the cultural life of the "ūlūs qizilbāsh" is his

Majma' al-Khavāṣṣ which gives short, witty accounts of the lives and works of poets who wrote in Chaghatāī Turkic (as well as in Persian or Arabic).[76] Even though some fine cultural institutions flourished, accompanying the ideal of a common qizilbāsh community, the real political unit of qizilbāsh life was the uymāq, and, even more important, the extended family unit.

The letter of 'Alī Qulī Sulṭān also refers to the uymāq. Uymāqs (*aimaks* in Chaghatāī), literally, "tribes," were organized in the same fashion as the īl, but on a smaller scale.[77] An uymāq was a grouping of two or more genealogical units that normally had no blood relationships through the paternal line but which quite frequently intermarried. Despite these links by marriage, the association remained an artificial one. It was originally based upon the relative ranking and power of all the different qizilbāsh families.[78] In the sources the Bayāt tribe, for instance, appears as one of the smallest uymāqs, having only a few individuals. In reality, however, chiefly families with some paternal relationship to a Bayāt lineage were numerous. A sept of the Dhu'l-Qadr was known as the Bayāt-oğlū, while the entire Chāūshlū clan of the Ustājlū uymāq was nothing more than a rather large subsection of the Bayāt tribe.[79] The Qājār uymāq was also formed from a considerable number of Bayāt ruling families. Similar affinities existed between the Shāmlū and the Afshār. Both, for example, shared individuals from the Īnāllū. The real institution in the qizilbāsh system was not the uymāq itself, but the various ruling houses or families of which each consisted.

The combination of ruling families into larger units was not entirely artificial. 'Alī Qulī Sulṭān's letter indicates that any such uymāq and the qizilbāsh ūlūs had an officer, the rīsh sifīd, whose main function was to maintain a balance between the different elements of the uymāq and the hold of his family over the prime position in the uymāq. These were not formalized functions, and the office itself was more like an honorarium granted to the most powerful and highly-placed individual in the tribe. Murshid Qulī Khān Chāūshlū was the rīsh sifīd not only of the Ustājlū tribe, but, because he held the highest position normally granted to a qizilbāsh, the *vikālat,* (office of the *vakīl* [chief counselor]), he was also rīsh sifīd of the ūlūs qizilbāsh.

The complexity of the organization thus outlined in 'Alī Qulī Sulṭān's letter reflects the ambivalence of the power struggles in the reign of Ṭahmāsp I. The uymāq system permitted innumerable possible interpretations of the relationships it encompassed. If a powerful person was attacked, all those less powerful who depended upon his bounty were necessarily affected. The downfall of Murshid Qulī Khān Chāūshlū in the year after 'Abbās I's accession was unaccompanied by any strife, probably as the result of the grave error committed by the vakīl, whose confiscation of royal property endangered the security of his entire family.[80]

Lesser amīrs frequently sought to advance at the expense of their superiors. The year before the deposition of Murshid Qulī Khān, there had been a plot by several chieftains to take the vakīl's life. One of these chieftains was Mehdī Qulī Khān Dhu' l-Qadr, who actually attempted the assassination. His nephew, Ya'qūb Beg b. Ibrāhīm, a propertyless amir who had been sojourning at the royal court awaiting the opportunity to attain rank and holdings, now found his chance: as his uncle was fleeing the royal palace after the failure of his assassination attempt, he confronted him and killed him on the spot without hesitation or any apparent remorse. He was rewarded for his gruesome deed with a grant of the family patrimony in Shīrāz. He also took rightful possession of his uncle's family, wealth, and household.[81]

Usually such extraordinary measures were not taken, and most of a deposed chieftain's relatives and protégés were stripped of their offices and even killed. After Murshid Qulī Khān was deposed, all those who had obtained office through his intercession lost their positions. The *mīr-i dīvān* (chief minister), a political appointee of Murshid Qulī, was forced to pay a fine in excess of 8000 tumans.[82]

The great Afshār conglomerate in Kūh-Gīlū was torn apart by the armies of 'Abbās I between 1590 and 1595, a period which witnessed two massive revolts there spearheaded by the Arashlū. The Afshār were broken up into smaller units and dispersed into different localities in Iran, such as 'Urūmīya, Mughān, and Khorāsān.[83] The breakup of patrimonial estates all over Iran led to the creation of at least one new group, the *Shāh-savan* (those who love the shah), who were among the intisāb-i shahī.[84] The name should not be interpreted so literally, however, for it refers not only to those who devote themselves to the service of the shah, but also to those who receive protection and a livelihood through their relationship with him. The new group was formed in northern Azerbaijan in the reign of 'Abbās I out of the defeated remnants of the Īnāllū, Begdīllū, Ṭālish, and Takalū tribes. The formation of this new grouping, supposedly more dependent upon the central government, was a coup against the long-established scions of qizilbāsh society, since several qizilbāsh groups were placed directly under the control of individuals of undistinguished ancestry, many of whom were whispered to be highwaymen, or, at least, *qazāqlār* (independent chiefs), who were willing to bolt from under the dominion of accepted authority and sell themselves to the highest bidder. This was the attitude of the qizilbāsh, at least, who were normally given possession of any new converts to the Safavid cause.[85]

The ever increasing complexity of the uymāq system led the central government to seek out new sources of power and new loyalties among a lower order of notables. By bypassing the old and complicated family loyalties of the qizilbāsh, 'Abbās I cut across family lines and political alliances in an attempt to reduce the power of the great amīrs, but in so doing, he merely created new loyalties and new intisāb groupings inside and outside the uymāqs. 'Abbās accomplished this by creating new intisāb groups, by promising members of established families rewards for turning against each other (and by limiting the number and size of awards to be given to qizilbāsh), and by nurturing the most ambivalent elements in the system such as encouraging the division of family domains among all the sons of a powerful chieftain and allowing them to compete. By wreaking havoc among the great households and causing their properties to be divided up and dispersed, ʻAbbās I strengthened his own position, but by not eliminating intisāb groupings altogether, he allowed the groups which would later divide Iran among themselves to survive and begin rebuilding.

Kinship Societies and Intisāb

This survey of intisāb groups and their relationships with one another between 1524 and 1629 has shown how destructive clashes between these groups could be. But what effect did these intisāb groups have upon the organization of the pastoral groups and other communities that claimed kinship affinities? It has already been noted that intisāb groupings could have two organizational patterns: one based upon kinship relationships and one based upon political or power alliances.

Nasaba, the Arabic root from which the word "intisāb" is derived, means "to be related genealogically." It can also mean "to harmonize, to agree, to be in agreement, to be in conformity, to be related by marriage, to derive one's name from, to stand in the same relationship."[86] The term intisāb means "membership, affiliation" and can mean membership in a political, religious, or genealogical group.[87] The same dichotomy is evident in the term *ʻaṣabīyya*, which can mean either "zealous partisanship, party spirit," or "tribal solidarity, clannishness."[88] The intisāb relationship can conceivably be based upon both aspects of the term, that is, upon genealogical association and political affiliation.

The claim of genealogical relationship to a certain individual was interpreted in a negative sense in Safavid society, however. A powerful person who fell from the shah's grace caused the fall not only of his protégés, but also of all individuals claiming ancestral connections with him, regardless of their actual political contact with him. The downfall of Chuha Sulṭān Takalū, for instance, caused many Takalūs to flee into Ottoman service, even though most of them had no actual political relationship with Chuha Sulṭān.[89] After the Afshār and Dhu' l-Qadr dispute of 953/1546–1547, the Dhu' l-Qadr, under Ḥusain Qulī Khalīfa, had gained the favor of the shah and, as a result, the Afshār were systematically excluded from participation in the Georgian campaign, despite their relationship to Sıvındık Beg Arashlū Qurchībāshī ('chief of qurchīs').[90] The Afshār qurchībāshī of Muḥammad Khudābanda lost his position and his life after the Afshār revolts in Khūzistān during the reign of ʻAbbās I. Even though he was an Īnāllū from Kermān and probably had nothing to do with the revolt, the very fact that he was of the same name as the Īnāllū and Arashlū rebels was reason enough for them to execute him.[91] The relative status of other individuals in one's family or tribal group, that is, the group from which one's name was derived, had significant bearing upon one's welfare.

Actual intisāb relationships varied widely. Ottoman and Safavid concepts of intisāb were fundamentally very close. In both, intisāb involved "a tacit relationship established by mutual consent between a powerful individual and a weaker one." The weaker member attempted to further his master's position and wealth, while the master, in his turn, treated the weaker member as his client or protégé.[92] Usually there was no genealogical affinity between master and client in either the Ottoman or Safavid system.

The career of the qurchībāshī of Ṭahmāsp I, Sıvındık Beg Arashlū shows how little genealogical relationship meant in terms of power relationships. Sıvındık Beg's clients included members of numerous qizilbāsh and non-qizilbāsh groups. He had affiliates among the Rūmlū, including Ḥasan-i Rūmlū, the author of *Aḥsan al-Tavārikh.*[93] He assisted these individuals in their careers and they, in turn, defended him against his enemies. Despite Sıvındık's hostile relations with Ḥusain Qulī Khalīfa Dhu' l-Qadr, the muḥr-dār and a determined rival, Sıvındık, had a sizable contingent of Dhu' l-Qadrī clients who accompanied him on campaigns.[94] When Sıvındık's own brother Mehdī Qulī Sulṭān rebelled against Safavid rule in 946/1539–1540, he ordered an army to seize Shūshtar and execute him.[95] The significance of Sıvındık's personal relationships is clear—the strongest bond of solidarity was to be found in diversification of one's ties. As the patriarch of the Afshār, Arashlū, and others, it was incumbent upon Sıvındık to establish personal ties with individuals from rival groups outside the Afshār. In so doing he protected not only his own position, but also the welfare of his relatives and clients. If any client or family member threatened the security of the group by treachery or rebellion, it was his duty to take measures against the threat and to eliminate the individual himself, if necessary. Relationships of this type were the key to stability in Safavid Iran and prevented destructive civil wars between different groups.

The intisāb system was an ambivalent one in Safavid Iran. It could be interpreted in terms of genealogical affiliation or political confederation. The ambiguity that resulted from giving loyalty to one's kinship group and one's political allies caused serious problems, even during the reign of 'Abbās I, when the qizilbāsh were largely excluded from high, governmental positions. 'Abbās I had minimized the ambivalence inherent in the qizilbāsh intisāb system by replacing the qizilbāsh with a corps of slaves who had been taken from their families at an early age and had no ties with their relatives.[96] The new slave corps developed its own intisāb relationships, but only on a unilateral plane and remained divorced for the most part from family connections. Whatever ambivalence remained was largely the product of the isolation of the qizilbāsh aristocracy, among whom the traditional modes of political and genealogical association remained. The corps of slaves, which was patterned to some extent upon the Ottoman *kapı kulları* (slaves of the Porte), and the qizilbāsh possessed their own distinctive political systems, and this distinction permitted the survival of the ambivalence in two exclusive and separate institutions. From the time of 'Abbās I only in the office of quchībāshī did the two forms of intisāb come together. As a result the alternatives for political disruption became temporarily limited.[97]

NOTES

1 *LP*, p. 60.
2 Ibid., pp. 60 ff.
3 C. E. Bosworth, "The Political and Dynastic History of the Iranian World (1000-1217)," *CHI*, V, 83-84.
4 *SīNā*, p. 33.
5 See, e.g., *Āyanda*, nos. 8-9, pp. 600 ff.
6 *LP*, p. 77.
7 *TMG*, pp. 339-340. This economic institution existed in Iran. The Mongol chiefs brought very little livestock with them. Most important, however, they brought an idea of pastoral property management.
8 *LP*, pp. 78-80. This relationship foreshadowed the connection between the qizilbāsh amīrs and the Turkmen pastoralists.
9 Ibid., pp. 77-78.
10 Ibid., pp. 82-89.
11 *TMB*, p. 249. For a later period see also: "NRPMI", passim.
12 M. G. S. Hodgson, *The Venture of Islam* (Chicago: University of Chicago Press, 1974), pp. 404-405.
13 *LP*, pp. 89-90.
14 *SECII*, pp. 521-522.
15 Raschid-Eldin, *Histoire des Mongols de la Perse*, ed. E. Quatremère, (Amsterdam: Oriental Press, 1968), p. 137 n. 15 (not n. 12 as Petrushevsky states in *SECII*, pp. 521-522).
16 Citing *TJG* (Ms of an unknown library, f. 109r).
17 Rashīd al-Dīn, Ms used by Quatremère, f. 303r.
18 *LP*, pp. 101-103. Ismā'īl I Ṣafavī appears to have levied such dues at Guzār-i Khalkhāl in 905/1499-1500 (*AT*, p. 12).
19 Martin, "Seven Safawid Documents," Documents II and especially VI.
20 *DLT*, II, p. 115, "tiyul."
21 V. Minorsky, "Tuyūl," *EI*², IV, 799, after V. Radloff.
22 The terms *timar* (Ottoman) and *tiyül* (Turco-Mongol), both derived from the verb *timäk*, in this instance reflect steppe practices.
23 *MK*., which is in Chaghatāī.
24 *AT*, pp. 138-139; *TAAA*, pp. 105-106, the Yomut tribes of the Yaḳa and Ukhlū.
25 *DLT*, III, 158. *Bay* meant wealthy person. The distinction was between the flock owner, who was referred to as *bay*, and the laborer or shepherd, who was called chūbān or "çoban"–originally an Iranian word.
26 *TAAA*, pp. 781 ff.
27 *DK*, p. 47.
28 Ibid.
29 Ibid., p. 49.

[30] Ibid.

[31] The place names indicate the territory near Lake Van and on into Georgia and Azerbaijan, that is, the region near the Bayāt. Greek influences, notably from the epics of Homer, are evident. As indicated above, adaptation to an Iranian environment is also evident.

[32] This changed during the reign of Ismā'īl I when numerous tribal rulers were subjugated by the Safavids and in part, came to form the leadership of the new Safavid order.

[33] *LHP*, p. 46; *Ismā'īl*, pp. 14-21; Heribert Horst, *Timūr und Hoğä 'Alī*, Akademie der Wissenschaft (Mainz: Franz Steiner Verlag, 1958), which doubts these traditions.

[34] *TM*, p. 189.

[35] J. S. Trimingham, *The Sufi Orders in Islam* (London: Oxford University Press, 1973), p. 68. T. Gökbilgin ("Kızılbaş," *İslam Ansiklopedisi*, 6 [1955], 789-795) states that the kızılbaş had their origins in a pre-Islamic Iranian order.

[36] E. Esin, "The Turkish Bakšhi and the Painter Muḥammad Sīyāh Kalam," *Proceedings of the XIth Meeting of the Permanent International Altaistic Conference* in: *Acta Orientalia*, 33 (1970), 100-114; Speros Vryonis, Jr., *The Decline of Medieval Hellenism in Asia Minor* (Berkeley and Los Angeles: University of California Press, 1971), pp. 271-275.

[37] *BOD*, p. 47.

[38] Ibid., pp. 64 n. 4, 211-213.

[39] S. J. Shaw, *History of the Ottoman Empire and Modern Turkey*, Vol. I, *Empire of the Gazis* (London: Cambridge University Press, 1976), p. 77.

[40] Erika Glassen, "Schah Ismā'īl, ein Mahdi der anatolischen Turkemenen?" *ZDMG*, 221 (1971), 61-69; V. Minorsky, "The Poetry of Shāh Ismā'īl I," *BSOAS*, 10 (1942), 1046a ff.; *Ismā'īl*, pp. 46-49.

[41] *AT*, pp. 56-59.

[42] Ibid., p. 58. Perhaps this was an indication to Ismā'īl that he would face the same problems with the ḳızılbaş that the Ottomans had faced.

[43] Shaw, *Ottoman Empire and Modern Turkey*, Vol. I, 77-83.

[44] *AT*, pp. 1-67, suggests that Ismā'īl earned the respect of the majority of the Iranian Turkmen very grudgingly and that the Turkmen aristocracy submitted only to force of arms or threats.

[45] Little information is available for specific Safavid followers before this time.

[46] *AT*, p. 14; *Ismā'īl*, pp. 42-43.

[47] *AT*, p. 12.

[48] Ibid., p. 13.

[49] Ibid., p. 3 n.b.

[50] Ibid., p. 12, Guzār-i Khalkhāl.

[51] Ibid., pp. 4-5.

[52] Ibid., p. 49; *SN*, II, 146; plus innumerable Ottoman sources.

[53] The distinction between Ḥasan Khalīfa Takalū, who appears to have been an ascetic, and his son Shāh Qulī Bābā Takalū, who revolted to gain political and economic ascendancy in his province, is a case in point.

[54] Military chieftains such as Ḥusain Beg Lala became the chief religious leaders of the state while well-trained theologians were rejected.

[55] Ibid., p. 13.

[56] Ibid., p. 59-60.

[57] Manṣūr Beg Afshār in 908/1503, Muḥammad Dhu'l-Qadr, the Bāyandur "tribe," the Qājār subordinates of Abīya (or Ayba) Sulṭān Qājār, Amīr Beg and the Mauṣillū, and so on. See: *AT, TAAA*, and *Ismā'īl*, all of which have significant genealogical information.

[58] *RC*, pp. 61–118.
[59] See above, chap. 1.
[60] Ibid., pp. 91–95.
[61] Ibid., pp. 95–100, 106.
[62] Ibid., p. 100.
[63] Ibid., pp. 108–112.
[64] Ibid., p. 97.
[65] Ibid., pp. 134–135. The enemies of Ḥasan's family are easily identifiable throughout *AT* since the author frequently went out of his way to degrade them.
[66] Ibid., p. 143.
[67] *KhT*, pp. 37–38.
[68] R. M. Savory, "The Safavid State and Polity," *Iranian Studies*, 7 (1974), 182–186, 197–200.
[69] "PO" (1), p. 91–105.
[70] *TAAA*, p. 47.
[71] *KhT*, pp. 41–42.
[72] Ibid., pp. 34–35.
[73] Ismā'īl I used the term "shah" for both secular ruler and God, while his predecessors had used the term mostly for God. ("PSI", 1026*a*, poem 4; 1042*a*–1043*a*, poem 15; 1044*a*, poem 101; 1046*a*, poem 168).
[74] *KhT*, p. 32.
[75] "PSI", 1010*a*, 1012*a*.
[76] *MK*, pp. 29–38, 102–130. The paintings of Ṣādiqī Beg and his contemporaries frequently depict the ideals and cultural values of this qizilbash society. See *ASh*, pp. 41–100.
[77] The distinction between "īl" and "uymāq" later weakened and finally the two terms became synonymous.
[78] See below, chap. 4.
[79] Bābā Ilyās Beg Bayāt and his descendants were the same as Bābā Ilyās Beg Chāūshlū and his descendants. Compare *AT*, p. 234, with *TAAA*, p. 445.
[80] *KhT*, pp. 48 ff.
[81] Ibid., pp. 39–40.
[82] Ibid., pp. 48–49.
[83] L. Bellan, *Chah 'Abbas I, Sa vie, Son histoire* (Paris: 1932), pp. 66–67; Kasravī, pp. 68–73, after the revolt of the Afshār, the Shāmlū replaced the Afshār; Nikitine, pp. 72–74; *TAAA*, pp. 500 ff., 524 ff.
[84] R. Tapper, "Black Sheep, White Sheep and Red-Heads, A Historical Sketch of the Shāhsavan of Āzarbāijān," *Iran*, 4 (1968), 63-65.
[85] The tribal legends of the Shāh-savan relate that Yūnsur Pāshā, founder of the tribe, came from Anatolia in the reign of 'Abbās I and that he received parts of Qarāja Dāgh and Mughān from 'Abbās (Tapper, "Black Sheep," pp. 65–66). This story probably recounts the large number of Jalālī refugees who settled in the area and pushed the qizilbāsh out.
[86] Hans Wehr, *Arabic-English Dictionary*, ed. J. M. Cowan (New York: Spoken Languages Services, Inc., 1976).
[87] Ibid., p. 960.
[88] Ibid., p. 615.
[89] *AT*, pp. 108–112.
[90] Ibid., p. 143.
[91] *KhT*, pp. 68–69.
[92] Shaw, *Ottoman Empire and Modern Turkey*, Vol. I, 166.

[93] *AT*, pp. 156-157.
[94] Ibid., p. 156.
[95] Ibid., p. 133.
[96] *TAAA*, p. 1106.
[97] *TM*, pp. 116–118.

3

Development of the Iranian Economy 1000-1500

Pastoralism, urban production, and agriculture were closely integrated economic sectors in Iranian life. While pastoral, urban, or village peoples possessed distinct social institutions or economic patterns, each entity was generally mutually interdependent with the others. Pastoralists herded animals, sometimes caring for the animals of wealthy townsmen or accepting the flocks of villagers. In return for their services, both villagers and great personages provided them with grazing rights in certain areas along the migration routes of the pastoral groups. The urban economy also received a boost from the grains the villagers sowed and harvested and from the animal byproducts from the flocks the pastoralists raised. This is the prototype picture of the Iranian economy handed down in certain scholarly works.[1] To what extent is this appraisal correct? To what extent is this theoretical approach false?

The primary fault of the theory, given in capsule form above, is that it presents a set of conditions that may have existed in the nineteenth or early twentieth centuries but that did not necessarily apply to previous periods. Most research on pastoralism in pre-nineteenth-century Iran has been done on pastoral tribes as they existed in the nineteenth century. Preexisting social and economic conditions are examined only insofar as they reflected later trends.[2] Questions about earlier periods are not fully answered and, as the result of a modernist bias, pre-nineteenth-century Iranian historical study suffers either from truncation or isolated spurts of scholarship. The present chapter approaches the problem by providing a developmental framework through which future efforts at developing a more coherent analysis of the Iranian economy may proceed.

The Iranian Economic Base

Before the importation into Iran of economic forms belonging properly to the steppe, various geographic and topographic factors had produced what might be termed a unique Iranian economic pattern. It should be noted from the outset that these economic forms persisted through time and continued to exist even after the Turco-Mongol invasions had introduced new ones. The basis of the Iranian economy, that is, the economy that has existed on the Iranian plateau and in the mountain rim of Iran from very early times, was the dualistic organization of one primary economic unit, the village or any equivalent community. The dual functions of the primary unit were cultivation of the soil and stockbreeding. The latter, while subsidiary to agriculture, formed an important activity.[3] Just as geographic conditions varied from region to region, so too did the dualistic organization of village economies in Iran. In certain areas agriculture was more important than stockbreeding. In others, livestock and livestock products were more important than agriculture. Mineral conditions in the soil determined the intentions of any stockbreeder.

The regions of Iran best suited to stockbreeding were those where milk-producing vetches and other milk-producing ground covers grew in abundance. Such plants grew in the mountains surrounding the Kermān basin,[4] along the Alburz, the Zagros, in the Mughān steppe, and in the region between the Syr Darya and Amu Darya.[5] These regions have traditionally been the dairy centers of Iran. Here milk, cheese, and other milk products have generally been emphasized over wool.

The best wool-producing regions of Iran were located on copper-rich soils. Copper stored in the liver of the sheep and circulated throughout its body by the blood, ensures the normal growth and crimping of the wool.[6] The areas of Iran with the highest concentration of copper include Kāshān, the Kermān region, the Sabzavār / 'Abbāsābād region, and the area between Tabrīz and Gīlān.[7] These areas also happened to be the main carpet-producing regions of Iran as well as the greatest centers of wool export. There are five major breeds of sheep in Iran, all of which have been used for breeding there since about 3000 B.C.[8] The best wool-bearing sheep have thick, curly wool, also called "secondary hair", which may or may not grow beneath a "primary" coat of long, straight hair.[9] The best breeds of wool-bearing sheep are the fat-tailed Baluchi of the Kermān / Kāshān region and the fat-tailed Dānadār, a small, black sheep with coarse and luxuriantly lusterous wool, indigenous to northeastern Iran. The fat-tailed Kurdī and Mughānī sheep are less valued as wool producers, and in fact the long hair rather than the short curly wool is used primarly for weaving domestic items. The least important wool-bearer is the Zil sheep, found in the highlands of Gīlān and Māzandarān.[10]

Nondomestic use of wool in Iran was rare before the end of the sixteenth century. Even as an item of trade on the international market, wool from Persia was only a fraction of one percent of such great, wool-consuming regions as England in the seventeenth century.[11] As early as the first century A.D., European merchants with an eye for wool extolled the qualities of the Kermān (Caramanian) or Baluchi sheep above all others.[12] Wool was a marketable item, nonetheless, since both Polo and Fryer noticed large amounts of raw and, less commonly, refined wool for sale in Persian marketplaces. This trade in wool, though less substantial and less attractive than that in silk, was a source of income for some of the local notables in the wool-rich zones of Iran.

Most of the alluvial fan villages of Iran were heavily involved in pastoral activities because the plains and/or valleys were reserved more fully for agriculture and also because most soils in the plains would not support the necessary plant life. These alluvial fan villages located at the base of the mountains engaged heavily in agriculture, using the *qanāt* system, which required location on the alluvial fan of a mountain, as the means of irrigating the crops. These villages often retained permanent hamlets on the pasture sites of summer quarters located in the mountains.[13] The practice of maintaining a pasture establishment deep in the mountains developed at a very early date. Records from as early as the sixth/fifth century B.C. indicate that the Kurds produced milk products as well as grains.[14] Xenophon in the *Anabasis* notes that the Kurds, whom he called Gordyaeans, knew of mountain passages where they took their flocks.[15] Until the early seventeenth century, the Lurs were primarily agriculturalists and, unlike the Kurds, from as early as the twelfth century A.D.[16] tended to farm out the task of flock tending to Afshār pastoralists. Among these village settlements on the alluvial fans, where the dual mode of production predominated, an animal was prized for its meat and milk products. Domestic sheep were bred with wild Urial sheep in order to obtain a richer milk.

The agricultural economies of the plateau were normally less involved in a double system of production. Where large collectivities of animals were to be found, they were pastured in or near the villages. In great cities, garden farming and the occasional maintenance of single animals was most common. In outlying villages, fields surrounded a small cluster of permanent dwellings which were erected around a walled compound or courtyard. During the winter animals were kept in one of the buildings in the courtyard. During the summer they were put out to pasture. Great lords and patrons, such as the qizilbas̲h, maintained such walled compounds in the cities as well. Badr Khān Afshār, the first qūrchībāshī of ʻAbbās I, owned such a house in Qazvīn. It resembled a small fortress, since its walls were used to protect those inside in times of danger.[17] Pīra Muḥammad Khān Ustājlū also owned a house or *kārvānsarāī* on the road between Qazvīn and Kushk̦ early in the reign of ʻAbbās I. It had a courtyard surrounded by buildings and a wall. He extended his hospitality to allies or friends who were traveling the road by allowing them to keep their animals in his stables and to pitch their tents in his courtyard.[18] The leading proprietors of the field properties around villages also maintained similar dwellings in or near their village(s). Villages were also walled compounds, though of a larger size. Where the community consisted of only a few families, the walled compound enclosed every dwelling and served as a fence to keep animals in at night and as a defense against attack.

Larger villages possessed walls mainly as a defense. Those who were wealthy enough built houses with courtyards.[19]

Villages or smaller communities were the central core of the agricultural systems of Iran. Agricultural produce was their bulk item. Unfortunately, the organization of the Iranian agricultural system before the nineteenth century has only been studied poorly. Scholars have focused most of their attention on the sometimes intensive defoliation of the Iranian countryside, the result of stripping off the ground cover and of salinizing the soil through the use of the *qanāt* irrigation system. The best descriptions of these processes are by Paul Ward English, H. Bowen-Jones, and H. Bobek,[20] but they provide little information on the period prior to the nineteenth century. The few works available for earlier periods, such as that of I. Petrushevsky, are so concerned with ideological issues that they use figures and statistics mainly to support a preconceived theoretical approach.[21] The ideal mode of agricultural organization for the agriculturists was to settle in concentrated areas rather than in dispersed and isolated holdings. Proprietary rights to the land were reckoned according to plowland or shares of water. The size of the plowland (*juft*, *zūj*, or *yūgh*) varied from region to region, but in general it was as much land as one yoke of oxen could plow within a certain amount of time. Smaller units of land were called *lang*s, one lang being equivalent to one-half of a juft. The system was employed from a very early date and was marked by the communal or collective organization of all these individual plots for the usufruct of the community. The open field system was employed in addition to the closed-field system.[22] Land was owned either by landlords who possessed large landholdings or by peasant proprietors who held bits of land dispersed in patches among the holdings of the lord. A significant majority of the rural population consisted of landless agricultural laborers (*khūsh-* or *khīsh-nishīn*, literally "squatter on plowland"), who worked the land for its owners in return for some type of payment.[23]

From late Sassanian times agricultural land was increasingly held by private owners. The revolts of Mazdak and Bābak represented efforts to resist the trend, but eventually communal ownership of property was phased out. Almost at the moment that personal rights to agricultural land were established, invaders from the steppes of Central Asia brought a new concept of property and thereby partially transformed the Iranian economic system, twisting it to meet their own ends.

Economics of the Steppes

"Steppe economics" might be defined as the organization of any economic unit, such as the family or the extended household, to adapt to the demands of large geographic units called plains or steppes. Such an economic organization involves the breakdown of social and economic sections into imprecisely distinguished units in which there is only a vague sense of landed property.

The vast plain stretching through Central Asia, beyond the Ural Mountains into Russia, the northern Balkans, Hungary, and Poland was the steppe proper. The inhabitants of the steppe organized their economy differently from the peoples who lived to the west, east, and south of them in the so-called centers of civilization. In eras of great turbulence and economic dislocation, the steppe peoples brought their economic habits and organizations into the areas they invaded. Contrary to the view of many classicists, they did not entirely lose their cultural background, at least not until some of it had been fused with the indigenous cultures of the regions they settled in or took by force.[24] In Iran, the process of fusion was particularly painful because the striking geographical contrasts of the land permitted the lengthy survival of distinct and autonomous cultural units. Steppe economic traditions were retained with particular tenacity in Iran because prevailing conditions did not permit perennial animal husbandry in the same pasture.[25] The specific Iranian interpretation of this geographic arrangement into a coherent economic system was analyzed above. This section will describe what economic systems the Turks and the Mongols brought into Iran and to what extent these systems were imposed upon the Iranian economic base. In any event, it must be noted at the outset that the economic systems of either Iranians or Turks was of necessity geared to the geography and the topography of Iran.

The economy of the steppe was guided by one incontrovertible fact—that there were few distinct boundaries anywhere in the steppe. This made pastoralism, which had more flexible concepts of ownership than agriculture, a primary alternative for anyone seeking a living there. Yet agriculture was never entirely ruled out as a means of producing a livelihood. In fact many of the tribes which were considered primarily pastoral engaged heavily in it in order to supplement their diets.[26] Wherever agricultural settlements wished to proliferate and become productive, it became necessary to establish a definite set of boundaries, or at least roughly defined buffer zones. Down through the seventeenth century, agriculture in northeastern Iran—Khorāsān—suffered time and again from the least economic ripple in the steppes to the north. Regions of Khorāsān could be said to be geographic extensions of the Central Asian steppes and in Safavid times were inhabited by Turkmen pastoralists. Agricultural patterns were adapted to the demands of a pastoral economy and formed a significant segment of the Central Asian economy.

The economic forms of Central Asian pastoralism may be divided into two broad categories: (*a*) multivariate resource utilization and (*b*) precipitated resource utilization. Multivariate resource utilization was an economic form adopted by steppe peoples who had no distinct region under their control. Most students of the great invasions of Europe, the Middle East, and China have mistaken this multivariate form of livelihood as "wandering," but, in reality, this method of obtaining a livelihood represented an organized, if not planned, effort to establish a means of support during a period when a particular tribe or group of tribes did not have a designated homeland or a more patterned pastoral economy. Most of the Turkic tribes that entered the Middle East in the eleventh century possessed such a multivariate economy. The drive of the Oghuz Turks into Anatolia, for example, which culminated in the Ottoman expansion into the region of Thrace in the 1360's, also retained the most distinctive elements of the multivariate economy.

Precipitated resource utilization, on the other hand, was applicable to those pastoral communities which held more or less distinct regions and possessed migration routes between summer and winter campsites which were well-established by habit or custom. In reality it is difficult to distinguish the two prototypes since each unit residing in the steppe was constantly in flux and the situations of the tribes or other communities relative to one another changed rapidly and frequently. The reason any distinction is possible at all is that changes viewed along a time continuum produce different results from changes viewed along a cultural continuum. In the historical development of any tribal economy, there was at least one period when it was forced to adapt to emergency conditions. When the emergency persisted for some time, the tribe or community was forced to develop an economy which could float freely and continue to develop outside the exigencies of patterned pastoralism. The less urgent factor, that is the lack of boundaries, on the other hand, enabled specific patterns of economic utilization to be developed within more or less better defined territorial regions.[27]

Multivariate pastoralism is the fullest utilization of the economic resources of the several regions which any tribe or tribes entered in the course of nonpatterned movements away from the region(s) in which they were established previously. This required the maintenance of an economic unit as free as possible from dependence upon the land. More than one type of livestock animal (mainly cattle, sheep, goats, and camels), each a possible source of food, shelter, and clothing, was maintained in the event that any one type died out suddenly or failed to produce as expected. Raiding and large-scale warfare also played an important role since available economic resources might be insufficient owing to failure of the food supply through panic consumption, overly heavy utilization of the food supply, or the demise of the animals.[28] The wasteful extremes coincident to this form of pastoralism required that the peoples engaged in such movements stop at some point and adopt either precipitated pastoralism, or, if available, some other economic activity.[29] The military and political structures involved with this form of pastoralism were inflicted upon Iran more than once (the Oghuz invasions of the eleventh and twelfth centuries and the Mongol invasions). As soon as the effects of the initial impact of the steppe invaders had passed, those migrants who could had to establish themselves in particular economic zones, since Iran was the geographic opposite of the steppes and possessed large plains bounded by rugged mountains. Those groups unable to assimilate were pushed westward into Anatolia and Syria or were forced by economic necessity to limit their movement.

Precipitated pastoralism was a distinctive form of pastoralism which required the narrowing down of the economic variates and the field of migration. The source of food for the livestock was generally known, being secured by custom or by law. The property concept of this form of pastoralism was little more specific than that held up as the ideal in multivariate societies. The difference between the multivariate and the precipitated forms is that communities employing precipitated economic forms possessed rights to a certain more or less defined parcel of land. A vague notion of proprietary rights over the land was formulated in precipitate systems either by habit or custom and, in the more advanced stages of assimilation with subjected societies, by law.[30] The flow of economic activities began to take on a more specified channel, and relationships between different groups became more clearly defined.

The core unit of wealth in communities employing precipitated pastoralism was the amount of grain and fodder needed to support one household and usually its sheep and pack animals. Wherever such economic communities were linked with military organizations, they produced the wealth that supported the military. Just as there were specific channels of production in precipitated pastoralism, there were also specific, traditionally established patterns of migration and cohabitation on the land with agriculturalists. Multivariate pastoralism was nonspecific in these terms by its very definition and may be contrasted to more precipitated forms. Precipitated pastoralism involved semiannual transportation of all belongings and livestock to either a summer pasture in the mountains or a winter pasture in the plains.[31] It became easy for military elements outside the group or associated with the larger tribal group to which the producing household units belonged, to control the economic cycles of these migrating units in their more restricted economic activities. It also became possible for the precipitate pastoralists to focus their wealth at two points, where other economic activities such as farming, weaving, and food preparation were also located. Precipitated pastoralism was capable of permanent establishment since it employed specific patterns of transport, economic livelihood, and cohabitation on the land with agriculturalists. Multivariate pastoralism, on the other hand, was temporary by nature and possessed less concentrated aims.

The Growth and Development of Steppe Economics in Iran, 1000–1500

The Byzantine writer Matthew of Edessa notes the first attack by Turkish raiders on Armenia:

> In the beginning of the year 465 a calamity proclaiming the fulfillment of divine portents befell the Christian adorers of the Holy Cross. The death-breathing dragon appeared, accompanied by a destroying fire, and struck the believers in the Holy Trinity. The apostolic and prophetic books trembled, for there arrived winged serpents come to vomit fire upon Christ's faithful. I wish to describe, in this language, the first eruption of ferocious beasts covered with blood. At this period there gathered the savage nation of infidels called Turks. Setting out, they entered the province of Vaspuracan (in eastern Anatolia) and put the Christians to the sword. . . . Facing the enemy, the Armenians saw these strange men, who were armed with bows and had flowing hair like women.[32]

This rather graphic description of the first Turkmen raid into Byzantine-held territory marks the entry of the first group of multivariate pastoralists into the Middle East. The powerful terms in which Matthew of Edessa portrays the Turks is indicative not only of the reputation the Turks had established for themselves by this time but also of the violence that actually accompanied this and other raids. These bands of raiders and freebooters were "composed of horsemen equipped with bows and arrows who wore clothing of skins and wool and who moved about practically unencumbered by impediments, although they kept their herds close to them. An example of this kind of warrior is the group of 200 men who in 1038 captured the town of Nishapur under the command of Ibrāhīm Īnāl."[33] Soon afterwards, the troops of Tughrūl Saljūqī entered Nishapur, taking it from Ibrāhīm Īnāl. The soldiers of Tughrūl bore armor, and C. Cahen, in the article cited above, has taken this as an indication of the first appearance of armor among the Oghuz.[34] The notion that wild raiders could suddenly become organized and disciplined troops is incorrect. The people Ibrāhīm Īnāl led were desperate, rootless individuals, that is, multivariate pastoralists, who were searching for a livelihood. The raiders who entered eastern Anatolia and are mentioned by Matthew of Edessa were also desperate people who had been pushed first to the south and then to the west.[35] Overcrowded conditions on the steppes and irreconcilable conflicts between power elites ruling in Central Asia had forced the uncontrolled migrations which burst forth into Iran in the early eleventh century. There were too many peoples claiming rights to and attempting to use the same sources of livelihood, the same pastures, and the same water supplies. Of the competing parties, some or many groups would lose, fall into the conditions of poverty, and be forced to move out. Those who won out were best able to control pasture and water rights. Their control of other sources of wealth enabled them to build up armies with more sophisticated weapons and trained soldiers. With them they edged out their less fortunate competitors. The echoes of this unrelenting competition for economic stability in Central Asia are recorded in the oral epics of *Dede Korkut*, particularly in the story of the rebellion of the Outer Oghuz.

This story relates how the Outer Oghuz revolted because Salur Kazan had allowed the begs of the Inner Oghuz tribes to pillage his tent and carry off its valuables before they arrived. More than any other in the *Dede Korkut* cycle, this story passes on the memory of that great economic emergency which initiated first the southerly and then the westerly movement of many tribes which could no longer compete.[36] The wealth of the steppes was seized by those best able to defend their right to it since there were no distinctive geographic boundaries to aid in the task. The conflict over economic resources was recorded by the anonymous author of *Ḥudūd al-'Ālam*, who on one occasion states that the Kimäk and the Oghuz shared the same territory which was the winter pasture of the Oghuz and the summer pasture of the Kimäk.[37]

The Mongol invasions of Iran were no less destructive than the early incursions of the Oghuz since the Īl-khān leader brought not only his army, but also his royal flocks, herds, and family as well as the flocks and families of his troops. The scale of migration seems to have been less extensive than that of the Oghuz earlier, including the movements of actual Mongols. Only such groups as the Jalāyir and the Hizāra Mongols established definitively pastoral economies within the conquered regions. A host of Turks, mostly Oghuz, plus other assorted elements, made their way into Iran after being dislodged by the Mongols. It was these groups which spread out in every direction, using the economic resources of the region to their own benefit and subverting the rights of agriculturalists and precipitated pastoralists to their own. These Turkish movements through Iran were recorded in the numerous legends which ascribe Mongol origins to such tribes as the Qājār and the Afshār.[38] The story in Āşıkpāşāzāde's *Tārīhī* about the Kayı origins of the Ottomans also draws from the memory of those times even though it is falsified. Āşıkpāşāzāde states that the ancestor of Osman I was forced out of the region of Māhān in Khorāsān by the Mongol attacks, that from there he moved across Iran into Iraq and finally into Anatolia.[39] While the genealogical relationships portrayed in these stories are falsified, they all represent actual occurrences, the base of which was the full-fledged establishment of these tribes as an accepted sector of the Iranian economy (and, in the case of the Ottomans, as the major ruling sector of the Ottoman Empire).

The assimilation of the Turkish or Turkic-speaking tribes into the Iranian economic system did not mean the total loss of the old economic concepts brought from Central Asia. The iqṭā' system was being formed before the Saljūq conquest of Iran, but the Saljūqs developed and molded the system to meet financial exigencies in a particularly Central Asian manner. Iqṭā' administrative units developed from the need of the Saljūq army to support itself; the soldiers, their families, and whatever livestock they possessed, especially war-horses. Although the lowest common denominator of the system was called by various names in different periods–iqṭā', *tīyūl*, *tīmār*, or ūlkā, all were units of wealth "cut off" from the revenues of the state to support a soldier or several soldiers and to provide whatever they needed to maintain a livelihood and a military institution. Sometimes the grants of these administrative units involved the concomitant grant of pasture rights. Sometimes the latter were given out separately, but as time passed, the two rights appeared to be intertwined, since the soldier necessarily had to support his war-horse. One of the clearest indications that ūlkās were handed out for the purpose of supporting animals, particularly animals used for military purposes, is found in a chronicle written early in the reign of 'Abbās I. Its author states that the holders of nonmilitary soyūrghāls (exempt holdings) were now responsible for the payment of the tax known as the *qaimat-i asp* ("horse-value").[40] The abstraction of the Central Asiatic system of land allotments discussed in Chapter 2 is clear and obvious in this arrangement. The equivalent of a certain amount of pasture land was used as the unit of taxation. Pasture land was not, however, actually given to the soldier.

The survival of this particular administrative tradition into Safavid times and later was no mere accident, and the interrelationships involved were not merely the formal survivals of bygone institutions. Turkic invaders from the steppes had brought concepts of economic organization which they imposed upon that part of the countryside where the land and the topographic layout permitted their importation. In some cases the same economic norms were imposed upon the subject peoples who in consequence were forced to abandon village-centered pastoralism for the precipitated forms of pastoralism. In other cases, where tribes using precipitated pastoralism also tended the flocks and herds of villagers in their areas, an economic void had to be filled, and, as a result, the pastoralists were annihilated, forced into settlement, or deported to other regions in later times. The Afshār tribes of Kūh-Gīlū long had the responsibility of caring for the flocks of their Kurdish, Arab, and Lur affiliates in the region.[41] When in the Safavid period a major portion of the tribe was forced to resettle very far to the north around Lake 'Urūmīya, the Lur tribes of the area were forced to fill the void by taking their own animals to summer pasture in the mountains. Since the migration route was very long, the steppe system of migration was employed rather than the Iranian method of establishing two villages.[42] The distinction between the two forms of economic organization did not represent "national" differences, but differences based upon the distinct cultural experiences and developmental backgrounds of Iranian communities and Turkic-speaking inheritors of the modes of life brought in from the steppe at various points between the early eleventh and the fourteenth centuries.

Even though the continuity of the steppe economy is evident from the above, economic life must not be viewed as a static existence. Once the initial shock of invasion had passed, the multivariate groups, having encountered apparently insurmountable obstacles and having used up all the temporary resources available to them in that area, were forced to restrict their activities and formulate economic patterns which belonged distinctly to precipitated resource utilization. Multiple possibilities continued to be followed wherever they existed, but pastoralism continued to form the basis of the economy. All resources within a specific region were used to their utmost on a calculated time cycle. Multiple variates were not adopted beyond this specified region unless economic difficulties forced the consideration of outside economic activities, including raids, full-scale wars of conquest, or full migration outside the area.

No specific timetable can be given for the assimilation of the steppe economy into the broader Iranian economy. Invaders and future settlers moved into Iran in waves. The Oghuz invaders of the early eleventh century moved through Iran as if through a sieve and then went on into Anatolia. One large group of Afshār tribesmen remained in Khūzistān and Kūh-Gīlū, where they on occasion resisted Saljūq authority.[43] Other Oghuz groups moved into the area around Lake Van, to northern Syria, and northern Azerbaijan. In 1185-1187, one-and-one-half centuries after the initial Oghuz invasions, another large party of Oghuz emerged from Central Asia and eventually established themselves in Kermān province.[44] One-half century later, the Mongol invasions began, causing another large movement of Turks and some Mongols into Persia. Then, within another century, the followers of Timūr-i Lang followed their leader into Iran. In this way niches in the pastoral ecosystem of Iran were slowly filled by the surplus labor of Central Asia. Even as late as the sixteenth century, the Yaḳa and Ukhlū tribes (the Yomut Türkmen) took possession of the steppe bordering upon Astarabad and became a buffer between the Üzbeks and the Safavids.[45] Eventually, once this movement ceased, both in terms of specific tribal movements and the general pattern of movement, a new and integrated economic system was established in Iran. This new economy was a cross between the economy of the steppes, imported from Central Asia and implanted wherever conditions warranted, and the Iranian agriculture-based economy. A whole series of interrelationships grew up between both sectors as the pastoralists settled more securely into precipitated patterns. It must be noted here that the conversion was not total. In many regions, control of the pastoral activities remained in the hands of the Iranians who continued to send their animals to distant pastures. Where Central Asian pastoralists were forced to stop their journey and abandon multivariate economic pursuits over a long range, they adopted the more restricted prerogatives required for settlement and cooperation with the villagers. The fused system that resulted possessed distinctive characteristics.

When settlement into a specific economic pattern was achieved, the pastoralist became a counter of wealth, responsible for producing the necessities of life, such as food and clothing, which were then exploited by the leaders of the group(s) and their families. These leaders might be responsible for providing a percentage of the income to someone in a position higher than themselves, and so on through the chain of authority. The whole of Persia was a network of these chains, but the income flow upward was scarcely regular and never the total of what was required. Percentages of the income were taken out by those in intermediate positions through lawful and unlawful means. Some beneficiaries were permitted to keep the total income of the economic unit(s) granted them while others were required either by law or by the command of their superiors to pass on a portion. Pastoralists, like villagers, were now the lowest common denominator in the system, and when they, in cooperation with villagers and local authorities, refused to pass the wealth on or were unable to produce a surplus, the political system, which was dependent upon that wealth, had to take extraordinary measures up to and including extortion or was forced into breaking apart the field of its control among local authorities. Since the problem was chronic, an intermediate layer of subrulers, both military and nonmilitary, administered the wealth at a point closer to its source in order to obtain part of it for themselves as repayment for their services. This network has been labeled the *amīr-ayyān* (lit., 'amir-merchant') system,[46] but it included more than just the amirs and the wealthy members of the mercantile community. Persons who did not fit these categories headed such units of production both on a small and on a large scale. The proliferation of smaller units was particularly noticeable in border zones, where the governments of the interior had little control over economic matters. Nonetheless the amirs did form a rather large plurality within the system, partly because they possessed the might to enforce their wishes and partly because they held a powerful economic position in relation to the economic counters which they controlled. Some of the amirs were descendants of early Turkish invaders, others were Iranian, such as the Sharvanshāhs, whose line extended back into pre-Islamic times, or such as the Safavids, while still others were Kurdish, Afghān, or Baluchi. In any event, the network of control did not belong to one "class" (amīr-ayyān) or one particular ethnic group. The same fuzzy areas found in the network as a whole tended to be repeated in the smaller units as well, including the qizilbāsh uymāqs of the Safavid period.

The qizilbāsh tribes were the successors of the Turco-Mongol tribal chieftains who had ruled Iran in the preceding centuries. In many cases there were direct genealogical links with the chiefly families which had formed part of the Āq-Quyūnlū and Qarā-Quyūnlū tribes. Most notable among these were the Mauṣillū branch of the Turkamān uymāq, the Purnāk branch of the same uymāq, and the Qājār tribe, all of whom had intermarried heavily with the Bāyandur tribe.[47] These qizilbāsh chieftains, from whatever family they came, represented the more or less final cementing together of Central Asian and Iranian traditions and systems. In many ways they were the originators of economic bonds which continued to exist down to the beginning of the twentieth century, even though in later times there were changes in certain parts of the system. They represented a zenith in the development of the various Iranian ecosystems where steppe pastoralism had transplanted village pastoralism. They performed the function of organizing the economic efforts of the producing elements, often in a harsh and exploitative way, to their own personal benefit, but, without them, the segments they controlled would have degenerated into economic chaos. In order to reduce the harshness of their exactions and to weaken their control over the economy of Iran at its most local levels, 'Abbās I attempted to remove them to isolated posts to separate them from their traditional holdings,[48] but the newcomers in each district eventually took up where their predecessors had left off. No matter how successful 'Abbās I had been, the exigencies and the pluralities of the economic and topographic organization of Iran made control, of necessity, a function of many, not just a few or even one.

The Qizilbāsh "Household" as the Unit of Organization

To this point, the examination has centered upon the gradual merging of steppe and village economic systems into one coherent whole. Since society was hierarchically organized, however, the economy also had to follow suit. It was not possible to have a centrally planned or centrally controlled economy. Control was difficult enough on the local level, as will be seen shortly. The denominator used to express the hierarchical utilization of the economy was "household" and, despite certain difficulties, the same term is used here for qizilbāsh holdings to mean (*a*) the institution required to manage the productive forces and (*b*) the total of all the productive forces subject to the command of the qizilbāsh chieftains. The term must not be construed in the sense of the Greco-Roman ideal as it was passed on to Muslim scholars. The qizilbāsh household was a part of the economic reality it sought to control, not an ideal system.

An idealized version of the concept of household may be found in the *Akhlāq* of Nāṣir al-Dīn Ṭūṣī. The significance of Ṭūṣī's reasoning is not the degree to which he echoes the traditions of the classical scholars he emulated through Muslim continuators, but the degree to which he portrays the household as more than a physical plant, as a particular combination of "wife and husband, begetter and begotten, servant and one served, possessor of property and property itself."[49] He attempts to reflect the reality of the society in which he lived. The term he uses to express this sum of relationships is *manzil*, and, taken on the most apparent level of meaning, he portrays the physical ordering of affairs among the members of the household.[50] Even though he expresses the sets of relationships in ideal formulae, he indicates the hierarchical systems which composed the sinews of the actual "households" he perceived in his own time. The household organization he describes can also be construed as a model of government. This is most significant for the present study since the qizilbāsh household was often a combination of private enterprise and public institution. The techniques of ruling provinces or segments of provinces (*ḥukūmat*) might be considered an offshoot of the techniques used to manage the household (*ḥikmat-i manzilī*). In Safavid times the governors of provinces and smaller economic and/or administrative units were called ḥākims in their roles as private and as public administrators of their regions. An example of this can be selected almost at random from any Safavid source. The image of 'Abbās I at work in his palace, Chihil Sutūn, after his assumption of power clearly shows that he considered himself the orderer of affairs almost as if they were private matters. His palace was a private residence, and great pains were taken to prevent outsiders from entering it.[51] The qizilbāsh chieftains, his subordinates, were also the heads of private institutions of distinctly smaller proportions, and the dispensation of these private institutions depended upon the good will of the shah and their ability to maintain independent economic organizations.[52]

Sound economic theories backed Ṭūsī's conceptualizations of the household as the basic unit of the economy. The aim of the regulator of the household (*mudabbir-i manzil*) was to maintain an equilibrium (*i'tidāl*), a concept Ṭūṣī ultimately derives from Neoplatonism.[53] On the most mundane level of interpretation, Ṭūṣī sets forth the soundest business practices when he points out that no particular economic unit can remain totally self-sufficient but must achieve a balance of income and expenditures before an economic balance can be achieved. This concept leads Ṭūṣī to formulate another idea based on the term "i'tidāl" in its meaning of "moderation." For him the household in its most extended economic form was an institution in which an economic surplus was produced, distributed, and consumed. Ṭūṣī states in a rather fatuous manner that the role of helpers or servants was to help maintain the process of food production.[54] Ṭūṣī's model is still dangerously close to the concept of *oikonomos* in Greek and Western thought.[55] The similarity of the Classical and the Persian systems is evident from the fact that both endeavor to maintain the economic organization in an hierarchical fashion.[56] Of course the two economic approaches differed both in time and in place as well as in forms of labor organization, concepts of property, and in actual terms of production.

The Classical Western and the Persian approaches to theories of economic organization differ most conspicuously in the conceptualization of things to be regulated. Western thinkers have always regarded pastoralism as an extension of the agricultural function. Very few modern economists have perceived pastoralism as a subject worthy of a separate discussion.[57] The qizilbāsh, like any other minister of wealth in Iran, perceived or utilized a system in which pastoralism played a significant but separate role. The chieftain's household was the exploiter of both agricultural and pastoral societies and the link of both to the market place.[58] The total sum of these functions was the household proper.

Evidence that the qizilbāsh households linked marketplaces in the urban areas, the communities of precipitated pastoralists, and agriculturalists in the hinterland may be found in documentary sources and in the chronicles. Qāḍī Aḥmad Qumī continually refers to the domiciles that the great amīrs retained in the capital city and to kārvānsarāīs that some possessed along major highways.[59] These impressive dwellings were combinations of economic centers (in the capital city often located near the bazar), fortresses, centers of education and the arts,[60] and living quarters for the amīr, his family, his allies and protégés, and their households. In the provinces, where the qizilbāsh chieftains were the local governors, the household took on an impressive military character. When, as was frequent, the citadel was located in lightly or nonurbanized areas, the fortress served as both market and military strongpoint. A real "command" economy was formed, in which the consumption patterns of the ruling group(s) and their supporters were dispersed among the production units themselves. The lists of dues and levies frequently encountered in documents from the Safavid period attest to the existence of thirty-odd, and perhaps more, different tax levies, of which a major portion permitted consumption on the spot of both perishables and nonperishables.[61] The administrator of these smaller provincial units had to travel constantly in order to be effective. As a result the economic surplus was continually drained out of the local economies in support of these provincial institutions. An indication of this support in monetary terms may be seen in the array of provincial offices listed in *Tadhkirat al-Mulūk*,[62] which gives the relative support allotted to each district and the number of service troops permitted each commander. The data provided are useful not as absolute figures, but as relative consumption indicators required for the maintenance of the institutions in each district. It should be pointed out that actual consumption rates were probably higher, because the figures represented the amount needed to support only the "service" contingents. The private armies, or "non-service" troops each chieftain maintained were financed by dues paid him in his role of landlord or proprietor of his district. Extraordinary levies were legally required in certain areas of the chieftain's ūlkā, while other areas might be immune.[63] Amīrs located in remote spots, or other chieftains revolting against central authority, often levied extraordinary taxes where they were not allowed to do so. Amīra Sīyāvash Khān Ṭālish, ḥākim of Khalkhāl, and his ally Ḥamza Khān Ṭālish made illegal demands upon the resources of the village, and their treatment of the region was so harsh that the economic organization of the village was wrecked.[64] Consumption of this type, even on a medium scale, did not permit the development of a central economic system and militated against the formation of larger communities.

The scattered nature of the economy limited the availability of resources, even to the royal family. In 996/1587, ʿAbbās I could not grant a number of amīrs regions to administer, so he bestowed *anʿāmāt*, ("consignments of movable or precious wealth") upon them. The number of landless qizilbāsh amīrs must have been extremely high at all times due to the "scatter" phenomenon, since innumerable amīrs were forced into the service of others in order to make a living.[65] One crass means of advancement to higher positions was to murder opponents. Yaʿqūb Beg b. Ibrāhīm Khān Dhu'l-Qadr had been a landless amīr at ʿAbbās I's court until he killed his uncle, the ḥākim of Shīrāz, for his part in the attempted assassination of the vakīl in 1588. His reward was the post his uncle had held at Shīrāz as well as his uncle's possessions and family.[66] Such fratricidal conflicts were common in the sixteenth and seventeenth centuries. In 946/1539, the ḥākim of Shūshtar, Mehdī Qulī Sulṭān Arashlū revolted against the rule of Ṭahmāsp I, thus threatening the power and influence of his brother, Sıvındık Beg Arashlū qūrchībāshī. His brother's reaction was to send an army under the command of his own son, sieze Shūshtar citadel, and order his brother killed.[67] A power struggle between different branches of the Kermān Īnāllū had been developing during the course of the sixteenth century. The descendents of Valī Khān Īnāllū emerged the victors.[68] While control of the urban market systems was at the core of most of these struggles, the major reason for their length and complexity was the inability of the parties to agree on the apportioning of the isolated units of production/consumption in the hinterlands.

The households of the qizilbāsh chieftains were also centers of employment for numerous individuals not involved in military affairs. To some extent this was because they emulated the royal court, but it was also because the wealthiest chieftains always needed more Persian administrators and servants to help administer their large estates. The household of ʿAlī Qulī Khān ʿAbdillū Shāmlū, beglārbegī of Hirāt to 996/1588, was a fine instance of such an organization. His house was a state within a state as was indicated by his marriage alliances with potential enemies of the Safavid government. He was married to the Georgian princess Hūrī Khān Khānum[69] and to Jān Āqā Khānūm, the daughter of Murād Beg b. Dānā Khalīl Bāyandur Qājār.[70] The one-time wealth of the beglārbegī of Hirāt is not indicated in the *Tadhkirat al-Mulūk*, which assigns one of the lowest income standards to that district.[71] The household of ʿAlī Qulī Khān led all the qizilbāsh households in sheer wealth and power. Few qizilbāsh chieftains possessed so many highly placed and well-paid servants as ʿAlī Qulī. He even had a librarian, Yūl Qulī Beg Shāmlū. The very existence of such a personage indicates that the ruler of Hirāt not only possessed an extensive library which required a librarian, but they held an important place in the cultural life of Iran, both as patrons and as producers of artistic and scientific works.[72] In their role as the governors of a crucial province, the Shāmlū also possessed a dīvān consisting of several vazīrs led by a *dīvān-begī* ("head of council of state").[73] In addition, 'Alī Qulī Khan had a *sufrachī* (keeper of the table and of the dining cloth), whose function was to supervise the proper provisioning of the household and the storage of food. 'Alī Qulī Khān's sufrachī, Dūra Beg "Kirāmī," was also responsible for supervising service at dinner and perhaps for providing entertainment as well, since he was a musician.[74] Numerous other servants of both low and high rank also served the Shāmlū chieftain since he maintained more than one fortress in the city of Hirāt, as well as innumerable other foundations. A blow to the power and wealth of the Shāmlū was meted out in 966/1588, when the Üzbeks took Hirāt by storm and reduced the power of the Shāmlū.[75] Even earlier, however, the Ustājlū had defeated the forces of 'Alī Qulī Khān and had forced them to submit to the rule of 'Abbās I.[76] Other great chieftains also possessed households of similar proportions. The ḥākims of other large cities such as the Dhu'l-Qadr governors of Shīrāz had their own vazīrs down through the early part of 'Abbās I's reign, when Fārs was turned over to the administration of the household of 'Abbās I, who appointed a slave administrator.[77] Other officers dependent upon the ḥākims of great urban areas included the holders of tīyūls in rural districts, the kalāntars, *dārūgha*s ("provost"), *'āmil*s ("tax collector"), and kadkhudās.[78] They were not members of the governors' households in any physical sense, but since they oversaw the collection of taxes which were partly or wholly destined to remain in the hands of the governors and their retainers and since they regulated affairs in the marketplace in the name of the governors, they were an extension of the ḥākims' personal administration.[79] These local officials were, however, "chosen by the local population" and functioned in their behalf just as much as they represented the local chieftain.[80] Such officials were also active among groups of pastoralists and in the villages. The heads of migrating tīras were often entitled kalāntar, or more commonly rīsh sifīd (or its Turkish equivalent, āḳ saḳāl). Each village had a leader responsible for administering affairs in the name of the chieftain. The village headman was also called kadkhudā or rīsh sifīd. Like their urban counterparts, these officials were responsible for regulating local economic matters.

Very little precise information is available on the productive forces controlled by the qizilbāsh. No precise ledgers or other such business accounts have survived, if, indeed, they ever existed. Students of the Medieval European or Early Modern European economic systems are blessed with an abundance of primary materials. In some instances records of ancient Persian economic matters have survived in finer detail than records for the period after the Mongol invasion (down through the eighteenth century). The full extent of the economic foundations under the control of the qizilbāsh chieftains is uncertain. To assume that 'Abbās I was able to place strict limitations on their political power by curtailing their economic powers is not warranted.

Only the greatest amirs were affected by his actions. The vast majority had been and continued to be the possessors of small or medium-sized estates in rural areas remote from great market centers. Amīrs of the stature of Amīr Khān Mauṣillū, Sıvındık Beg Arashlū Qūrchībāshī, 'Alī Qulī Khān 'Abdillū Shāmlū, or Murshid Qulī Khān Ustājlū were rare. Most qizilbāsh always had to seek the support of some great personage or institution.[81] The most common form of dependence was that of a lesser amīr upon a greater one. Süsenī Beg Mauṣillū, a distant relative of Amīr Khān, had been forced into the service of another chieftain: "His [Süsenī Beg's] beginnings came as the greatest of the shah's qūrchīs. Each one of the qizilbāsh champions knew him as a brave man, but, finally, as the result of the persistent use of wine and opium, and much gambling, he had to sell his services as a professional guard to other begs, and his life was spent in this manner."[82] A cluster of impoverished or middle-income retainers assembled around the greatest chieftains. A rather large body of independent border chieftains with no specific (genealogical) relations with qizilbāsh families were assigned to the guardianship of one or another of the uymāqs. These chieftains went under the general name "qazāq" or "qazāqlār."[83] In 920/1514, Valī Khān Beg-i Qazāqlū was one of the Turkamān amīrs who participated in the battle of Chaldiran.[84] 'Alī Khān and Shamsī Khān, both chieftains of Qarā Bāgh and qazāqlār, were enrolled as Shāmlū chieftains even though they were not even remotely connected to the Shāmlū.[85] A set of Persian clients (*mavālīs*) also were dependent upon the great chieftains or upon the chieftain's tribes for a livelihood.[86] Whether this class was extensive or not cannot be determined exactly, but the majority of the Persian administrators seem to have advanced into the Safavid administrative system at large through the grace of a great patron. The varied systems of dependence were very extensive and included both qizilbāsh and non-qizilbāsh. The networks of dependence were signs that the economic organization could not support many independent chieftains and their households. There were a few powerful qizilbāsh masters who exacted loyalty and obedience from a large mass of both Turkish and Persian subjects of every degree and rank. The changes wrought by 'Abbās I were the result of the need to curb the growing power of his greater amīrs. In order to do this he weakened the chieftains by forcibly deporting those dependent upon them to other areas of Iran, by attacking them militarily and destroying their institutions, and most of all by imposing a class of new administrators over their heads and forcing them to become dependent upon them in their own turn.

The series of relationships between lesser and greater chieftains is only a sign that the productive forces within the diverse sectors of the Iranian economy were not strong enough to support a large class of independent military chieftains. Even where the qazāqlār existed, the phenomenon was due less to continuous economic stability than to their ability as chieftains to manipulate political loyalties to their own benefit. Wherever income figures exist, as in

Tadhkirat al-Mulūk, they probably represent standards of payment rather than actual payment, and therefore signify only the relative standing of each group. Even if the figures represent actual payment, there is not enough other data on the basis of which a continuum can be devised.

The Organization of the Qizilbāsh Command Economy

The qizilbāsh uymāq system might be termed a "command" economy, that is, an economy based on the real or imagined necessity of maintaining a military organization. A command economy was not a military despotism, but rather the subjugation of local economies to the economic needs of the military institution.[87] In such an economy the market may either be concentrated in one particular locality or it may exist in a more dispersed form. The greatest qizilbāsh houses were able to gain control of some part of the central markets in the cities. The Ilyās-oğullari were able to maintain the Dhu'l-Qadr hold over Shīrāz for almost a century.[88] The Shāmlū held on to Hirāt despite the policy of 'Abbas I. The majority of qizilbāsh chieftains were not able to utilize the centrally located market systems in the cities but were forced to adopt a different consumption pattern.

The dispersed market of the nonurban areas of Iran consisted of innumerable, localized economic units, the pastoralist and the agriculturalist societies, which had no means of forming an extensive economic association. The degree to which the market was scattered over the countryside varied from region to region, and, even though the ideal of the producing units was self-sufficiency, the inability to remain at a constant level of economic independence required the formulation of some small, but inconstant markets. The continual lack of an organized, centrally located market system was accounted for by the mode in which the predominant sector of the local economy, the landlords and their retainers, exploited the wealth of their regions.

Taxation was a mode of consumption rather than a means of obtaining revenues for the support of the state (table 1). Even the central government was nothing more than a consumer. The position of the provincial and the central governments as both public and private institutions made a public revenue system almost impossible. The collection of money in such a system resembled fiscal organization, but in terms of this particular society, where the difference between public and private was shadowy, it was little more than an indirect means of consumption. A more direct means of consumption was the levy of goods, some of which were consumed directly on the spot where they were collected. Items providing for immediate use included the various services used by traveling officials and troops as well as food for humans and animals. Other levies including the requisitions of food stores and animals, were made for consumption in the near future. The chart below gives

TABLE 1

The Persian Administration as a System of Consumption

1 Levy of cash or equivalent	2 Levy of kind *a.* Immediate	 *b.* Near immediate
Ṣad-yik, 1 percent tax	*'Alāfa*, food	*murgh* (requisition of fowl
Ṣad-do, 2 percent tax	*'Ulufa*, fodder	
Ṣad-chahār, 4 percent tax	*Qunughlū*, for entertainment of envoys	*gusfand*—requisition of sheep or goats
Yārghū, levies for the investigation of crimes	*Bīgār*, forced labor	*qilān*—labor service
Kad va sar shumār, family and poll tax	*Shikār*, hunting tax	*qubchūr*—requisition of cattle
Khāna-shumār, house tax	*Ulāgh*, levies of animals for couriers	
'Aidī va naurūzī, New Year levies	*Ulām*, forced guide service	
Levies For the *'āmil*, tax collector	*Sāvarī*, presents	
'Ushr, one-tenth of the crop	*Sāchūq*, entertainment dues	
Commissions for the *ṣadr* and the *vazīr*	*Pīshkish*, gifts	
Purchase tax	*Mushtulūq*, levies for announcement of good news	
Valuation and measurement taxes and commissions for them	*Ahdāth*, production tax	
	Yāmbardār, levies for the post	
	Dast-andāz, gratutities	

Source: *LP*, pp. 102–103; the arrangement is mine.

a summation of the specific types of consumption. Some levies represented in this chart *may* belong in more than one category. Each tax, levy, or requisition has been placed in its particular category because it represents either an obvious component of that category or because it illustrates an interesting point generic to that category. The various percentage taxes and *'ushr* (one-tenth of the crop) obviously represent levies taken in kind, but since they were not intended for immediate or near-immediate consumption, they have assumed the form of a cash equivalent. Any of the other taxes or levies in column 1 could have been collected in kind, but unless the official demanding it wished to consume his tax on the premises (in the form of food, fodder, clothing, or other items), it was usually taken in cash or the equivalent of cash.

Table 1, col. 2*a* represents items consumed on the spot by officials and small parties of soldiers, of which the items *'alāfa* through *ulām*, inclusive, are the most representative types. The *ahdāth* was a levy which could be made payable in cash or kind, but it so obviously consisted in the consumption of locally produced material that it could not be considered a long-term fiscal equivalent. Both *sāchūq* and *yāmbardār* were characteristic forms belonging to this category, while the four remaining impositions (*sāvarī*, *pīshkish*, *dast-andāz*, and *mushtulūq*) were occasional levies which probably consisted of the extortion of goods on the spot. Column 2*b* contains listings which were meant for more than short-term consumption but which did not fall in the category of long-range fiscal planning or salary-distribution as illustrated in column 1.[89]

The long-term fiscal equivalents represented in column 1 were payments made in cash or in agricultural produce, though rarely, it seems, in pastoral produce (except for wool or hides), since meat, milk, and cheese were extremely perishable items. Except for *qilān*, the items of payment in column 2*b* were levies of animals on the hoof in the form of herds or flocks. The animals were kept alive and migrated with the army or the column of official travelers, and were butchered as the need arose. Requisitioned fowl were placed in cages which were strapped onto pack animals. They were not tended in the same manner as four-legged creatures. Labor service was required to tend these animals during the march and for other duties connected with the march, such as the maintenance of roads or the blazing of paths through rugged territory. Since the effective administration of each provincial unit required the administrator to travel continually throughout his territories,[90] the services provided by the levies in column 2*b* were continually imposed. Such provisions kept on the hoof, so to speak, did not require large migrations of flocks or herds, unless large armies were involved, and cannot be classified as a form of pastoralism (system of production), only as a pattern of consumption. The items in column 2*a* might be cash, agricultural produce, or pastoral produce, in short, any item destined for almost immediate consumption.

Specific figures which could indicate the rates of consumption of each item are unfortunately not available. They would give a fuller indication of the survival of steppe practices under the aegis of the qizilbāsh administrators. The combination of an administrative system originally geared to administer agriculture-oriented societies, with pastoralist societies having different conceptions of property, would lead necessarily to the creation of a hybrid point in the molding of the two traditions of economic organization into one. Physical orientations toward a form of life loosely based upon steppe patterns of production and consumption continued down through the nineteenth century, but as time went on, various tribal organizations made a fuller adjustment to the tempo of agricultural societies. The concepts of property that first arose in the steppes of Central Asia and were transferred into Iran between the eleventh to the fifteenth centuries remained as a conspicuous element of the Iranian system down to the early twentieth century. Its clearest expression and its integration into the Iranian economic system came during the Safavid period.[91]

The concept of "household" is not inappropriate in this connection since it reflects the hierarchical utilization of labor, production processes, and consumption. The only means of controlling a dispersed economy was through the smaller units such as the household (in its extended sense), not through larger capitalistic methods of organization.

Conclusions

The economic organization of Iran after the eleventh century was based upon the hierarchical control of three separate economic entities: the urban market, agriculture, and pastoralism. Pastoralism as a separate entity has existed in Iran only since the eleventh century, though it had previously been an extension of the agricultural economy of the Iranians. Between 1000 and 1400 a steady flow of pastoralists into Iran led to the development of a new economic sector. The need to integrate the new pastoral systems with the agricultural economy required the imposition upon the entire system of a new concept of property which would allow the coexistence of land-oriented properties with economic systems which emphasized the value of movable property over land. The high point in the integration of these economic organizations was the formation of the qizilbāsh institution(s) which were staffed by descendants of the Turkish and Mongol chieftains who had entered Iran in times past. These individuals were frequently poor soldiers who possessed no patrimony, while others, more fortunate, headed great households which controlled a dispersed economic institution possessing an organizational network which covered segments of the agricultural economy as well as the pastoral economy and had an outlet in the urban marketplace. 'Abbās I weakened or destroyed the greatest of these households but he could not revolutionize the rural economy of Iran without dire consequences for the agricultural base. He could not eliminate qizilbāsh administration since it integrated the two economic systems and thus, until the twentieth century, promoted the fullest vitalization of the rural production potentials of Iran.

Mercantile Development and the Reorientation of the Iranian Market System under 'Abbās I

The qizilbāsh chieftains lost their supreme position during the reign of 'Abbās I. Their economic power was broken by a series of disastrous civil wars and then by the reforms of 'Abbās I himself. The uymāq chieftains were part of a social and economic scheme that was greater than the uymāq system. Their power to resist the reforms had been sapped by the excesses of vitiating wars, and they themselves no longer had the financial means to withdraw into independent isolation or to rebel openly. During these years a new economic policy was promulgated in Iran, and, though it was never able to overcome the traditional economic systems (pastoralism/agriculture) or eradicate the economic bases of the uymāq system, it was for a time able to overshadow other activities. The new commercial spirit was marked by a number of features.

First, 'Abbās I was able to redirect the silk trade from its traditional route through the Ottoman Empire. He did this by establishing a mercantile order composed mainly of Armenians. They took the trade through Astrakhān, maintained world-wide trade connections, and acted as a professional class of merchants and traders in the international market.[92] Between 1513 and the 1620s, the trade in Iranian silk dropped enormously in Bursa, leaving the coffers of the Ottomans emptier each year.[93] Silk and other trade items were taken across the Caspian Sea to Astrakhān and from there portaged to points west. The rerouting of this trade, while it may not have saved cash, allowed the Safavid Empire to maintain an independent mercantile revenue beyond the reach of the Ottoman Empire.

The competitive economic stance 'Abbās I adopted may have saved Iran from the imperial adventurism of the Portugese, but, since it was not maintained in successive reigns, the English, French, and Dutch assumed ever more control of the Indian Ocean/Persian Gulf trade routes. As long as 'Abbās I reigned, Iranian commerce and craft industries were on a solid competitive basis with the British, French, Portugese, and Dutch. European merchants were forced to deal on the terms set by 'Abbās I, who allowed them privileges, but who was also strictly out for his own advantage.

While silk was the keystone of his new economic policies, 'Abbās realized that it alone would not enable him to retain a competitive position in the international market. He therefore cornered the trade in various other items. He outbid the Dutch, for instance, for the right to the trade distribution of

Chinese porcelain. Hand in hand with this, on the basis of Chinese models and with the assistance of Chinese technicians in the initial stages, he developed the porcelain industry of the Safavid Empire.[94] The European merchants also seem to have been interested in Persian woolens: they bought several head of "Caramanian" (Kermānī) sheep and shipped them to England for breeding purposes, a venture which apparently failed. Most items in the wool trade, though, were completely finished by the time they found their way into the hands of Europeans (either the "East India" merchants or the dealers in the European markets themselves). The buying of raw wool does not seem to have been permitted since this would have represented a profit for the qizilbāsh houses, which managed to maintain a strong interest in the wool trade. Only in the late seventeenth century and in the eighteenth did the British and French establish "factories" in Kermān and begin direct dealings for wool with the Īnāllū Afshār chiefs.[95] About this time carpets, shawls, and other wool items began to find their way to Europe in greater numbers.

The success of 'Abbās I's policies was not due entirely to any genuine "industrial revolution" even though 'Abbās I was able to initiate certain technological advancements in some industries. But, as with so much else in the fickle vacillations of trade and the oscillations of international trends, no force in either the Persian Gulf or the Indian Ocean was strong enough to prevent the success of his economic programs. Unlike the Mediterranean-embracing Ottoman Empire, Iran was not subjected to the economic imperialism of European commerce nor, as far as can be determined, was it forced into an economic slump. One might even say that the upsurge of the economic interests of the Safavid Empire was permitted by the European powers since they had not been able to establish themselves in a strong position in India or the Persian Gulf. The English East India Company was able to found its first trading post in India only in 1613, while the English and the Dutch were competing anxiously with the Portugese for the prizes of Empire. 'Abbās I appeared at a time when the Portugese were losing out to the other Europeans and before the English and Dutch could establish strong positions. As late as the visit of Fryer in the 1670s, the European presence on the Persian Gulf was directed by individual merchants with little or no loyalty to the East India Company. Many who did get to Iran were mere adventurers like the Sherley brothers, or were on official business other than private ventures like Sir Thomas Herbert, or were individual merchants seeking their own livelihood.[96] The weak presence of European imperialist ventures at the beginning of the sixteenth century enabled 'Abbās I and his immediate successor Ṣafī I (1629-1642) to nurture a strong economic system that could extract itself from the control of a tribalized rural economy. When, toward the end of the seventeenth century, European mercantilist control began to suck out many of the raw products of the area, the economic advances made by 'Abbās I and his independence from the uymāqs began to fade away. A rather unique situation was caused by the resurgence of European economic power in the Indian Ocean and the weakening of 'Abbās's reforms. Since 'Abbās had shattered the tribes, no single one of them was able to regain power. As a result the eighteenth century represented a lapse into chaos, not a "resurgence" of tribal power, as has been claimed.[97]

A second aspect of 'Abbās I's economic policies was the loosening in some areas of the qizilbāsh grip over nonpastoral economic systems, notably over urban economies. The city of Iṣfahān was suddenly transformed from a series of disconnected market areas into a uniquely unified market center. 'Abbās brought the scattered economic structure of Iṣfahān into a more unified and coherent whole by connecting the markets of the various sections of the isolated urban units into one continuous bazar.[98] The success of this urban reclamation project meant that the notables who had controlled the old, isolated marketplaces could no longer silently defy royal authority or a more centralized economic system. The Iṣfahān bazar became the core of a developing network of such bazars throughout Iran, a network each unit of which was coming increasingly under the influence of 'Abbas's economic reforms. The provincial marketplaces, however, did not fall into line so neatly as the Royal Bazar in Isfahan. The provincial notables, many of whom were also qizilbāsh, continued to control affairs in their local marketplaces. Urban economic systems were given the chance to develop independently of the control of tribal leaders, though, and this development began the process by which the uymāqs and their subtribes began to lose power and formal position within the economic superstructure of Iran. Tribalism remained a powerful factor in Iran down to the beginning of the twentieth century, but it never again assumed the major role it had during the period from the Mongol invasions to the early years of 'Abbās I. His economic policies effectively minimized and "de-officialized" the tribal leaders and the power of the forces backing them. After him, the tribes, while still important political, social, economic, and military forces within Iran, never quite found an established position within the official structure of the government. This meant that their respective positions were weakened vis-à-vis themselves and in their relationships with the newly-independent urban and agricultural communities. They sank to the same level as the entities they had so imperiously ruled.

NOTES

1 Paul Ward English, *City and Village in Iran* (Madison: University of Wisconsin Press, 1966), pp. 30-39.

2 Such works are too numerous to list here. The major authors are Gene Garthwaite and Pierre Oberling. The former is very sophisticated in his approach and has put out some fine works, but he does not go past the nineteenth century.

3 *LP*, pp. 350-358; Martin, "Seven Safawīd Documents", pp. 196-200, shows that certain areas such as Khalkhāl were as heavily involved in stockbreeding as in cultivation.

[4] English, *City and Village in Iran*, pp. 12-14.
[5] H. Bowen-Jones, "Agriculture," *CHI*, I, 592-598.
[6] SAWB, pp. 183-184.
[7] J. V. Harrison, "Minerals," *CHI*, I, 501-505.
[8] Kent V. Flannery, "The Ecology of Early Food Production in Mesopotamia," in *Peoples and Cultures of the Middle East*, ed. L. Sweet (Garden City, N.Y.: The Natural History Press, 1970), pp. 46-47; SAWB, pp. 4 ff.
[9] SAWB, pp. 45-47.
[10] Ibid., p. 153.
[11] Ralph Davis, *English Overseas Trade, 1500-1700* (London: Macmillan, 1973).
[12] Strabo, *The Geography* (Cambridge, Mass.: Harvard University Press, 1966), pp. 151-155; Marco Polo, *Travels* (London: J. M. Dent, 1926), pp. 55-57; John Fryer, *An Account of East India and Persia* (London: Hakluyt Society, 1912), II, 159-164, 369; III, 1-9.
[13] English, *City and Village in Iran*, pp. 128-134; *LP*, 350-358.
[14] A. T. Olmstead, *History of the Persian Empire* (Chicago: University of Chicago Press, 1960), p. 241.
[15] Xenophon, *The Persian Expedition* (Baltimore, Md.: Penguin, 1967), pp. 133-134.
[16] *BK*, pp. 58-60.
[17] *KhT*, p. 39. See *LP*, pp. 8-9.
[18] *KhT*, pp. 39-40.
[19] English, *City and Village in Iran*, pp. 18-29.
[20] Ibid., pp. 30-39; H. Bowen-Jones, "Agriculture," *CHI*, I, 565-598; H. Bobek, "Vegetation," *CHI*, I, 280-293
[21] "SECII", passim.
[22] A comparative study of the open-field (champion or champagne) system and the closed-field (woodland) system is very revealing. All areas of Iran had an open-field system and labor was collectively organized if ownership of the land was not. Individual ownership of an isolated plot, though not unheard of, was rare. See George C. Homans, *English Villagers of the Thirteenth Century* (New York: Norton, 1975), pp. 51-82.
[23] *LP*, pp. 2-4, 4-8.
[24] For a more detailed discussion of the ramifications of this passage, see Gy. Györffy, "Système des résidences d'hiver et d'été chez les nomades et les chefs hongrois du Xe siècle," *Archivum Eurasiae Medii Aevi*, 1 (1975), 45-154.
[25] *LP*, pp. 2-4.
[26] Otto Maenchen-Helfen, *The World of the Huns* (Berkeley and Los Angeles: University of California Press, 1973), pp. 174-178; "KSOTM", pp. 225 ff. See also R. Browning, *Byzantium and Bulgaria* (Berkeley and Los Angeles, University of California Press, 1975) pp. 30 ff, who shows that the Slavs were primarily agriculturalists in their segment of the steppe and that they were ruled by successive waves of pastoralists.
[27] *HA*, pp. 94 ff., 311 ff. This work clearly shows that economic regions in the steppes were only artificial impositions and that they frequently overlapped.
[28] "KSOTM", pp. 213-225.
[29] S. Vryonis, Jr., *The Decline of Medieval Hellenism in Asia Minor* (Berkeley, Los Angeles, London: University of California Press, 1971), pp. 258-285, has an in-depth, well-documented study of such processes in Anatolia.
[30] *TAAA*, II, p. 360, notes that according to Shari'a law, since Muḥammad Begdīllū left no male heir, at his death, his property passed to his uterine brother (برادر اعیانی).
[31] Since this method of pastoral organization was extremely common in the Eurasian steppes as well, it must be pointed out that many groups had both summer and winter pasture in the plain.

[32] Vryonis, Jr., *Decline*, pp. 80-81.

[33] Cahen, "La Tughra seljoukide," *JA*, 234 (1943-1945), p. 167.

[34] Ibid., p. 167.

[35] The movement of the Oghuz from the Altai into Central Asia is traced in C. A. McCartney, *The Magyars in the Ninth Century* (London: Cambridge University Press, 1968), pp. 242-243. The drive west eventually resulted in the establishment of various precipitated pastoralist groups in the Zagros Mountains, northern Syria, and Anatolia.

[36] *DK*, pp. 182-189.

[37] *HA*, pp. 99-100.

[38] Fasā'ī, pp. 1-2.

[39] Āsıkpāsāzāde, *Tārīhī*, 'Alī Bey, ed. (England: Gregg International Publishers, Ltd., 1970), pp. 3-4.

[40] *KhT*, pp. 41-42.

[41] *TAAA*, p. 275; *Āyanda*, pp. 597-598.

[42] Kasravī, pp. 68 ff.; *TA*, pp. 10-18; *TAAA*, pp. 500 ff., and 524 ff.

[43] *Āyanda*, pp. 597-598; *SN*, p. 33.

[44] Muḥammad Ibrāhīm, *Saljūqīyān va Ghuzz dar Kermān*, ed. Bāstānī-Pārīzī (Tehran: Tahurī, 1964).

[45] *PZP*, p. 17. The Yaḳa moved into the Astarabad steppe in the reign of Ṭahmāsp I; *TAAA*, pp. 105-106, 580, 581-583; *AT*, pp. 138-139; *KhT*, p. 46; Wolfgang König, *Die Achal-Tekke* (Berlin: 1962), pp. 11 ff.; William Irons, *The Yomut Turkmen* (Ann Arbor: University of Michigan Press, 1975).

[46] M. G. S. Hodgson, *The Venture of Islam* (Chicago: University of Chicago Press, 1974), pp. 95-112.

[47] *AQ*, passim, pp. 207-209, 210-211.

[48] "PO" (1), p. 100.

[49] Nāṣir al-Dīn Ṭūṣī, *The Nasirean Ethics*, trans. G. M. Wickens (London: George Allen and Unwin, Ltd., 1964), p. 154.

[50] The mystical conception of the household as the earthly representative of a divine order and of the head of the household as the earthly representative of God is not considered here since it is beyond the scope of the discussion.

[51] *KhT*, p. 38.

[52] *KhT*, pp. 34-35. For Ṭuṣī's statement on the combination of public affairs with private techniques, see Ṭūṣī, *Nasirean Ethics*, p. 155.

[53] The term *i'tidāl* is a complete philosophical syllogism by itself. The allegorical connotations of the word will not be discussed here.

[54] Ṭūsī, *Nasirean Ethics*, pp. 153, 155-156.

[55] M. Plessner, *Der Oikonomikos des Neupythagoräers Bryson und Sein Einfluss Auf die islamische Wissenschaft* (Heidelberg: 1928).

[56] See M. I. Finley, *The Ancient Economy* (Berkeley, Los Angeles: University of California Press, 1973), pp. 17-21.

[57] The exception is Fernand Braudel, *The Mediterranean and the Mediterranean World in the Age of Phillip II* (New York: Harper and Row, 1966).

[58] A fairly decent theoretical approach may be found in John Hicks, *A Theory of Economic History* (London: Oxford University Press, 1969), pp. 1-41.

[59] *KhT*, passim.

[60] *MK* shows the extent of qizilbāsh participation in the composition of poetry.

[61] Martin, "Seven Safawid Documents," pp. 203-204.

[62] *TM*, pp. 100-105. A fuller discussion of the implications of this revenue system follows in the next chapter.

[64] *TAAA*, pp. 299, 306, 312-313; Martin, "Seven Safawid Documents," pp. 200-201.
[65] For instance, Süseni Beg in *MK*, pp. 118-119.
[66] *KhT*, p. 39.
[67] *AT*, p. 133.
[68] *TK*, pp. 303, 372.
[69] *TAAA*, p. 135. This marriage was arranged by Ismā'īl Mirzā Safavī.
[70] *AQ*, pp. 178, 222.
[71] *TM*, p. 102.
[72] *ASh*, p. 66; *MK* no. 105, p. 107.
[73] *TAAA*, p. 1069, Āqā Beg Dīvān-Begī.
[74] *MK* no. 119, p. 122. Dūrạ Beg was himself a poet.
[75] *TAAA*, pp. 386-388; *KhT*, pp. 42-44.
[76] *TAAA*, pp. 302-305.
[77] The descendants of Ilyās Beg Dhu'l-Qadr are cited on numerous instances in the chronicles, see *TJA*, pp. 268-269.
[78] *PZP*, p. 61.
[79] "ISP", pp. 81-86.
[80] Ibid., p. 80.
[81] See the sections on intisāb above.
[82] *MK* no. 114, pp. 118-119.
[83] W. Barthold/G. Hazai, "Kazak," *EI*², IV, pp. 848-849.
[84] "PO" (1), p. 90.
[85] *TAAA*, p. 671.
[86] Mavālī-yi Turkamān was enrolled in the Turkamān tribe as an honorary member after years of service as a client, *MK* no. 129, pp. 129-130.
[87] Hicks (*A Theory of Economic History*, p. 14) states incorrectly that command economies were despotisms. A despotism was a far more effective and efficient state than any qizilbāsh institution could have been.
[88] *AT*, p. 32 (Ilyās Beg), p. 64-65 (Khalīl Sulṭān b. Ilyās), pp. 72-73 ('Alī Beg), p. 94 (Murād Sulṭān and Ḥamza Sulṭān), pp. 125-126 (Ghāzī Khān), p. 171 (Ibrāhīm Khān). Other Ilyās-oğlū governors of Shīrāz are mentioned in *KhT*, pp. 38, 39-40, 82-83, and *TAAA*, pp. 380-384 (Bunyād Khān, Ibrāhīm Khān, Mehdi Qulī Khān, and the last Dhu'l-Qadr governor, Ya'qūb Khān, who was executed in 1590).
[89] Consult: Martin, "Seven Safawid Documents," p. 204, as well.
[90] The condition of the communications system in medieval Europe was at the same or at a slightly higher level than that of the systems of communication in sixteenth- and early seventeenth-century Iran. The comments of Marc Bloch (*Feudal Society* [Chicago: University of Chicago Press, 1961, pp. 60-65]) are appropriate, but only from the vantage that similar physical circumstances required the existence of decentralized social and economic systems.
[91] If statistics are unavailable for a more scientific evaluation of patterns of production and consumption, then the study of the technologies of production and distribution are lacking even more for sixteenth- and seventeenth-century Iran and will only be studied cursorily in the next section.
[92] Fernand Braudel, *The Mediterranean*, pp. 50-51.
[93] Halil Inalcik, "The Ottoman Economic Mind and Aspects of the Ottoman Economy," *Studies in the Economic History of the Middle East*, ed. M. A. Cook (London: Oxford University Press, 1970), pp. 209-215.
[94] Hans E. Wulff, *The Traditional Crafts of Persia* (Cambridge, Mass.: M. I. T. Press, 1966), p. 149.

[95] *Farmāns* concerning the English trade, British Museum: B. M. Sloane, #1237; B. M. Harleian, #109. Jean Chardin, *Travels in Persia* (London: Argonaut Press, 1927), pp. 100 ff.

[96] Auguste Toussaint, *History of the Indian Ocean* (London: Routledge and Kegan Paul, 1966), pp. 101-149. Additional information can be obtained from A. T. Wilson, *The Persian Gulf* (London: George Allen and Unwin, Ltd., 1954), pp. 110-191.

[97] A. K. S. Lambton, "The Tribal Resurgence and the Decline of the Bureaucracy in Eighteenth Century Persia," *Studies in Eighteenth Century Islamic History*, ed. Thomas Naff and Roger Owen (Carbondale: Southern Illinois University Press, 1977), pp. 108-129.

[98] Lisa Golombek, "Urban Patterns in Pre-Safavid Iṣfahān," *Iranian Studies*, 7 (1974), pp. 18-40; Ali Bakhtiyar, "The Royal Bazaar of Isfahan," *Iranian Studies*, 7 (1974), pp. 320-322.

4

Qizilbāsh Uymāq System

An uymāq was nothing more than a great ranking system implanted within Safavid society at large. Hierarchy was the predominant postulate upon which contemporary writers such as Iskandar Beg Munshī, Ṣadiqi Beg, and Ḥasan-i Rūmlū based their perceptions of society in general and of the uymāqs in particular. They were members of uymāqs and belonged to a hierarchical world, fraught by internal divisions and internal upheavals caused by internal and external pressures.[1] The label "uymāq" should not suggest that the differences between uymāq and nontribal societies are the same as those between uncivilized and civilized communities. The similarities between uymāq and nontribal societies were indeed far-reaching since the tribal system in Iran formed part of the larger social community. The Safavid social system was fundamentally akin to European and Asiatic societies existing at that same time in that they too were hierarchically ordered, though the internal elements of these societies differed in many ways. The uymāqs were continually reordered within their hierarchical frameworks as power within the uymāq shifted from one group to another. Each uymāq was not a kinship unit, but the arrangement of several kinship groups around one or more great households. Even though the smaller units were patrilineal and agnatic kinship groupings at the core, the system in which they existed was not a kinship organization.[2] A hierarchical conceptualization of social precedence, labor, and unit organization pervaded even the lower level nuclear households which were responsible for performing various tasks and duties. When there were struggles between the upper-level households, the groups at the base of the uymāq system were drawn up into the dispute willingly at times, not so willingly at others.[3]

The Safavid uymāq system was a stratification of a certain segment of the upper layers of society–the military order–into a recognizable and clearly distinguished network of rankings. Social stratification by order "consists of a hierarchy of degrees each one distinct from the other and organized not according to wealth nor consumption capacity, nor yet by role in the process of production of material goods," but rather according to the esteem and rank associated with certain social functions.[4] The strong link between the substrata of economic formations and social position within the hierarchy must not, however, be overlooked. Individuals of high rank in the social hierarchy very definitely were landowners.[5] In this capacity and according to their own needs they organized the labor and the production system on their land. In the case of the uymāq chieftain, the proprietorship of productive forces also included the special economic category of pastoralism and pastoral production, which existed apart from the agriculturally based economies. The uymāq system generally, and its member units, cannot be considered a class system, for that can only develop in societies with a well-organized market economy.[6] While there was tension in the uymāq system between the less wealthy majority at the bottom of the hierarchical order and the ruling elite, it was not possible to organize the struggle into a coherent or meaningful opposition to the overprivileged. The bases of production and the system of distribution were too dispersed for the society to establish a consistent struggle between two dialectical extremes. V. Minorsky's view that the qizilbāsh uymāqs suddenly began to fail as the result of deliberate attempts by the Safavid rulers to break down and dilute the influence of the great tribes is inaccurate: the great tribes had always been divided into many lesser rankings.[7] The attacks of 'Abbās I upon the qizilbāsh were not, therefore, attacks upon whole uymāqs or categories of uymāqs, but attempts to divert power from the great core families of each uymāq to lesser families that would then become more independent. The belief, found in the works of Minorsky[8] and others,[9] that the uymāqs represented a class or portion of a class, is incorrect in the sense that these writers use the term "class" to designate a social demarcation that cannot be clearly marked off (in the case of V. Minorsky) or a relationship with a marketplace that was nearly nonexistent (in the case of the others).[10]

The qizilbāsh uymāq system was in essence a military order, but members of qizilbāsh families also pursued activities proper to other orders of Safavid society. As time passed, the tendency to engage in nonmilitary activities increased, and more individuals who would previously have been amīrs involved themselves in other matters. The evidence in this regard may be very contradictory, however, since those who did not receive positions within the military bureaucracy in the earlier periods worked in other capacities, but not as literati or artists, who could have recorded their activities more fully. In the early period, mainly before the accession of Ismā'īl I, some qizilbāsh were undoubtedly members of the religious, educational system, but their position in the Safavid hierarchy was an honored one.[11] As early as in the period of Shāh Ṭahmāsp, many qizilbāsh, such as Ḥasan-ī Rūmlū and Iskandar Beg-i Turkamān, may have entered government service as scribes or in some other capacity. Others, seeking alternative forms of military service, entered the corps of qūrchīs.[12] Some uymāqs even had a division of labor: one grouping of families trained and controlled the qūrchīs, another tended the provincial holdings of the uymāq.[13] Nevertheless, it is evident that a major prerequisite for the maintenance of a station in the qizilbāsh elite was military service.[14] Even more important than the military service was possession of a higher position within society at large. A particular social rank might be inherited, and more rarely as time passed, it could even be earned. The route to such a status was meritorious military service, usually in the qūrchī or qizilbāsh military establishments, both supported by *khāṣṣ* revenues (the shah's personal household income).[15]

Individuals who failed to perform military service or did not serve as military leaders were not even mentioned by the majority of chroniclers and writers (except by Ṣādiqī Beg in *Majma' al-Khavāṣṣ*). As a result there are big gaps in our genealogical information. The chroniclers and writers reported about those who served the Safavid state, about a few rebels, not, however, about their descendants when they did not serve the Safavids, and about a few qizilbāsh who eventually landed positions in the administrative structure of the Safavid state or of local uymāq institutions. With a few exceptions they did not mention individuals not in these categories.

The great void in the sources cannot be filled easily. They do, however, permit us to glean some information about individuals who would normally have been qualified to serve by hereditary links with a qizilbāsh family and who did support military institutions. In the reign of Muḥammad Khudābanda, Ḥasan Khān b. 'Abd al-Laṭīf Khān Kūh-Gīlūya Afshār became the independent ruler of part of Khūzistān and paid allegiance to no ruler, Safavid or Ottoman.[16] Qazāqlār were also mentioned on occasion, as were Jalālīs, who were reluctant to accept anyone's rule.[17] Even great qizilbāsh chieftains such as 'Alī Qulī Khān 'Abdillū, Amīr Beg Mauṣillū, Amīr Khān Mauṣillū, and Murshid Qulī Khān Ustājlū continually sought alternative outlets to service under the Safavid shah, but their endeavors were cut short and their rebellions undermined. While the chronicles record their revolts, they give little information about those individuals submerged at the lower levels of the qizilbāsh order who sought alternatives to employment in the increasingly more standardized institutions of the uymāq system. The base economic units under the control of the uymāqs (such as villages, pastoral tribes, and even urban quarters) are even less well represented. The names of individuals at the lowest levels of society are not mentioned at all,[18] and their numbers, when given, are exaggerated.

The problems enumerated above show how difficult it is to examine the organization of the uymāq system in precise terms. The blank spaces in the evidence clearly indicate that something was happening outside what was considered the norm. Individuals at the peak of their social power began to attach new and differing values to their status. This resulted in revolt. Similar changes were occurring in the degrees of society arrayed below the qizilbāsh and slave orders of Safavid society. Suddenly large numbers of rootless and dispossessed people appeared on the scene: the Jalālīs, the Shāh-savan, perhaps even the Yaḳa Türkmen in Khorāsān, all representing an influx of peoples from Anatolia and Central Asia. Their emigration to Iran caused an uprooting of the local Persian population (including many Kurds) in places like Khorāsān, Astarabad, Azerbaijan, Shirvan, and Georgia. The increase in banditry and other forms of social unrest became evident even in the ranks of the qizilbāsh, some of whom were named after rebels of the period.[19] The crises of these times are examined more fully in chapter 9. It must be noted that as time went on the uymāq system was subject to a growing imbalance that in the end made the uymāqs partially or wholly dysfunctional.

The "uymāq" of Safavid chroniclers was a collectivity of semirelated genealogical units arranged in hierarchical power relationships around a central unit—a family or clan. The particular organization developed by the qizilbāsh uymāqs represented the zenith in the tribal evolution of Iranian society.[20] The methods an uymāq used to administer the diverse regions of Iran were more complex than anything that had preceded the uymāq system since it involved a fuller assimilation of pastoral/agricultural networks into one and also because the hierarchical chains that commanded the resources of the local economies became increasingly elaborate.

The diluted nature of each uymāq came more and more to the forefront as the member groups of the uymāqs became attuned to the local communities they controlled. Some became so disparate that they disappeared in all but name. The Rūmlū uymāq almost totally ceased to exist after a brief interlude of power in the first three-quarters of the sixteenth century. Only a few individuals with the name Rumlū appeared in government service late in the reign of 'Abbās I and throughout the course of the seventeenth century. As late as 1829, a small, pastoral tribe, bearing the name "Ay Rūmlū," existed in the province of Yerevan, though its connection with the Safavid uymāq is unknown. In the nineteenth century one or two Shāh-savan *tīra*s also bore the name Rūmlū. The Shāmlū rulers of Khorāsān, who had been extremely powerful under Muḥammad Khudābanda and even under 'Abbās I, succumbed to a series of crushing defeats. Their holdings based on Hirāt had represented the highest income level of all the uymāqs and provincial governorates in the reign of Ṭahmāsp I, but by 1725 the province they had held was, before its collapse, the lowest of all revenue prospects in the Safavid Empire.[21] Groups of pastoralists and parcels of land or pasture that had belonged to the Shāmlū eventually went over to other tribal groups such as the Yaḳa, Yomut and the Jalāyir. The Afshār, Qājār, and Ṭālish uymāqs were tenacious enough to survive eras of reform and defeat, though in a mangled form, but eventually they formed new power relationships. Families, such as that of Qāsim Khān Afshār,[22] rose from the lower levels of their uymāqs to positions of leadership. These families often had little relationship to the deposed ruling families other than the fact that they had once served them.

In Iran the Bayāt tribe consisted of two subsections—the Āḳ Ūlūs (White Nation) and the Ḳarā Ūlūs (Black Nation). The Āḳ Ūlūs consisted partly of Anatolian refugees who had come to Iran late in the fifteenth and early in the sixteenth centuries to serve the Safavid family. They were located in areas along the Safavid-Ottoman border and at Hamadān. Āḳ Ūlūs chieftains controlled Kurds and other groups of Iranian speakers around Hamadān, some of whom in time came to speak tribal Turkish or Āzarī and to consider themselves either part of or subject to the Bayāt tribe. The Ḳarā Ūlūs, mainly the family of Bābā Ilyās, did not come from Anatolia, but were Chaghātaī (Central Asian) Turks who entered Safavid service at an early date.[23] Turkish nationalist scholars persist in making wholesale identifications of these tribes with Anatolian Turkish tribes who traced their ancestry back to Oghuz origins.[24] Such clearcut ethnic delineations cannot be made because the Safavid qizilbāsh drew on various sources of manpower from the beginning. Even after the order was closed, other sources of manpower were continually sought out. This was nowhere so evident as in the case of several qazāqlār chieftains who were enrolled in the Shāmlū uymāq although they definitely had no genealogical links to the Shāmlū.

If there was no blood tie between the various groupings of any uymāq, what principle of unity held them together? That is a difficult question to deal with. As has already been pointed out, the basis of political and social organization was intisāb. Within an insitāb organization, relationships often developed between individuals of different uymāqs. Another principle closely allied to intisāb was the ideal of ʻaṣabīyya, the obligations of individuals or family groups in any one uymāq to support one another according to the priorities of uymāq solidarity (*bi jahat-i taʻsub-i uymāqīyāt*). Iskandar Beg notes that Pīra Muḥammad Khān Ustājlū along with Silmān Khān b. ʻAlī Mīrza revolted in accordance with this principle.[25] Amīr Khān Mauṣillū, the most powerful cheiftain of the Turkamān uymāq, was obliged, unwillingly it is implied, to take up the cause of his harried fellow tribesman, Murtizā Qulī Khān Purnāk, beglārbegī of Mashhad, who was being squeezed out of his holdings in Khorāsān by an Ustājlū/Shāmlū alliance there.[26] A fine account of the unraveling of these ʻaṣabīyya relationships as a result of Amīr Khān's actions can be found in the book by Don Juan of Persia (Ūlūgh or Ūrūch Beg Bayāt). When in 1585 the Turkamān uymāq began a general revolt, they caught Muḥammad Khudābanda, the shah, off guard. He was busy directing siege operations around Tabrīz. Realizing this, the Turkamān chiefs moved on Qazvīn and attempted to sieze the government of the Iranian Empire. When Qazvīn was taken, they looted the city, or at least the houses of their enemies but eventually a force was sent from Tabrīz in which Ūlūgh or Ūrūch Beg Bayāt and his family served.[27] He writes in regard to the Turkamān capture of Qazvīn:

And I think I hear one who is reading this book asking for explanation of the reason as to how it came about that Qazvin, the most important city of Persia was so easily taken by foe and friend in turn. Him, my reader, I would answer quoting the Spanish proverb: "The worst thief is he who is of the household." The immense population of Qazvin, as is the case with the population of every capital city in all countries, is made up from peoples of all parts, and the Turkaman tribesmen always had many friends and relations among them. There were therefore as many hands to open the city gates to them as there might have been to close these gates against them. This, too, is why it is never possible to keep the secret of the court of one prince from the knowledge of those at the court of the prince, his neighbor, for the gate of egress must be left unclosed in the city-wall of every king's capital.

Ūlūgh Beg's house was plundered in the Turkamān sack of Qazvīn. In retaliation, Ūlūgh Beg's four cousins immediately joined the royal army to avenge their relative and themselves. When the Turkamān chieftains sent an envoy to convince them to abandon the shah's army, they reacted violently and threw the man and his party into a ditch. They were not only upholding the virtues of 'aṣabīyya by doing so, but also ensuring a mutual pact of alliance between themselves and their cousin Ūlūgh Beg.[28]

The task of maintaining a strict neutrality between the various uymāqs or subsections of uymāqs was difficult to say the least. Muḥammad Khudābanda had been very unsuccessful at holding a neutral position, thus threatening the security of his realm. 'Abbās I was extremely successful in using the means at his disposal to achieve a political equilibrium. At his accession in 1587, he executed a number of recalcitrant or culpable chieftains in his audience hall in the palace of Qazvīn. Instead of using members of the Sufi bodyguard, who were from qizilbāsh households and usually performed such tasks, he used slaves to block off all the exits and to execute designated individuals.[29] He used the slaves rather than the Sufis in order to preserve the security of the state and to relieve 'Abbās from the added pressures of dealing with civil wars between different qizilbāsh factions. The maneuvers associated with this execution indicate that the Safavid central government was little more than a great household among other households and that it possessed its own 'aṣabīyya organization and intisāb relationships outside itself with other chieftains—a relationship characterized as intisāb-i shāhī. A more precise delineation of this 'aṣabīyya organization was developed for the central government during his reign by 'Abbās I, who attempted to exclude qizilbāsh chieftains from the more important functions of the state and prevented them from expropriating the state for themselves.

The organizational unit of a qizilbāsh uymāq was the hierarchical chain descending from the khans down to the various social/economic units. Precedence of rank was an important element in retaining the equilibrium of the uymāq since too many chieftains of equal rank vied with and too frequently destroyed one another. The most powerful uymāqs possessed an office held by their most powerful individual and entitled the *rīsh sifīdī* (office of rīsh sifīd).[30] The name implies that age was an important criterion, but this was not necessarily the case. The office belonged to the head of the greatest family, not always to its eldest member. It was important that the head of the family have the experience to hold the office effectively and be young enough to pursue matters with constancy and vigor. The title of the office-holder, *rīsh sifid*, was borrowed from the designation of an oba chieftain who managed the activities of the families under his protection, notably arranging their semiannual migration and monitoring their economic productivity. This word is probably the translation of the Turkish āḳ saḳāl. The main difference between the oba chieftain and the uymāq chieftain was status—the latter had a much higher economic and social position than the former. The uymāq rīsh sifīd not only supervised the economic welfare of the uymāq, he also held the political destiny of the entire uymāq in his hands. The same political and social functions belonged to the āḳ saḳāl of an oba, but on a more restricted plane and in more mundane matters.[31]

Not every uymāq had an office of this nature because within the uymāq too many chieftains with nearly equal powers were constantly competing for positions and power. The Rūmlū, Takalū, and Dhu' l-Qadr possessed no discernible rīsh sifīd who was empowered to unite the various threads of their respective uymāqs into a workable polity. The survival of the Turkamān uymāq into the reigns of 'Abbās I and his successors was astounding indeed, since the uymāq united households (the Mauṣillū and the Purnāk) which had always been vicious rivals for the control of empire. Only the tenacity of Amīr Beg Mausillū and his grandson Amīr Khān b. Ghulābī (II) and the increasing weakness of the Purnāk was responsible for the equilibrium within the uymāq.[32] Nonetheless, Amīr Khān committed the fatal error of rebelling at an importunate time. When he was finally taken into custody by Ṣultān 'Alī Beg Bayāt even his own brothers and sons plotted with the Shāmlū and Ūstajlū enemy to assassinate him.[33] Uymāqs such as this disappeared gradually and would have disappeared even without the reforms of 'Abbās I. Those uymāqs that were too widely dispersed and in which the offices and functions of branch families were well defined tended to survive longer (for instance, the Afshār, the Qājār, and even the Shāmlū). Among the various houses designated as Afshār, the Arashlū and Gündüzlü held the office of qūrchibāshī in the reigns of Ṭahmāsp I, Ismā'īl II, (1576-1578), and Muḥammad Khudābanda. The last Afshār to hold the office was deposed in 1590.[34] A much clearer example was the Shāmlū control of the position of the *ishīk-āqāsī-bāshī* (commander of the ḥaram guard) late in the reign of 'Abbās I and in the period of Ṣafī I.[35] The ability of certain uymāqs to retain a successful hold over their own spheres of influence was not due to better cooperation between various branches or members of the same branch. Offshoots of the

Afshār managed to survive four centuries of fratricidal strife, the reforms of 'Abbās I, Nādir Shāh (1726-1747), and others, as well as the vagaries of political, social, and economic change.[36] The Qājār uymāq also outlasted innumerable changes.[37] The Afshār and Qājār tribes retained a central organization, a concept of 'aṣabīyya, and an office of rīsh sifīd or a less formal equivalent which enabled them to endure in one form or another even after the efforts of 'Abbās I and successive dynasts to drive them from positions of power and destroy them.

It has been established to this point that the uymāq was a very real part of the Safavid socioeconomic system. Most uymāqs were so disparate, however, that they functioned as power units only when certain branches were less powerful and dependent upon a central element. The power of any uymāq was maintained only as long as one of its leading members, the rīsh sifīd, maintained the prestige and power of his own position.[38] The most capable leaders maintained a fine balance within their uymāqs, distributing wealth and possessions like reigning monarchs. Few rīsh sifīds were able to sustain long periods of control. Their powers were generally delegated to people who were in theory their inferiors within the system. In fact, these individuals in lower positions had the ability to make their influence felt by withdrawing their support and therefore always retained the option of independent rule for themselves.

The account recorded by Don Juan oversimplifies the process of subordination and independence among the ranks of the uymāq leaders, but a slight hint at the dynamics of the system can be gleaned from this passage: "The Khans, though their offices are considered hereditary, for they hold them as of their own property, are liable to be dismissed by the king at his pleasure, should they anywise be found in fault, for they are but his servants; and indeed all the Khāns and governors who serve the state holding positions of importance are liable to be dismissed at any moment."[39] The real indicator of the subordination/independence syndrome within any uymāq is the size of the administrative bureaucracy serving the uymāq chieftain(s) or the rīsh sifīd. Many chieftains possessed only themselves and a body of troops (mounted and afoot). But some great chieftains, rīsh sifīds like Khān Muḥammad Chāūshlū, Ḥusain Beg Lala and his 'Abdillū (or 'Ubaidilū) descendants, Murshid Qulī Khān Chāūshlū, Manṣūr Beg Afshār (Kūh-Gīlūya) and his descendants in Shūshtar and Dizfūl (even beyond 1597), as well as other great chieftains possessed their own dīvāns over which a vazīr presided. They administered their uymāqs or segments of uymāqs as rulers and could thus attain to the political power of their superiors or to that of the Safavid state itself. Beneath these great leaders were their own sons, relatives, and unrelated branches of the same uymāq subordinate to their rule. Each of these individuals or units were at varying stages in the development of administrative organizations of their own or were a part of the already existing institution of the rīsh sifīd. These individuals, too, were viable alternatives to the rule of the rīsh sifīd. Ya'qūb Khān Dhu' l-Qadr, for instance, killed his own uncle and took over the government of Shīrāz in 1588.[40] Afshār power in the Kūh-Gīlūya region was continually in a state of dysfunction since power was shared by several groups. In 904-905/1498-1500, when Manṣūr Beg was independent sovereign of the Kūh-Gīlūya, he was the head of a highly complex, hierarchical power structure. Manṣūr Beg was the ḥākim. Beneath him were two retainers, Pīrī Beg Afshār and Ashraf Beg Afshār, who in turn had their own personal subordinates, Pīr 'Alī Beg, the governor of Sāva, Pīr Muḥammad Beg, and Qīya Beg.[41] The streamlined version of the Afshār hierarchy presented by Ḥasan-i Rūmlū does not give the clearest indication of Afshār power relationships at the time, but does show that power was arranged according to hierarchical arrays. When Manṣūr Beg affiliated himself with the Safavids three years later, he brought his whole institution into the Safavid state. Ninety years after the Kūh-Gīlūya had come into the Safavid service, the Afshār organization had become so complex, that crossed patterns of authority crippled and incapacitated the order of the Afshār household there. The sinews of the hierarchical organization had branched out into so many arrays, each competing with the others, that the means of social and economic control became entangled in the many branches and the system ceased to function effectively. The destructive civil wars of the 1580s and 1590s in Kūh-Gīlūya were the result of vicious competition among the members of the uymāq holding portions of the patrimony who fought each other for control of the entire patrimony. In the end these civil wars proved the undoing of the Afshārs in that region since, exhausted from fighting each other, they were unable to resist the efforts of the central government to implement a more direct control of the area.[42]

The independence/subordination syndrome played a very important role in the Safavid uymāq system. The uymāq might be characterized in a lopsided fashion as a system continually in a condition of dysfunction. If a power impasse did not actually exist between members of the uymāq, the threat of a standoff could always be used to obtain concessions from those holding power in the uymāq. When reconciliation became impossible, the system was cleansed by violent internecine conflict or the different branches which were at odds with one another broke apart and formed other alliances. This was the dynamic that gave the uymāq system strength. It is labeled here the "independence/subordination" syndrome. The extreme examples of this syndrome were the qazāqlār groups in Chukhur-i Sa'd, Azerbaijan, and Georgia, the leaders of which continually shifted their allegiance from the Safavids to the Ottomans and back again.[43] The term "qazāq" represented a singular way of life best described in the Köroğlu (Goroglī) stories.[44] The steppe tradition, discussed earlier in chapters 2 and 3, was well represented in the qazāq clusters which existed in the shadow areas of the Safavid Empire

These qazāqlar groups constantly shifted loyalty from one state to another, refusing, in the long run, to bow to any authority. The same impulses toward independence tore apart the large qizilbāsh uymāqs, causing them to be remolded along new lines in the late sixteenth and early seventeenth centuries. A surging compulsion toward independence among the lower level tribal groups tore away at the traditional structure of the qizilbāsh uymāqs and to some extent eradicated the intermediate steps between the Safavid government and the lower tribal groups. Higher level tribal authorities existed outside the pale of the central government and no longer performed official functions. Once the policies of 'Abbās I began to give precedence to the lower level authorities within the qizilbāsh system—that is, to those khans who controlled smaller portions of a patrimony or to those who were normally the retainers of the greater chiefs—it became evident that the lower level chiefs merely stepped into the shoes previously filled by greater personages. In some cases the local chiefs were capable of raising themselves to heights of prominence equal to that of their former masters.[45]

The other part of the syndrome, that of subordination, represented the full establishment of an equilibrium within an uymāq or segment of an uymāq, as well as a balanced relationship with non-uymāq societies subject to the rule of the uymāqs. These relationships are more clearly indicated in the subordination of chieftains acting as retainers to a major uymāq authority and in the development of an administrative system staffed by a regular bureaucracy of administrators and scribes.[46] The following chart gives the spectrum of offices available at the uymāq level. It is not intended to be an absolute format for uymāq organization, but rather a spectrum that indicates the various possibilities available to each uymāq chieftain who commanded a large household institution. These offices were not found in every uymāq, and, indeed, some uymāqs probably had offices or informal positions not indicated in this listing. A very serious lacuna in the chronicles in relation to the uymāq organization has made it difficult to provide more details than this. Even documentary evidence is lacking which could illuminate this very dank corner of Iranian history.[54]

The material summarized in the chart on the next page indicates an intermixture of Iranian social systems at an institutional level. It does not bear out the oft-repeated claim that the Turkish and Persian societies were mutually antagonistic. The main tensions within society at this time were between hierarchical units (the uymāqs and others), represented by major households governed by rīsh sifīds, and the internal tensions within the hierarchical units themselves caused by the need to maintain institutions of coercion (the offices of dārūgha, kalāntar, and the provincial governorates).

Also important, the evidence connects the uymāqs with the smaller communities at the base of the system, the obas and the villages which possessed their own internal hierarchies based upon the ownership of property and the

Uymāq Offices Rīsh Sifīd (Elder)[47]	
Office held by Turkic-speaking chief or descendants	Office held by Tājīk administrator
Ishīk-āqāsī-bāshī (commander of the ḥaram guard)[48]	Vazīr (chief administrator)[49]
Ḥākim (governor or military administrator, commander of provincial fortress)[50]	Khazīna-dār (treasurer)
Sufrachī (keeper of the table and of the dining cloth)	Various munshis and mustaufis (scribes and secretaries)[51]
Yüz-bāshī (commander of a hundred men) and on-bashī (commander of ten men) (commanders of provincial troops under the rīsh sifīds or the ḥākims)	Kalāntar (town provost)[52]
Dārūgha (provost)[53]	Kadkhudā (village head, also called āķ saķāl or rīsh sifīd)
Āķ saķāl (elder) or rīsh sifīd of migrant obas	

division of labor. The chief representative of the small community within the uymāq was the āķ saķāl, the most experienced individual in his group and the one capable of managing matters. His status was less elevated than that of the rīsh sifīd of the uymāq. The elders of these local communities were merely the chief individuals among equals, while the rīsh sifīds of the uymāqs, being high-ranking military commanders and/or administrators, had progressed far beyond such a relationship. Beneath the rīsh sifīd of the oba or village were a number of families who had entrusted the supervision of their affairs to him. During migrations, for instance, it became necessary to have the direction of one chief who was an expert at determining the best path through the mountains. More than one such guide for any one group would lead to a chaotic migration and ultimately to accidents or even death. The heads of families were the "equals" to whom the rīsh sifīd was beholden. These men, and any male relatives of the proper age who lived in their household, were the common owners of flocks or herds (and in the villages, the owners of a plot of land).[55]

The major owners of animals in the uymāq were the qizilbāsh chieftains. Their wealth as the greatest flock- and herd-owners gave them a central position in the uymāq since they were able to employ many individuals as flock tenders and shepherds.[56] Their military status enhanced their ability to control such wealth. The men and families who served them as flock tenders and preparers of sheep and animal products (wool: carpets, saddle bags, clothing; food: milk, cheese, yoghurt; and others) were supervised by the independent system:

Qizilbāsh ruling elite
  Independent flockowners
    Dependents of various types
      (*a*) heads of families owning fewer than a certain number of sheep and forced to sell their services to others
      (*b*) *Chūbāns*, who own nothing and whose main function consisted in tending the animals of others. These could be boys, young men, or villagers seeking seasonal employment.

It is impossible to say for certain whether the qizilbāsh ruling elite arose from the category below it, the independent flockowners, but it is probable that the very early qizilbāsh elite, if indeed it could have been called an elite, were independent flockowners or even dependent laborers who served the Safavid murshid. By the late fifteenth century it was evident that the murshid headed not only a religious organization, but that his followers included military chieftains.[57] During the course of the fifteenth century, the qizilbāsh network set up by the early Safavid murshids became transformed into an uymāq system, and the religious hierarchy gradually gave way to a tribal hierarchy. As the religious organization of the Safavid Order gradually disappeared, the uymāq systems, which had been a part of the system from the beginning, began to grow in importance until they actually became institutions with immense secular power within the Safavid state.

NOTES

[1] Works which treat hierarchical organization from a sociological or historical standpoint are rare. See: Roland Mousnier, *Social Hierarchies, 1450 to the Present* (New York: Schocken Books, 1873); and (*SS*), pp. 33-152. One of the best works on a case study is *CA*. The next two chapters employ a great deal of comparative material to elucidate certain phenomena in the qizilbāsh system.

[2] L. Krader, "Principles and Structures in the Organization of the Asiatic Steppe Pastoralists," *Southwest Journal of Anthropology*, 11, 2 (1955), 85-87, explains the Mongol and Turkish social organization in similar terms. Paternal descent, that is, the kinship structure, was considered like a bone (*yasun*) or part of a skeleton which was ordered and arrayed according to a particular pattern.

[3] Krader, pp. 87-89. *DK*, pp. 27-28, provides another allegorical explanation of the hierarchy at the core of the Turco-Mongol tribal system. In the opening story, Bayindir

(Bāyandur) Khān, who himself has a many-colored pavilion, distributes the Oghuz notables possessing certain qualities into tents of a certain color, each color being associated with a particular quality. The color of each tent signifies the status of each chieftain residing in it in relation to the desired quality (in this case, the possession of a male heir). Mousnier, *Social Hierarchies*, p. 23, "In India, at the beginning of the Vedic period, there were in the Rig Veda three orders of 'colours'. . . ."

[4] Mousnier, *Social Hierarchies*, p. 23. This does not mean that controls over the whole economic system or segments of it were lost to elements within the hierarchy, a point Mousnier completely neglects.

[5] *SS*, p. 85.

[6] Mousnier, *Social Hierarchies*, p. 35 capitalistic societies. See also Jacques Heers, *Le clan familial au moyen age* (Paris: Presses Universitaires de France, 1974), p. 8, and E. J. Hobsbawm, "The Crisis of the Seventeenth Century," *Crisis in Europe* (New York: Doubleday and Co., Inc., 1967), pp. 32 ff.

[7] *TM*, pp. 17-18.

[8] Ibid., pp. 14-23.

[9] Including many Marxists.

[10] See Chapter 3.

[11] *MK*.

[12] *TM*, pp. 17-19. Fewer chieftains held higher positions at the beginning of the seventeenth century.

[13] The Qarādāghlū, for instance: *TAAA*, pp. 756, 819.

[14] *Ash*, p. 64 Ṣādiqī Beg, for example, served for some time as a cavalryman in an Afshār army.

[15] Other means were probably available as well, but there are no data to support the claim that there was widespread venality of office or position in the qizilbāsh system when the intrinsic value of "being qizilbāsh" declined.

[16] *TAAA*, pp. 274-275.

[17] Ibid., pp. 791-801, for instance, for Jalālī/Kurdish revolts against Safavid rule in 1610–1611.

[18] A significant exception is the revolt of the people of Tabrīz reported in *AT*, pp. 197-198. At least two representatives of *zūr-khānas* were involved, as well as various quarter chieftains or leaders of groups of artisans or families.

[19] Whether the name Köroğlu came to have the significance it later had is not capable of being ascertained, though several amīrs possessed this name. The name Delü was also common. See: Nora Chadwick and Victor Zhirmunsky, *The Oral Epics of Central Asia* (London: Oxford University Press, 1968).

[20] The early Qājār monarchy was little more than the formation of one particular uymaq system into an imperial system. The formation of the Qājār dynasty in no way represented the final peak of uymāq development in Iran since by mid-century the old uymāqs, even that of the Qājārs, were losing their grip over their holdings. With the formation of new uymāqs in the 1880s a thoroughly Iranized tribal system developed in Iran.

[21] *TM*, p. 102.

[22] *TA*, pp. 10, 17-18; *TAAA*, p. 1018; Nikitine, pp. 72-74. In 1576-1578 Qāsim Khān b. Ṭahmāsp was made cogovernor of Mauṣil with his father. From there Qāsim eventually established control over 'Urūmīya. Until 1878 his descendants in one line or another continued to govern the area from Dim-Dim fortress and other forts in the area.

[23] So, not only was the Ustājlū uymāq a conglomeration of unrelated subtribes, but the subordinate tribe of the Bayāt was organized in a similar fashion.

[24] Faruk Sümer, *Safevi Devletinin Kuruluşu ve Gelişmesinde Anadolu Türklerinin Rolü* (Ankara: Güven Matbassı, 1976); idem., *Oğuzlar, Türkmenler* (Ankara: Ankara Üniversitesi Basımevi, 1967).

[25] *KhT*, p. 39
[26] *TAAA*, pp. 258-260.
[27] *DJ*, pp. 194-201. The quotation below is from *DJ*, pp. 200-201; *TAAA*, pp. 276 ff.
[28] *DJ*, p. 198.
[29] Ibid., p. 210; *KhT*, pp. 208-211; *TAAA*, pp. 377-386.
[30] *KhT*, p. 32; *Ismā'īl*, p. 63.
[31] For this office see: *TAAA*, p. 223.
[32] *AQ*, pp. 207-209, rivalry of the Purnāk and the Mauṣillū under the Āq Quyūnlū Sulṭāns; "PO" (1), p. 91; *SN*, I, p. 448; *TAAA*, pp. 139, 223: Amīr Khān b. Ghulābī (II) was the first rīsh sifīd of the Turkamān uymāq in the Safavid period, pp. 258-263; 'Aṣabiyya priorities required Amīr Khān Mauṣillū to defend Murtizā Qulī Khān Purnāk against the Shāmlū, p. 276, and *DJ*, pp. 175-176, describe the position of the Mauṣillū in relation to the entire uymāq.
[33] *DJ*, pp. 175-176 and *TAAA*, pp. 322-329.
[34] *AT*, pp. 130, 140; *KhT*, pp. 27, 49, 50.
[35] *TAAA*, p. 440.
[36] *TA*, pp. 1-10; Nikitine, passim.
[37] A. K. S. Lambton, "Kadjar," EI^2, IV, 387 ff.
[38] Mehdī Qulī Khān b. Alvand, a relative of Sıvındık Beg Qūrchibāshi Afshār rebelled against Safavid rule in 946/1539–1540. Sıvındık Beg considered this a threat to his position at the Safavid court and personally commanded Mehdī Khān's brother to attack Shūshtar and execute Mehdī Qulī Khān. F. Sumer, *Oğuzlar*, p. 283.
[39] *DJ*, pp. 45-46.
[40] *KhT*, pp. 39-40.
[41] *AT*, p. 11.
[42] Kasravī, pp. 68-72; *TAAA*, pp. 274-275; *KhT*, p. 76; *TA*, pp. 10-17. See the next chapter for an explanation of crossed patterns of authority.
[43] *TAAA*, pp. 671, 882. Shamsī Khān Qazāqlar became a member of the Shāmlū uymāq.
[44] For the Köroğlu epics see: A. Chodzko, *Popular Persian Poetry* (London: 1842) and *OECA*, pp. 57-60, 300-304, which relates the historical background of this personage during the Safavid period. For the Kazāk phenomenon in Middle Eastern and Central Asian border areas see: G. Hazai, "Kazāk," EI^2, IV, 848-849, which has a bibliography, as well as Philip Longworth, *The Cossacks* (New York: Holt, Rinehart, and Winston, 1968), of value even though it tends to romanticize the Slavic Cossacks.
[45] See chapters 5–8 for detailed examples of this trend.
[46] Most uymāq chieftains, notably the rīsh sifīd, were patrons to Tājīk administrators who moved up through uymāq ranks and eventually into the service of the central government.
[47] For the rīsh sifīd of a whole uymāq see: *KhT*, p. 32; *TAAA*, pp. 275-276 Afshār, pp. 358-363 Turkamān, pp. 293-295, 302-305, pp. 361-364, 366-372, 380-387 the Ustājlū under Murshid Qulī Khān Chāūshlū. For further information see: *DJ*, pp. 207-208, *KhT*, pp. 27, 42, 48-49. For the rīsh sifīd of part of an uymāq, see *KhT*, p. 34 Ḥusain Beg Shāmlū, rīsh sifīd of the 'Abdillū.
[48] *KhT*, pp. 90, 91 Mehdi Qulī Sultān Shāmlū at Hirāt.
[49] See n. 32, above.
[50] *DJ*, pp. 45-46.
[51] *TM*, pp. 85-100. Some offices listed as part of the central government were also duplicated or imitated on the local level.
[52] *VP* 2, p. 292–"le prévôt de la ville."
[53] "ISP," pp. 84-85; *VP* 2, pp. 302-303, "chef du métier."

[54] Martin Dickson, "Shāh Ṭahmāsp and the Üzbeks" (Ph.D. dissertation, Princeton University, 1958), p. 8: "Since the internal structure of the uymaq(s) is not sufficiently known, one cannot judge how open movement upward was within the ranks."

[55] Cf. Karajuk in *DK*.

[56] *DK*, pp. 47-49.

[57] *Amīnī*, p. 68, Shaikh Ḥaidar was responsible for militarizing the Safavid order.

5

Formation of Qizilbāsh Family Estates and the Decline of Qizilbāsh Power

The Ṭālish Chieftains

In the qizilbāsh system the notion of family was important among the ruling elite. The nuclear or stem family was for the qizilbāsh, far more meaningful than the tribal organization. Indeed, sometimes the family became too unwieldy and its members placed their own personal fortunes ahead of the fate of the family unit. The familiar conceptualization of the uymāqs as solid, unbreakable units organized on a tribal pattern was not feasible. The dispersal of familial or patrimonial power over broad stretches of territory did not permit such perceptions as 'asabīyya to be practical or enforceable methods of organization, even on the level of the nuclear family. The adoption of Persian administrative systems and the fusion of Mongol and Turkic administrative elements with the Persian administrative organization enabled familial rule to maintain a more stable position within Iran. Nonetheless, a combination of purely social and economic phenomena (as described in chapters 9 and 10) with a flourishing steppe mode of organization did not permit family rule in Iran to remain stable for very long. Short periods of social and perhaps economic stability ended in violent whirlwinds of destruction time and again as stability enabled the ruling families to grow in size. With more people sharing the same or nearly the same amount of produce and revenues, it was not possible to maintain unified rule over the family domain. Iranian history is filled with such cycles of growth and decline leading to an increase in the size and number of ruling families, collapse of the revenue base supporting the ruling houses, and the breakup of the families into smaller units more easily supportable by the revenue-producing substrata of society. These cycles predominate from the Saljūq period on, but they grew vicious after the Mongol conquest. The weakening of the Persian administrative tradition and the molding of that tradition to fit Turco-Mongol concepts of family rule were partly responsible for the worsening of these cycles of growth and decline. One of the most violent episodes in this long history of growth and sudden reversal was the disruption of the Āq Quyūnlū domain. Power was distributed among such a wide spectrum of individuals and families that there was no way the Āq Quyūnlū sulṭān could extricate himself from the disarray of families and individuals seeking to protect their own rights and powers. In the second half of the fifteenth century, from the individuals and families surviving the Āq Quyūnlū civil wars was formed the nascent qizilbāsh system.[1] As long as power was concentrated in the hands of a few individuals, it was possible for the new qizilbāsh elite, survivors in part of the old Āq Quyūnlū system, to retain a hold on their domains.

As the qizilbāsh uymāqs became increasingly complex and unwieldy, they began to disintegrate much as the households of Āq Quyūnlū chiefs had before them. Qizilbāsh chieftains began to receive smaller estates and consequently lower revenues which led to a decrease in their military power. This must be recognized as an element of crisis (see chapter 9). Every uymāq experienced such an emergency at one time or another in its history. Some uymāqs were able to handle the problem effectively, others were not and disappeared almost totally from involvement in the qizilbāsh political/military system. The latter were crippled by the internal problems uymāq chieftains faced in dispensing a fixed or nearly fixed amount of revenues to an increasing number of subordinates.[2] Unable to please everyone, they were confronted by mounting hostility within their own organization and even within their own immediate families.

Extortionate Practices and the Qizilbāsh System: The Example of the Ṭālish

One of the major elements of the steppe tradition that survived into Safavid times was the particular concept that the uymāq chiefs had maintained concerning revenue exploitation. The regions they controlled were exploited less as agricultural societies and were dominated more as if they were appanages of pastoral societies. The agricultural establishment existed to serve the chieftain in his perception of the world order. It was there to provide him with cash revenues, with fodder for his horses and those of his troops, with food, when requisitioned, for himself and his men; and with labor or military service which was sometimes exacted with a severity that ruined the economies of whole villages. The chiefs were merely exploiting the natural resources of the domain that they held by force or by inheritance, and they exacted dues as they needed them. This method of exploitation had the earmarks of a steppe economy (even where pastoralism was not prevalent), since in pastoral economies, the natural resource–livestock–could be moved to better pastures when fodder failed in the old ones.[3] Likewise, in the dispersed command economy of the Safavid Empire, chieftains who came from a steppe tradition (and who were indeed still the chieftains of pastoralists) would have few qualms about seeking out new resources to exploit if the old ones failed them or were insufficient to support them. In its flexible use of pasture this sytem of using natural or man-produced resources closely resembled the practices of the pastoral economies of Central Asia and Iran.[4]

Such a method of resource utilization has been considered the ultimate in barbarism and uncivilized behavior.[5] The management of domain in this manner has often been compared to pillaging or robbery, but this comparison is not entirely justified. At that time plundering was considered as legal or illegal depending upon the sanction one received to carry it out. The taking of pillage was considered as the rightful exploitation of the chieftain's property.[6] Plundering could also be construed as an unlawful act when the malfeasant took more than his due according to a previous arrangement with his chief, or when he extorted the belongings of those nominally under his care without his master's permission.[7] In the mixed Iranian system, where agricultural and pastoral economic complexes existed side by side, it was difficult to maintain a balance since the administrative rights of exploitation granted the chieftain were sufficient only in times when productive conditions were ideal. Administrative compilations such as the *Tadhkirat al-Mulūk* and other works that treat the administration of revenues even in part do not take extraordinary economic circumstances into consideration. The urgent need to balance the two productive forces in an equilibrated economic system was recognized only in the right of legislation given to the monarch or supreme ruler, who in theory was able to make adjustments to meet new circumstances. When the network of chieftains controlling the resources and wealth of the realm became too complex for the ruler to control, as in the time of the Āq Quyūnlū sultans from the 1450s on, and as in the Safavid Empire from the 1530s to the early part of the seventeenth century, the chief element of flexibility in the entire system–the right of the supreme ruler to legislate–lost its effectiveness. There was no longer any rhyme or reason to the political system, and the functionaries who were part of it were forced to take extraordinary action when they were no longer able to obtain whatever they needed to maintain their establishment.

The frustration of the Iranian economic system and the consequent arrest in the social life of Iran is best shown in the case of the Ṭālish chieftains in Azerbaijan. They ruled the Ṭālish district, belonged to the Ustājlū uymāq, one of the numerous groups to comprise the Kungurlū sept,[8] controlled a highly mixed economic structure, and were heavily involved in pastoralism. Even if they did not migrate with the pastoral tīras, they managed all aspects of the semiannual migration. Āstārā and Ardabīl were the centers of Ṭālish power, and here the chieftains resided the year round, except when off on campaign in the service of their master. Āstārā and Ardabīl were also the foci of the *qishlāq* (winter quarters) of the migrating tīras. The power of these chieftains was dependent upon the presence of the tīras around them in the winter camp just as the early Safavid shaikhs also depended upon their presence in winter camp before undertaking any rebellious or ambitious projects.

Just before Ismā'īl I came out of exile in 1500, he sent off to Ardabīl a message that he was coming, but 'Ālam Shāh Begūm, shocked at Ismā'īl's intentions, sent a message in reply. "She said (to the messenger): Go quickly to my son (Ismā'īl)! Tell him that it is not the time for his coming. The murids (the Ṭālish) have all gone to summer quarters and there is no one in the town. He must wait six months longer until the murīds will return from the yailāq [summer quarters]."[9] After wintering around Ardabīl and Āstārā, the tribes would move their flocks west and south into the Ṭālish highlands for the summer. They also controlled an agricultural substructure located mainly in the coastal plain leading to the Caspian Sea and on the alluvial fan of the highlands. Rain was particularly favorable to agriculture in this region. A number of streams watered the area. For the region around Ardabīl, Ḥamdallāh Mustawfī states: "Its climate is extremely cold; hence corn cannot be ground in the same year in which it is sown, and some remains for the next year; and except for wheat, no other grain is grown here. Its water is from streams coming down from Mount Sablan: and it is most digestible, for which reason the people here are great eaters."[10] Khalkhāl to the southwest was a dairy center which produced yogurt for export. It had extensive farm fields watered by irrigation systems. Two mills in the area also aided in the irrigation system, though it is not said whether they were also used for grinding maize or grains.[11] Adjoining regions produced grain crops as well as some fruit.[12] The whole region facing the Caspian Sea had the best natural vegetation in all of Iran and, due to its climate, was in the best agricultural zone in Iran.[13]

The earliest chieftains or members of any ruling elite to give their support to the Safavid shaikh in the period before the formation of the Safavid monarchy came from among the chiefs of the Ṭālish. Shaikh Ṣafī al-Dīn relied on their support. It seems possible that his ancestors also had political ties with them.[14] After 1334 the chieftains of the Ṭālish appear to have entered into a relationship of dependence with the Safavid murshid, Ṣadr al-Dīn b. Ṣafī, who supposedly "drubbed the heads of the Ṭālish army with gifts."[15] Although the passage is extremely vague and laced with polemical vituperation, Khunjī is clearly making reference to the development of some form of institutionalized dependence in which Ṣadr al-Dīn was the patron figure. Documents from the period of Timūr-i Lang clearly show that the Ṣafavid murshid was later a powerful landowner and that Timūr increased the wealth and prestige of the Ṭālish chiefs even more.[16] It is probable that Ṣadr al-Dīn had granted them some parts of his patrimonial domain in return for their support and political alliance. The combination of political and economic subservience with the religious doctrines of Khalvatīya Sufism brought about the practices that Faḍlullāh b. Ruzbihān Khunjī abhorred, notably the abasement of one's person in the presence of the shaikh. In fact Khunjī ascribed the origins of the practice of *proskynesis* in the presence of the murshid to the people of Ṭalish as well as to other groups in the expanding network of Safavid adherents in the period of Shaikh Junaid.[17] By the time of Junaid, these chieftains and the peoples they ruled were very definitely a part of a political and religious superstructure that formed an enclave on the edges of Āq Quyūnlū territory ready to resist central rule without hesitation. Junaid and Ḥaidar both may be credited with building up the military power of the Safavid house by developing an intricate political network supported by a large military organization comprised of levies of both pastoralists and village agriculturalists.[18] The core element in these developments was the cadre of Ṭālish chieftains who were in a position of hereditary subservience to the Safavid house.

The concept of uymāq is nebulous in the sources describing the earliest Ṭālish chieftains. This vagueness probably reflects the original state of the Safavid system, which relied more on several of a number of households, but not on arrays of households scattered about a geographically diffuse region. Only with the extension of the Safavid network into Anatolia, northern Syria, and the southern Zagros was it necessary to establish some means of geographical or tribal categorization. The Ṭālish, being the original followers of the Safavid murshid, did not conform readily to the uymāq mold. Even under Shāh Ismā'īl they probably refused to enter the Ustājlū uymāq. They were all of disparate family origins and cherished heritages of long service to the Safavid family. They were not conquered by force of arms as were the majority of the uymāq households under Ismā'īl I and therefore refused to be associated with other groups that were for all intents and purposes still unbelievers. Despite these fundamental differences, the amīrs of Ṭālish conformed to the pattern of uymāq organization. The chiefly houses held sway over a diversity of smaller groups, each with their own leaders, and controlled a mixed economic structure from which they obtained levies and subsidies. Even though revenue administration may at first have been organized on the pattern of *waqf* (endowment) units, they probably conformed more and more closely to the Turco-Mongol system, especially after the reign of Ismā'īl I. The earliest Ṭālish chiefs first mentioned in the sources, Dede Beg and Khādim Beg, are given a unique aura by the chroniclers.

Dede Beg Ṭālish, also called Abdāl Beg Dede, was the highest person in the hierarchy of the Safavid order. "Dede" and "Abdāl" were not his real names, but, like "Beg," titles that indicated his position. In the Safavid order the *dede* ("grandfather" or "elder") was the chief religious authority after the murshid and the chief delegate of the Safavid leader in both religious and secular matters. *Abdāl* referred to the spiritual hierarchy as defined in Khalvatīya doctrine and indicated that Dede Beg was considered to be among "the elect" of the Safavid hierarchy.[19] This chieftain was originally a retainer of Shaikh 'Alī, the brother of Ismā'īl I, though it seems logical that he may have served Ḥaidar Ṣafavī as well. Dede Beg was one of Ismā'īl's closest guardians, remaining with him from the moment of 'Alī's death in 1495 until the end of his self-imposed exile in Gīlān. Both his political/military functions and his status in the religious hierarchy were vestiges of the original system to which the Ṭālish chiefs adhered. The arrangement between Dede Beg and Ismā'īl I began to change with the successful campaigning of the period after 1500-1501. Dede Beg became the ḥākim of Qazvīn, Rayy, Sāvuj Bulāgh, and Khār and ruled these regions until 915/1509, when he was replaced by other chieftains, notably Zainal Khān Shāmlū. During this period, from 911/1505-1506 to 915/1509-1510, he was also the qūrchībāshī of the qizilbāsh military institution.[20] When in 916/1510 Marv was conquered, he received the governorate of the city. During the ensuing Üzbek invasions, he disgraced himself by fleeing the enemy. Ismā'īl I had him paraded before the qizilbāsh army in shame. He was subsequently pardoned, but the incident represented the growing chasm that was developing between Ismā'īl I and his older chieftains, like Dede Beg, who were probably unaccustomed to such great power and wealth and who became too self-indulgent according to the standards of discipline set by the Safavid order in pursuing their own affairs. For this reason Ismā'īl saw the danger in giving them too much power. The sources say nothing about Dede Beg after 1512. Presumably he was forced into a retirement that amounted to exile.[21] The very fact that he had held a unique position in the traditional hierarchy of the Safavid institution (a position that his family may have held for as long as two centuries if the trend toward family control was true also for his family) worked in his disfavor as the qizilbāsh system increased in size. Newly recruited chiefs were often of far higher social status than he had been. He did not conform to the ideals of personal bravery and military prowess that they idealized nor did he fit well into a broader uymāq-type structure since most of his experience had been in a more confined environment.

Khādim Beg Ṭālish, a chieftain of equal or secondary importance to Dede Beg, held a position that was the third most revered in the hierarchy of the Safavid order. As the *khādim* (literally "attendant, servant"), he was probably the keeper of the *tasbīḥ* (great rosary) of Ṣafī al-Dīn, founder of the order. He probably acquired some prestige for arranging ceremonies that the murshid attended, becoming like a chief or master of ceremonies.[22] Khādim Beg also had a reputation as a theologian of sorts, since later, after Ismā'īl I's conquests, he rose very high in the Safavid religious hierarchy. Like Dede Beg, he was strongly attached to the older Safavid system and participated in most of the great campaigns of Ismā'īl I. Unlike Dede Beg, he does not seem to have had difficulty in adapting to the new, expanded uymāq system. He became the *khalīfat al-khulafā* (chief religious agent of the Safavid murshid) in 914/1508, a position he held until his death in 920/1514 at Chaldiran.[23] That same year Ismā'īl conquered Arabian Iraq from Bārīk Beg Purnāk. Khādim Beg was made first ḥākim of Baghdad then governor of the whole province, a post which included the task of supervising the shrine at Karbalā. In addition to these functions, Khādim Beg was an important advisor to the shah and an amīr of the dīvān. Khādim Beg fit into the new institution established by Ismā'īl after the conquest of Iran far more successfully than Dede Beg. His success was attributable to the success of the Safavid movement itself. He did not have to be troubled by questions of status because most individuals who could have claimed to be his competitors, the Sunni ulama, had either been killed or exiled, and there were fewer qualified people to control positions requiring greater professional competence.[24]

In terms of the crisis of the qizilbash system, one of the problem areas discussed below in chapter 10 is evident in the foregoing discussion.[25] The early Safavid system employed by the shaikhs preceding Ismā'īl was a particularized one. The leaders in the organization were not drawn from the highest levels of the ruling elite, but mainly from local chiefly families of only moderate wealth. The social organization of these regional families and their patrimonial domains conformed more of less to the Safavid religious hierarchy. This was particularly true of the Ṭālish chiefly families, the fifteenth-century Takalū chieftains in Teke, as well as of numerous other minor groups that are not given fuller discussions in the sources.[26] In such a situation, where the different groups of mūrīds were scattered over wide distances and restricted by local organizations to the formation of a particularized system, the murshid deemed it essential to erect a more rigid hierarchical structure, especially in the center of activity, Ardabīl. It was no coincidence that the leaders of the Safavid organization beneath the murshid were given the titles appropriate to a paternalistic family organization. The institution was organized in much the same way as the communities of devotees that adhered to it. The dede was perceived as the patriarch of a number of families and thus as the guardian of the family heritage. Within the family environment he also had the religious function of preserving the "hearth" (*ujāq*), which symbolized the ritual or the ancestral fire.[27] In the Safavid order the dede was charged with organizing the *bābā*s (murshids of lower level groups) and passing on to them the pronouncements of the Safavid murshid-i kāmil. His position was comparable to that of the grandfather of a family because he ensured proper observance of respect for the spiritual orientation of the Safavid leader. The bābās were the delegates of the dede. They passed the message of the Safavid prince on to their followers, members of the patrimonial organization owing allegiance to the bābā. These bābās were the abdāls, the spiritual elect of their communities. The murshid-i kāmil chose the dede from among them.

At some point during the fifteenth century more and more the dede and some of the bābās became military leaders and secular chieftains. Heredity was a far more important qualification for succession to office than ability or piety. One manifestation of this trend was the inability of even the murshid-i kāmil to provide a soundly worked out religious doctrine. One look at Shāh Ismā'īl's poetry is enough to convince anyone that it was a hodgepodge of popular beliefs that combined pre-Islamic precepts with both Shī'a and Sunni Islamic ideals. The single most important idea to come out of the doctrine was the idea of family and the importance of genealogy:

> My mother is Fatima, my father is 'Alī; and eke I am the
> Pīr of the twelve imams.
> I have recovered my father's blood from Yazīd. Be sure that
> I am of Haydarian* essence.

and

> My sire is Ṣafī, my father Haydar. Truly I am the Ja'far
> of the audacious.
> I am a Husaynid and have curses for Yazīd. I am Khata'i,
> a servant of the Shah's.

This pronounced inclination toward dynasty at the upper levels of the Safavid system permeated down into the rank and file groups in the order. Furthermore, this growing tribalization of the Safavid order was accompanied by an increased militancy and secularization. In another poem, one evidently meant to be uttered by the murīd, perhaps in a community service, Ismā'īl focuses on the significance of the pastoral tribes:

> Thou art my king over the land [yurt] where the arrows (*okhlār*)
> are arrayed in review.[28]

This indoctrination in the value of the family and family group (*okh*, hence the okhlār of the poem) had the effect of creating a strong, unshakable belief in the intrinsic value of belonging to a particular 'aṣabīyya or intisāb community. Religious conviction most assuredly held a primary role in contributing to the establishment of a system in which family had an important part. The Safavid order itself was under the control of Ṣafī al-Dīn's family ever since its founding. As in the Shī'a theories concerning the Prophet's family, the belief that the special religious qualities of the founder were passed on through heredity became more and more pronounced among the followers of the Safavids. A true sense of dynasty can be perceived as early as the time of Ṣadr al-Dīn, who succeeded his father Ṣafī. The development of a conception of 'aṣabīyya can also be seen in the many references in Safavid polemical literature to fire and the passing of fire from father to son. Fire represented a

* Haydar is Shaikh Ḥaidar, Ismā'īl's father, and the first Imām, 'Alī.

number of things in the syncretic Safavid doctrine, above all the divine wisdom as it had been passed on to the family of the Prophet. It also symbolized the principle of family and the essence of all previous generations. The conception that fire, like the soul within one's body, was inherited from one's ancestors was an allegorization of the genealogical chain of being that was at the heart of the concept of 'aṣabīyya. In the third place, fire was perceived as the sign of world rulership.

Groups, like the Ṭālish and the Takalū, which owed allegiance to the shaikhs must have regarded their own major families as part of such a chain of being. Ḥasan Khalīfa Takalū was portrayed by one of his murīds as having a "fire" within his loins that would eventually be born into the body of his son Shāh Qulī Bābā. This fire was undoubtedly considered the divine wisdom the Safavid shaikh had taught him. It also represented the establishment of a Takalū ruling family that owed obedience to the Safavid leader. Other qizilbāsh ruling families must have had similar conceptions of family solidarity, but the further removed they were from fervent revolutionary ideas, the less significance did they attach to the idea of the genetic transferal of a preexisting spirit in the form of fire. Even among these "sceptics" some conception of intisāb in a broader familial or political sense predominated and allowed for the feeling that a particular intisāb grouping had all that was the best either in human or otherworldly terms, or both. Anyone not a member of such a grouping was considered an outsider worthy only of extermination. It was the motive of Shāh Ismā'īl to impress this chain of being upon the world. Those who refused to accept this mode of existence were to be eradicated mercilessly:[29]

> When the *ghāzīs* enter the arena, the outsiders
> will be utterly under their feet.

or

> I shall exterminate outsiders from the world.
> I am Khata'i, I have come to serve as a
> proof of truth.

or, in one line that betrays Ismā'īl's sentiment that he was the instrument of the avenging Mahdī, if not the Mahdī himself:

> An angel has descended from the skies. Good
> tidings to the men of mystic knowledge! Death
> has descended upon the outsiders, calamity has
> befallen the Yazīds.

The formative period of the qizilbāsh uymāq system is reflected in Shāh Ismāʻīl's poetry. The Ṭālish chiefs, like the other groups adhering to the Safavid credo, were subjected to a bombardment of such beliefs and were required to look upon unbelievers as enemies or outsiders to their community. Such extreme internalization of the family principle was a factor in Ismāʻīl's rise to power since it brought out the deepest devotion in his followers and gave his organization a unity that his opponents did not possess. In terms of the Ṭālish, though, it created an extremely limited sphere of control and an exceedingly rigid conception of their role in the hierarchical organization of the Safavid institution (order or principality). As chieftains who belonged to the group formerly labeled as outsiders began to enter Safavid service, it became difficult for the Ṭālish staffing the secular organization of the Safavid state to accept the newcomers.[30] The result of this confluence of attitudes was the formation of an atmosphere of tension sparked by the entry of competitors into the political system and the creation of a "culture shock" caused by the entry of these chieftains, who had continuously lived in a parochial environment, into a broader social environment. The problems Dede Beg Ṭālish encountered in the collapse of his career were indicative of this clash of interests.

The view that an established religious hierarchy was essential to the operation of society and government was not universally held after the first conversions of great chieftains to the Safavid cause. A new secular organization was developing that molded the Safavid precepts of family organization with Turkic concepts of social and tribal organization. While the need to impose a distinct social order upon society was regarded as most urgent by Ismāʻīl and his followers at the outset, the injection of hostile elements into the conquering qizilbāsh order transformed this belief and brought about the initial impetus behind the crises of later years since there was a gap in confidence existing between the two classes of chieftains. The tensions existing between the different amīrs was even cited as the cause of the defeat at Chaldiran by Ḥasan-i Rūmlū, who indicated that the word of Khān Muḥammad Ustājlū was not taken by a Rūmlū chief of staff and that the wrong tactics were employed in fighting the Ottomans.[31] It was no longer possible to reconcile the different views, though the traditional style uymāqs, which were smaller than the new uymāqs, were eventually absorbed into the greater tribal systems, just as the Ṭālish was eventually recognized as a portion of the Kungurlū Ustājlū.[32]

The Spread and Decline of Ṭālish Power in Northwest Iran

Out of the troubles encountered by the early Ṭālish uymāq emerged one family that was more successful than any of the others. This was the family and clientele of Bāyandur Khān Ṭālish, who is first mentioned in the sources in 946/1539-1540.[33] His ancestry might possibly be traced back to Mīrzā Muḥammad Sulṭān b. Ḥamza Beg, though any attempt to establish such a connection would be problematical.[34] This family developed such a powerful organization that one member, a peripheral kinsman named Ḥamza Sulṭān, was the possessor of a great compound in the capital city, Qazvīn, where he kept a treasury and an armed bodyguard.[35]

Bāyandur Khān became the governor of Āstārā in 946/1539-1540, after the former governor had been dismissed for rebellion. On an expedition to Gīlān in 1578, he and his son, Amīr Ḥamza Khān, were nominally under the command of Ibrāhīm Sulṭān Zīyād-oğlū Qājār and Nazar Sultān Ustājlū though in fact, they provided most of the troops, except for a body of Gaskarī infantry provided by Ibrāhīm Sulṭān. During this expedition, the Ṭālish khans attempted to establish their suzerainty over Gīlān (Lāhijān) at the expense of the rebellious governor, Khān Aḥmad.[36] Upon the successful conclusion of the campaign against the rebel chieftains in Gīlān, Bāyandur Khān and Amīr Ḥamza Khān were faced by a series of popular uprisings that were difficult to put down because the population of Gīlān fled into the dense wilderness areas of the Alburz range and joined the remnants of the rebel forces that had supported Khān Aḥmad. These revolts became especially vicious after about 1580. By 1587 the Ṭālish domain, now under the control of Amīr Ḥamza, extended from the Mughān steppe to the plains of Gīlān. Amīr Ḥamza's client and uterine brother, Amīra Sīyāvash, was ḥākim of Gaskar, while other Ṭālish chiefs were to be found in or around Lake 'Urūmīya, in Chukhur-i Sa'd, and on the Mughān steppe.[37] The accession of 'Abbās I and the victory of the chiefs of Khorāsān did not reverse the progress of the chieftains of Ṭālish. Amīr Ḥamza accepted 'Abbās I as shah and continued step by step to gather his forces and extend his power into Azerbaijan. He was in the process of becoming the most powerful figure in the province, though he was not without competitors or rivals. His personal holdings were extensive, comprising:[38]

a. A position of dominant power in Azerbaijan, where he supervised the affairs of the province.
b. The control of the citadel (*qal'a*) of Sindān (Shīndān).
c. The ūlkā of Langar Kinān.
d. The ūlkā of Jahān and Matā' in the region of Ardabīl.
e. Qizilbāsh cavalry.
f. 3,000-4,000 Ṭālishī foot soldiers.
g. An unrecorded amount of dues in cash, kind, and services from the pastoralists and agriculturalists of Ṭālish.

The power of Amīr Ḥamza's relatives and clients was being extended as well, and through them the influence and prestige of Amīr Ḥamza. Amīra Sīyāvash Khān was ḥākim of Gaskar, and he was given the ūlkā of Khalkhāl (shortly after the deposition of his master, however).[39] This growing power coalition was broken up, first by the defeat of Amīr Ḥamza at the hands of Qarāmānlū chieftains, who were his rivals for power in Azerbaijan, and then by the deposition of Amīra Sīyāvash Khān. An extraordinary document illustrating the latter event has survived and was published in 1965. The unraveling of public order that occurred at the time of Amīra Sīyāvash's deposition seems to have been part and parcel of the rebellion then brewing in the area. A Kurdish chief named Shāh Qulī Āqā-yi Sūrla had raided the ūlkā of Khalkhāl, looted widely, and caused the people to scatter from their property. The document states:[40]

A royal command has been issued: the dispersed peasants at Kazaj in Khalkhal, which has been fixed as the *soyurghal* of the descendents of the late Mawlana Kamāl al-Dīn Ḥusayn Khādim, wherever and with whomever they may be, are to return to their places and homes with every good expectation, and occupy themselves with agriculture, piety, and husbandry. No person is to impede or create difficulties for the aforesaid peasants; they should be allowed to return to their accustomed dwelling place.

The document further gives the exact extent of the administrative structure of the ūlkā of Khalkhāl just before Amīra Sīyāvash Khān's deposition. The Ṭālish chief controlled a kalāntar, a dārūgha, several 'āmils, and a number of *mubāshīrān* (bailiffs), and he had relations with the elders (here called *malik*s) of the villages and pastoral camps.[41]

Several problems discussed in previous sections are evident in this sequence of occurrences. The increasing power of the chiefs of the Ṭālish earmarked them as targets for rivals and disgruntled subchiefs who had very little hope of upward advancement. The competition for power and wealth that was so much a part of the "crossed patterns of power" complex (chapters 9 and 10) is nowhere so dramatically illustrated as in the fall of Ṭālish power after the accession of 'Abbās I. Jealous rivals, who in past years could do nothing but watch the progress of the Ṭālish chiefs, were able to cut them down to size as soon as they fell from the shah's favor. When the Ṭālish rebelled against the shah, the territories and revenues they controlled were pounced upon by discontented underlings who were constantly seeking just such an opportunity and by powerful competitors who sought their own elevation. It is evident from reviewing the difficulties facing the chieftains that they fell prey to a series of consequences arising from their rebellion. The immediate chiefs concerned lost all their prestige and power in the Safavid institution. Their holdings became fair game for anyone. With the state forces seeking to repress the rebellion and the bands of local (but unrelated) insurgents marching on their domains, these chiefs had to give up all their wealth and possessions. They probably experienced a severe reduction in the manpower that was willing to serve them in any capacity. The family of these chieftains, who were not all involved in the revolt, suffered a severe reduction in the extent of their domains, or, at least in the extent of the family domains. The ability of the Ṭālish family to resist more powerful groups like the Qarāmānlū, the state, or later the Shāh-savan in some areas and the Ustājlū in others was severely weakened. First of all, the Ṭālish no longer possessed a large military force with which to resist the greater powers. The broad provincial base from which they had levied foot soldiers and revenues was gone, and what remained was not wholly willing to support the family. Pastoral subtribes were scattered all over northern Azerbaijan, and, without a Ṭālish chieftain in control of the affairs of the province, they were incapable of resisting the growing power of the sectional groups like the Shāh-savan and the Qarāmānlū. All that remained to the Ṭālish chieftains was the mountainous district behind Ardabīl and Āstārā, and even this they held for a time only precariously.

The organization that the Ṭālish chieftains had established in northern Azerbaijan was dismantled by the agitation of lesser groups seeking to establish themselves in positions of power and authority. In the campaigns against Gīlān, the inhabitants of the province absolutely refused to accept the rule of the qizilbāsh chieftains. They rebelled and fled into the forests, where they conducted a grueling guerrilla campaign against their new Ṭālish overlords. For this reason, the Ṭālish were never able to establish a complete hold over Gīlān. The rebellion of the Gīlānī villagers was facilitated by closeness to the Alburz range and its many inaccessible recesses. The subject population of Kazaj in the ūlkā of Khalkhāl dispersed from the place of their habitation and occupation. They may not have taken up arms as the Gīlānī peasants had done, but they were either unwilling or unable to produce more food and other products due to the burdensome exactions of both the established authority, the Ṭālish chieftains, and the gangs of bandits led by uprooted or unassigned chieftains. Such forms of disaffection were thoroughly effective in decreasing the power of the chief who overburdened his subjects but was also a means of attacking the power of a rival chieftain. Whether this method of attack was part of Shāh Qulī Āqā-yi Sūrla's conscious plan cannot now be ascertained, but it seems to be one means by which such bandit chiefs obtained power.[42] Large numbers of small bands following leaders like Shāh Qulī Āqā-yi Sūrla existed and increased in number during the breakdown in public order that began at the death of Ṭahmāsp I (1576) and ended in the middle period of 'Abbās I's reign. Some of these small bands succeeded in breaking away from the overweening control of the qizilbāsh and in establishing an uymāq recognized by the Safavid shah.[43] In such cases the chiefs were able to carve out their dominions and maintain them independently from qizilbāsh control. Amīra Sīyāvash, however, was so distracted by the rebellion of his patron, Amīr Ḥamza Ṭālish, that he devoted the energies of his dominion to supporting the dire cirumstances of his overlord. When all was lost, he was no longer able to maintain public order. Disturbances broke out in the local regions comprising his ūlkā. Such breakdowns in the provincial system were not isolated phenomena, as will be seen in the coming chapters.

Conclusions

As a class, the rulers of the Ṭavālish represented a number of things. In the early part of their history, they were the leaders of the Safavid *tarīqa* (Sufi order), second to the Safavid murshid. But even at this time their power was almost entirely localized. As part of the upper echelon of the qizilbāsh hierarchy in the early stages of Ismā'īl's rise to power, they were able to rise to the highest positions in the religious institution of the nascent Safavid state, but as secular chiefs they were unable to compete with the organizations of the greater uymāqs, even when the latter had been cut down to size by 'Abbās I.

The chiefs of the Ṭālish remained as secular rulers over Āstārā and adjacent regions in Gīlān and Azerbaijan. They developed an extensive network of Persian functionaries who owed them allegiance. It is fascinating to note however, that these Persian leaders (see Appendix 16a-d) were masters of armies and served in the capacity of qizilbāsh generals (though they were not qizilbāsh chiefs). Quite frequently they held positions officially reserved for a member of the Turkic ruling elite. Amīra Sīyāvash was the ḥākim of Gaskar, for instance. The *Tārīkh-i Gīlān* cites many instances of Tājīk administrators holding the position of dārūgha. The amīrs of the Ṭālish were consistently unable to command sufficient resources to subjugate the rest of Gīlān or parts of Azerbaijan such as Khalkhāl. It was perhaps for this reason that Shāh 'Abbās permitted Amīr Ḥamza's brothers to succeed him in the rule of Āstārā. Even if they revolted, the most damage they could do would have been to hide in the dense forests of Gīlān and Ṭālish and to carry on a campaign of local terrorism and raiding.

The attitude of 'Abbās I is highly interesting as well. After Amīr Ḥamza Khān's revolt had been put down, the shah did not appear inclined toward exacting a stricter obedience from the Ṭālish amīrs. His actions confirmed the Ṭālish as patriarchal leaders of their community and holders of a patrimonial domain. He did not seek to bring an abrupt end to the traditions of the ruling family there. Instead of appointing a Tājīk or a slave to the governorship of the ūlkā of the Ṭavālish, he gave the domain to Amīr Ḥamza's son, Bāyandur. Later, when his son died, he turned the realm over to Bāyandur Khān's younger brother. This represented a traditional Turkic means of succession as well as the mode of accession most commonly used by pastoral peoples in Iran. In confirming the family of Amīr Ḥamza Khān as the possessors of the Ṭavālish, 'Abbās I seems to have sought a reconciliation with the pastoral segment of society in the Ṭālish, thereby confirming the traditional patterns of socioeconomic organizations in the region and permitting them to survive.

NOTES

[1] *AQ*, passim.

[2] The actual revenue amounts of the Safavid system between 1500 and 1629 are not known. Even if cash amounts were known, it is not certain that they would be accurate since half or more was paid in kind or services. Cash was also extremely rare. A. Banani, "The Structure of the Persian Empire in its Heyday," unpublished paper, pp. 1-13.

[3] This movement was certainly the motive behind the semiannual migration, but, if there was not enough fodder in summer or winter quarters, the normal area of fodder-cropping by the animals had to be expanded beyond its normal circuit. This worked well in places where population density and economic structure permitted. In Iran, since a major portion of the population was living under an agricultural cycle, bad fodder years for the pastoralists meant heavier exploitation by the pastoral chieftains of the agricultural produce, and probably, though not necessarily, destruction of some crops.

[4] *HA*, pp. 94-101. Some tribes shared the same pastureland in bad times, though not without occasional conflict.

[5] "SECII," pp. 483-537, for instance.

[6] *DK*, "How the House of Salur Kazan was Pillaged," pp. 42 ff.

[7] J. A. Boyle ("The Dynastic and Political History of the Il-Khans," *CHI*, V, 338-339) gives an instance where Arghūn Āqā was called to task for misappropriating funds. *TJG*, pp. 507-508, states that it was Arghūn Āqā's function to prevent misappropriation in the first place.

[8] *TAAA*, p. 387, identifies Allāh Qulī Sulṭān b. Ja'far Sulṭān as a member of the Ṭālish-i Kungurlū. This does not mean, however, that all the qizilbāsh chiefs of Ṭālish were Kungurlū, only those belonging to this particular family. Most of the amīrs of this district are simply designated by the *laqab* ("title") "Ṭālish" in the sources.

[9] *Ismā'īl*, p. 46.

[10] Hamdallāh Mustawfī, *The Geographical Part of the Nuzhat al-Qulūb*, trans. G. Le Strange (Leyden: E. J. Brill, 1919) pp. 83-84.

[11] In Ardabīl, grinding was evidently a task carried out by hand, at least where immense amounts of labor were required for grinding the maize products of the area. This seems to have been the case in Khalkhāl as well.

[12] Mustawfī, *Nuzhat al-Qulūb*, pp. 84-85.

[13] W. G. Fisher, "Physical Geography," *CHI*, I, *The Land of Iran*, pp. 41-42.

[14] *Amīnī*, p. 62.

[15] Ibid., p. 63.

[16] Heribert Horst, *Timur und Khoje 'Ali* (Wiesbaden: Franz Steiner Verlag, 1958) pp. 6-28.

[17] *Amīnī*, p. 67.

[18] Ibid., p. 71.

[19] *AAS* (p. 44) distinguishes between Dede Beg and Abdāl Beg.

[20] *BOD* (pp. 111, 251 and 259) gives a definition of these terms for the Bektashis, who were from a branch of the Khalvatīya parallel to the Safavids. See below, chapt. 10, the point dealing with the acceptance of a spiritual hierarchy.

[21] *Ismā'īl*, pp. 30, 33; *AT*, pp. 26, 29, 50, 54, 55, 65, 88; *TAAA*, pp. 24, 41; "PO" (1), p. 101; Sarwar, pp. 27, 28, 31, 33, 38, 45, 51, 56, 62, 63, 68, 70; *TM*, p. 191.

[22] For the title "khādim," see: J. Spencer Trimingham, *The Sufi Orders in Islam* (London: Oxford University Press, 1973) p. 201.

[23] The fact that the office of the khalīfat began to decline in importance was not necessarily a reflection on him. R. M. Savory, "The Office of Khalifat al-Khulafa under the Safavids," *JAOS*, 85 (1965), 497-502.

[24] *AT*, pp. 46-49; *TAAA*, pp. 24, 25, 31, 34; Sarwar, pp. 27, 31, 33, 38, 52, 54-55, 80.

[25] See p. 133, item 9, on the need to establish a hierarchy of the elect.

[26] For the Takalū, see *AT*, pp. 59 f.

[27] Ibid.

[28] "PSI," pp. 1042*a*, 1046*a*. For the genealogical principle as developed by the Safavid family, see: Zeki Velidi Togan, "Sur l'origine des Safavides," *Mélanges Massignon*, III, Institut Français de Damas, Damas, 1957, III, 345 ff.

[29] "PSI," pp. 1042*a*, 1046*a*, 1049*a*; *AT*, p. 59; W. Ivanow, *The Truth-Worshippers of Kurdistan. Ahl-i Haqq Texts* (Leiden: E. J. Brill, 1953) pp. 33-47, 146-148. Khān Ātish, ostensibly "the King of the World," appeared "from the midst of the fire." While this text is from the nineteenth century, it represents a cryptic allegorization of ancestor worship influenced by solar beliefs as well as Christianity, Ismā'ilism, and the preachings of the Safavids.

[30] Manṣūr Beg Afshār, Amīr Beg Mauṣillū, Bārīk Beg Purnāk, Muḥammad Khān Dhu'l-Qadr-oğlū, among others, are examples of the political converts to Shi'ism who converted not as a result of religious experience, but to preserve their wealth, power, and social status.

[31] Khān Muḥammad had the most experience of any Safavid general in fighting the Ottomans, whom he had defeated on numerous occasions. *AT*, pp. 68-73.

[32] Exactly the opposite results were obtained by Stone for the British Aristocracy, though he does admit that many of the greater aristocrats were totally callous in regard to religion. *CA*, pp. 332 ff.

[33] *AT*, p. 133.

[34] Mīrzā Muḥammad Sulṭān was an early supporter of Ismā'īl I.

[35] *TAAA*, p. 198.

[36] Bāyandur Khān's design on Gīlān can be traced back as far as 975/1568–1569, when he was on an expedition there. *AT*, p. 190.

[37] *TAAA*, pp. 141, 340; *TG*, p. 120.

[38] *TAAA*, p. 442; *TG*, pp. 140-141, 237-239. The Qarāmānlū were their greatest rivals.

[39] *TAAA*, pp. 449-451. He received Khalkhāl in return for services rendered in putting down a revolt in Gīlān. *TG* (pp. 120-122) indicates that Amīra Sīyāvash had originally been Amīr Ḥamza's enemy and had killed Ḥamza's retainer Shīrzād Sulṭān. The two must, however, have made an alliance later to counter the growing strength of the Qarāmānlū chiefs located in Ardabīl.

[40] Martin, "Seven Safawid Documents," p. 198.

[41] Despite these defeats, Amīr Ḥamza's family continued to rule in the Ṭālish down to the end of the Safavid dynasty, see *TAAA*, pp. 1070, 1086; *Dhail-i TAAA*, p. 16; *'Abbās-Nāma*, pp. 82, 108.

[42] The criteria provided for *mafia* in *PR*, pp. 37-38, does not apply here to Shāh Qulī Āqā, since the Kurdish chief was neither a "feudalist" nor a "capitalist." Nevertheless, Shāh Qulī Āqā appears to have had "an apparatus of coercion" that was very similar to that described in Hobsbawm, pp. 38-39.

[43] *TM*, pp. 16-18.

6

Fusion of Āq Quyūnlū Uymāq Households with the Safavid System

The Mauṣillū

The conquests of Shāh Ismā'īl did not bring about the utter eradication of the older social, economic, and political systems of Iran. The Safavid menace promised to establish a new world order, but the slashing sword of the world redeemer, Ismā'īl, could not uproot the traditions and the order of an entire society. The new Safavid shah failed completely to implement the religious ideals promised in his message, particularly the more radical ones. Even so, the dogmatism and rigid thinking that characterized the Safavid religious program had a significant effect upon the nascent Safavid social system. Those elements able to survive the sweeping conquests of the Safavids, and they were considerable in quantity, were pressed into categories and political systems reminiscent of the older Āq Quyūnlū and Timurid organizations. This arrangement was nothing more than a recreation or restoration of the older institutions. It did not constitute a resurrection of a fully resuscitated Āq Quyūnlū or Timurid social system. The former ruling dynasties and the social systems they represented had been destroyed or subjected to the will of the Safavid prince. The entire Bāyandur ruling family, as extensive as it had been, sank into obscurity as the result of years of civil war and battle against the Safavid threat. The Purnāk uymāq was so utterly wiped out by the years of warfare and by the Safavid conquests that their descendants in the qizilbāsh uymāq system were few and weak. Whole branches of the Mauṣillū clan were killed off or went into exile as the result of the Safavid conquests. The family of Amīr Beg Mauṣillū was able to convert to the Safavid cause, but few members of other branch families succeeded in converting and surviving. The Kūh-Gīlūya Afshār, perennial survivors, managed to survive the Safavid onslaught under the guidance of Manṣūr Beg Afshār, as did the Kermān Īnāllū, the Hamadān Īnāllū, the Chāūshlū (or Chuvāshlū) of Khorāsān, and a number of others. Like the Mauṣillū, these groups had all been trimmed down to a manageable size, and they fit well into the Safavid scheme since they were weak and incapable of resisting. Their acceptance of Safavid sovereignty, because it introduced concepts of power and authority that had not existed there previously in any well-defined form, fundamentally altered the structure of the Safavid ruling system.

The tendency toward rigidity that so strongly characterized the Safavid religious organization and doctrine had an important role in canonizing the religious principles of uymāq organization and in standardizing them in new sets of conglomerated tribal structures. The elements of the new uymāq structures were almost exactly what they had been for centuries, right down to the details of revenue exaction and administrative organization, but the system as a whole bore only slight resemblance to pre-Safavid structures. The Safavid monarchs, from the time of Ismā'īl I onward, did not apportion wealth or segments of the rule in accordance with the steppe tradition, as had most of their predecessors. The Safavids were less influenced by steppe practices than any of the ruling dynasties that had controlled Persia or parts of Persia since the Saljūqs.

The unique interpretation that the Safavid order and the Safavid dynasty gave to the institution of *shāhanshāhī* was mainly responsible for the break in steppe patterns of organization at the upper level of Safavid society. In the heyday of the Safavid religious order the term "shah" was used primarily as a name for God and little more. Ismā'īl I took this title for himself, partly to suit his role as the self-proclaimed manifestation of God, but partly as the title that a secular ruler would take. The merger of the religious and secular aspects of the term "shah" can be best illustrated from the poetry of Ismā'īl:[1]

> From Pre-Eternity the Shah is our Sultan, our
> pir and murshid, our soul.[2]

The religious and secular meanings of the word are so deeply intermingled in this passage, that they cannot be separated. The Shah, besides being "God," is also the Sultan or possessor of secular power, and the pir ('elder') or murshid, the religious head. In another passage Ismā'īl imparts a clearly secular and conventional meaning for the term shah:[3]

> Today I have come to the world as a Master
> [*serverim*] . Know truly that I am Haydar's
> son.
> I am Faridun, Khosrau, Jamshid, and Zohak.
> I am Zal's son [Rustam] and Alexander.

His self-characterization as the sum total of all the great heroes from the *Shāh-nāma* of Firdausī and as the hero from the romances of Alexander the Great must have fit the fancy of Ismā'īl the boy or young man. He perceived himself as a glittering warrior, as a champion defeating all foes. Even though such passages as this may be classified as the fantasy of a child or young man, a certain tone and political perspective is exuded by these statements, which appear frequently in the poetry of Shāh Ismā'īl. The continual reference to such epic or militaristic prototypes was not merely poetic license, it represented the politicization of the idea of shah. The Shī'a concept of dynasty and family, as idealized in the concept of Imamate, was the core of Safavid dynastic organization held by the various Turco-Mongol predecessors of the Safavids. The Safavid interpretation of the institution of shah idealized Shī'a authoritarian concepts and succession to the rule that were alien to the steppe tradition.

The primary change wrought by the introduction of a Shī'a conception of state was the rigidification of the rules of succession to the throne. The new dynastic principle brought a coherent structure to the management of affairs at the upper levels of the state and replaced the chaos that had resulted from dividing the rule among members of the ruling families of the Mongol successor states. This change at the zenith of Iranian society was not accompanied by similar changes at other levels. Ismā'īl I and his successors were not able to do away with the great families of magnates. These great power factions were trimmed down to manageable size by the Safavid conquest and were even reordered along new lines to ensure stricter obedience to the new ruling dynasty, but the families that had been the main power source for the Āq Quyūnlū and Timurid rulers of Iran continued to exist. In some cases the families were stripped of all their power, but some of them managed to retain their local power enclaves without abatement. The Kūh-Gīlūya Afshār under Manṣūr Beg held solidly on to their homeland, which was inaccessible in the Zagros highlands. The Mauṣillū, Īnāllū, Bayāt, Chāūshlū, the Kermān Īnāllū, and a host of minor Kurdish families were able to maintain an unbroken hold on their patrimonial domains. Some of them were rearranged into the greater uymāq groupings: the Mauṣillū were grouped with the Purnāk, other family groups joined the Turkamān uymāq. The Īnāllū, Arashlū, Gündüzlü, Uṣāllū, and the Khudābandalū were likewise assimilated into the Afshār uymāq despite their quite different origins. The establishment of the uymāq system was an attempt to subject the Turkic family systems to a more orderly arrangement. It was intended to prevent them from becoming unwieldy, complicated affairs, that eventually broke down into factions competing for control of a patrimony. The tremendous attraction of the Safavid family in the late years of the fifteenth century was due in part to the sound principle of succession that it offered, as opposed to the Turkic practices followed by the Āq Quyūnlū subject houses that led only to a profusion of struggling competitors.

The establishment of the uymāq system was not a success. The old administrative systems remained. The tribal magnate families continued to rule as they had, except that they now had to deal with a more consistent, better organized central government that, when functioning properly, could keep them in their proper places. Even when the Safavid shah was powerful, he could not transform the five-century-old tribal institutions that represented the molding of the steppe and agricultural systems of organization. Ismā'īl I realized the need to keep the families of the great magnates as a constraining influence in the economic and social organization of the provinces. Without them there was no means of administering the radically different economic formations of pastoralism and agriculture that were strongly rooted in each locality of Iran. 'Abbās I attempted to do away with these great provincial families and to replace them with slaves who would remain loyal only to him. But his policy was unsuccessful: the slaves became dynasts in their own right, began to organize themselves in the same fashion as had the uymāq households, and often made alliances with the heads of the uymāqs in their provinces. The establishments of Ismā'īl I and the reforms of 'Abbās I were minimally successful. Tribal magnates continued to manage the affairs of the provinces. Turco-Mongol steppe practices and administrative forms continued to be a major element in the rural organization (and even in the urban structure) of Safavid Iran.

The continuation of steppe modes of organization, albeit in modified form, eventually caused a whole array of problems which ran in cycles. Under Ismā'īl I the uymāq formations were on the whole stable, as they were between the mid- to late 1530s and 1576 and throughout the seventeenth century. Periods of extreme instability alternated with times of peace and prosperity. The long term pattern in these periodic times of troubles was a noticeable decline in the power and prestige of the tribal magnates. Between the end of the fifteenth century and the middle of the seventeenth, the Turkic chiefly families descended from a position of monarchical rule to one of provincial rule and finally to a position of extreme subordination to more powerful provincial authorities. During the course of this progressively developing crisis, the problems that assailed the uymāq households are those described in chapters 9 and 10 below. The chiefly families were unable to maintain a firm grasp over their patrimonial domains. Too many members of the family claimed rights that only a few of them could ultimately possess. When the great patrimonies were being subdivided, the lesser provincial families, like the Qarāmānlū, the various Kurdish, and Lurī groups, were able to establish themselves in a position of nearly equal power. The great Turkic magnates–the qizilbāsh households–were losing wealth and power to the lesser groups, who sometimes sought to annex the domains of qizilbāsh houses directly, as in the case of the Ṣūrla chieftain above. The loss of territory and the decrease in the military power of the qizilbāsh chiefs was also a significant aspect of the unraveling crisis. Even with the relative decline in the power of the qizilbāsh, the uymāq families continued to play a significant part in the local organization of Iran. Even in their desperate circumstances they continued to be a link between the agricultural, pastoral, and urban sectors of Iranian society.

The Rise and Fall of the Mauṣillū Uymāq 1500 to 1587

The Mauṣillū segment of the Turkamān uymāq was directly descended from an Āq Quyūnlū chiefly family. During the Āq Quyūnlū period, the Mauṣillū ruled a region further east than they did in the Safavid period. They controlled the region of eastern Anatolia between Mauṣil (Mosul) and Erzinjan, ruling the province of Mauṣil from the town of 'Āmid.[4] During the Ottoman-Safavid wars of the early sixteenth century, Khān Muḥammad Ustājlū was appointed governor of Dīyārbakr, and they were forced to move further east.

The early history of the Mauṣillū may be divided into three broad periods. During the first, the Mauṣillū, under the leadership of Ṣūfī Khalīl, became an influential force in the Āq Quyūnlū domain. They were so powerful that they even took part in choosing the successors to the Āq Quyūnlū Sulṭāns who succeeded Ūzūn Ḥasan.[5] Caught up in the political disintegration of the Āq Quyūnlū realm, the Mauṣillū were eventually able to hew out an independent *beglik* (principality) in their home province, where they remained as rulers until they submitted to Safavid rule in 910/1504-1505. Most branches of the family were eradicated or sank into obscurity during this time of troubles.[6] Only the family of Amīr Beg b. Ghulābī b. Tuqmāq b. Bektash survived into Safavid times in the paternal line.[7] The chieftain who epitomized the difficult circumstances the Mauṣillū faced at the end of the Āq Quyūnlū period was Amīr Beg b. Ghulābī (I). At the outset he was the Āq Quyūnlū governor of Dīyārbakr. Later he became the independent ruler of Mauṣil. When the Safavids defeated him, he entered their service. In recognition of his great power and influence as the independent ruler of Mauṣil, Ismā'īl I appointed Amīr Beg to the office of *muhr-dār* and at the same time also gave him Khorāsān as an ūlkā.[8] He fully represented the trend in the early Safavid state whereby the serried ranks of Āq Quyūnlū notables were fused into the developing qizilbāsh uymāq structure. Like many other former Āq Quyūnlū confederate chieftains who entered Safavid service, Amīr Beg brought with him a whole new society and community structure. Loyalties to the uymāq chiefs such as Amīr Beg became paramount and were interposed between the Safavid murshid-i kāmil and the rank and file mūrīds of the expanding Safavid order and state. In the case of Amīr Beg, the retention of former power associations and the increase in size of the Mauṣillū patrimony brought about by the security of Safavid rule led to his rebellion at the end of Ismā'īl's reign.[9] Amīr Beg survived only because Ismā'īl I died too soon to have him executed and because Ṭahmāsp I had been his ward. Amīr Beg died of an illness in 928/1522.

The Mauṣillū chieftains made the transition from Āq Quyūnlū to Safavid rule without hesitation. Not only did this imply their lack of interest in the Safavid message, but it also showed how ruthless they could be in achieving their goals. Their power channels extended out into Azerbaijan first,[10] and then, under Amīr Beg, into Khorāsān. Dīyārbakr was taken from them after the Safavid conquest and given to Khān Muḥammad Ustājlū before the Ottoman conquest.[11] During the course of the sixteenth century, Mauṣillū interests were moved back toward the west into Azerbaijan, where Amīr Beg's successors maintained an almost regal court.

As the Mauṣillū chiefs became increasingly involved in the affairs of Azerbaijan, they developed contacts with most of the major personages of the province. Ṣādiqī Beg Afshār, a client of the Mauṣillū, was able to make extensive contacts among the intellectual and cultural elite of Hamadān during his stay there at the court of Amīr Beg's grandson.[12] Ṣādiqī Beg's reference to the wide circle of contacts maintained by the Mauṣillū chiefs shows that by the third quarter of the sixteenth century the Mauṣillū had achieved a pinnacle in the western regions of the Safavid Empire. Their power had grown to such heights by the end of Ṭahmāsp I's reign that they became one of several powerful enclaves that directed the administration and political life of the Safavid Empire. Their strength had increased so greatly that they could challenge the Safavid shah for the throne and compete with other uymāqs, notably the Chāūshlū and 'Abdillū, for control of imperial resources. The vicious and complex civil wars that began at the death of Taḥmāsp I and continued down to the middle of 'Abbās I's reign were the result of the pernicious influences of uymāq enclaves, such as the Mauṣillū that had become too powerful. Amīr Khān b. Ghulābī (II) b. Amīr Beg was the most influential and impressive of the Mauṣillū chiefs in Safavid times. He was able to build the superstructure that placed his household into contention for empire. At first he was ḥākim of Hamadān. Eventually he advanced to become beglārbegī of Azerbaijan and ḥākim of Tabrīz. With his advancement also came a supreme position in the Turkamān uymāq and the office of rīsh sifīd of the uymāq. This office gave him a central position in the uymāq from which he could supervise the affairs of both the Mauṣillū and the non-Mauṣillū Turkamān houses like the Purnāk. He may not have gained supreme power over the other houses in the uymāq, but he was at the pinnacle of a system of alliances. The tentacles of Mauṣillū power moved out in every direction and brought Amīr Khān's institution into conflict with similar uymāq organizations elsewhere, notably the houses of Murshid Qulī Khān Chāūshlū and 'Alī Qulī Khān 'Abdillū. He was also at cross purposes with Khalīl Khān Kūh-Gīlūya. The struggle between the Mauṣillū and the Ustājlū/Shāmlū coalition of Murshid Qulī Khān and 'Alī Qulī Khān 'Abdillū came to a head in the mid-1580s. Amīr Khān had been attempting to maintain a hold on southern Khorāsān by retaining Murtizā Qulī Khān Purnāk as the beglārbegī of Mashhad. 'Alī Qulī Khān was attempting to seize the beglārbegī of Mashhad. He attacked and displaced most of the Mauṣillū/Purnāk confederates from their ūlkā holdings in Khorāsān-i Mashhad and, with the assistance of the Ustājlū[13] at first, managed to push the Turkamān out of Khorāsān altogether. The loss of this province was partially responsible for the rebellion of Amīr Khān in 1584 or 1585.[14]

Amīr Khān rebelled against royal authority because the shah, Muḥammad Khudābanda, could not provide security for the growth and development of uymāq power. This deficiency was demonstrated by the fact that Amīr Khān's subordinates had been pushed out of their offices, both in the central administration and in the provinces, and the shah had not lifted a finger to prevent the civil war that had enveloped Iran for some time. Amīr Khān's timing was poor, though, because the Ottomans invaded Georgia and pushed the Safavid forces out of Ganja. Azerbaijan was also threatened by the Ottoman push, Amīr Khān's family, his brothers and sons, feared for their own possessions and established a coalition against Amīr Khān. With their abandonment, Amīr Khān was left with only a weak supportive army. He was forced to surrender to the shah's envoy, 'Alī Sulṭān Bayāt, and was executed shortly afterward. Even though Amīr Khān's relatives had abandoned him, they were drawn into a current of events that could not be stopped. Soon after the death of the rīsh sifīd, they were forced into rebelling under the leadership of Amīr Khān's brother or son, Muḥammad Khān.[15]

Amīr Khān was succeeded by Muḥammad Khān, who had originally governed the ūlkā of Kāshān and had supported Amīr Khān until the time of Amīr Khān's revolt.[16] He was the central figure in the plot among Amīr Khān's relatives to depose the rīsh sifīd. Muḥammad Khān was named as Amīr Khān's successor to the rīsh sifīdī of the Turkamān uymāq, with the recognition of the other amirs of the uymāq, as well as their Takalū allies.[17] His power base was at the center of the Safavid realm in the region containing the cities of Qum, Sāva, and Kāshān. This strategic location facilitated control over the economic and administrative resources of the Persian state and enabled Muḥammad Khān to revolt in 1585, capture the capital Qazvīn, and take control of the Safavid government.[18] He initiated a purge of his enemies in Qazvīn by sacking their household compounds and taking their wealth for himself and by executing any enemy he found. An army formed from Afshār and Bayāt troops, led by Ḥamza Mīrzā, was diverted from Tabrīz, attacked the Mauṣillū force, and defeated it resoundingly. With this defeat, the confederates of the Turkamān uymāq were forced to leave their homelands in Azerbaijan and the Kāshān region and were placed in the Rayy-Dāmghān region in the interior of Iran.[19] Muḥammad Khān and his sons retained control of Kāshān until 1587, when 'Abbās I deposed them and relegated them to the status of powerless pensioners.[20]

Mauṣillū and Turkamān influence in the Safavid polity was utterly undermined with the fall of Muḥammad Khān Mauṣillū and his family. The Mauṣillū never again played an important role in Iranian history, and the uymāq called Turkamān broke apart. The bludgeoning of Mauṣillū armies and the confiscation of Mauṣillū properties brought the demise of the Turkamān uymāq as a political, social, and economic entity. A few pitiful notices by historians, chroniclers, and writers gave notice to the exasperated condition of the Turkamān chiefs after their defeat. Ghulābī (III) b. Amīr Khān, in exile at Bidlīs, the domain of Sharaf Khān, was ready to enter Ottoman service.[21] Other chiefs were reduced to the level of low-grade chiefs. Some entered government service as the direct dependents of the shah. Others, hoping for the return of better times, clung to minor and unremunerative ūlkā-holdings. Despair and hopelessness became paramount among the survivors and their descendants who remained in subjugation to the overbearing dominion of the Safavid state now buttressed by rival uymāqs. The forlorn condition of the members of the once-powerful uymāq was poignantly displayed in the hedonism of Süsenī Beg and in the insanity of Sulṭān Maḥmūd Khān b. Amīr Khān.[22] During the reign of ʻAbbās I the shattered semblance of Mauṣillū power lay dispersed throughout the administrative superstructure of Safavid Iran. There was no great concentration of holdings in any one particular province or region, and, as with their defeat by Ismāʻīl I, the Mauṣillū were placed in widely separated holdings or forced to share the revenues of one holding among themselves. ʻAbbās I demoted Muḥammad Khān and his son Valī Khān Sulṭān, who had been ḥākim of Kāshān in 1587, and gave them the usufruct of a few scattered places in Ḥabla Rūd, Hizār Jarīb, and a few other places in Iṣfahān, which they were to divide between them.[23] Thus demeaned, they were forced to accept a status greatly inferior to what they had been accustomed to. Some Mauṣillū retained military appointments at Sāva and Āva, for instance, though they were minor chieftains and played only minor roles in the Safavid system. In such circumstances the Mauṣillū eventually sank into obscurity.

CONCLUSIONS

The Mauṣillū family represented something quite different in their origins from the Ṭālish. The Mauṣillū who came over to the support of Ismāʻīl I were not part of the original Safavid order. Through sheer cunning and shrewdness, Amīr Beg b. Ghulābī (I) was able to gain the confidence of Ismāʻīl I, even from the moment of his initial subjection. He surpassed the members of the old-style religious/secular institution who had been both members of the Safavid administration and leaders of the Safavid order. His callous abandonment of the Āq Quyūnlū cause (and of those his kinsmen who continued to support the Āq Quyūnlū after 1508) brought his household great success. He and his descendants were able to develop a great uymāq institution, which was far greater than the Mauṣillū family had ever possessed under the Āq Quyūnlū. The triumph of the Mauṣillū was a sign that the qizilbāsh institution had undergone significant change very early in its history as an imperial organization. The traditional qizilbāsh houses like the Ṭālish were simply too parochial in their physical organizations as well as in the thinking of their leaders. They were unable to compete on the same level with the more cosmopolitan and cynical backgrounds of chieftains like Amīr Beg, who had obtained extensive experience in the management of great realms by the time they entered Safavid service.

The growing success of the Mauṣillū and the brilliance of the family's leading members merely brought the family into conflict with other great houses. The competition for wealth and domain that marked this rivalry with the other households was the force that compelled the Mauṣillū into ultimate impoverishment. After the steady advances made by Amīr Beg and his grandson Amīr Khān, the family began to experience setbacks. First Amīr Khān was unable to maintain a hold on southern Khorāsān and gave way to the pressures of the Shāmlū and the Ustājlū. Then Amīr Khān was isolated politically, forced to rebel, and killed. His death marked the loss of Azerbaijan as a provincial holding for his family. While some family members still held ūlkās in Azerbaijan, they, too, were harried by their neighbors and opponents after the fall of Amīr Khān. The amīrs remaining in Azerbaijan were ultimately forced into rebellion in 995/1582. The two amīrs who repented their rebellion (E.9 and E.13 in Appendix B) and returned to Safavid service were given ūlkās outside of Azerbaijan. With the death of Amīr Khān the bulk of Mauṣillū and Turkamān forces moved eastward toward Kāshān where they supported the rebellion of Muḥammad Khān, the new rīsh sifīd. This rebellion also ended in defeat and eliminated the last remaining Mauṣillū stronghold in Iran. Thereafter the Turkamān and the dependents of the Mauṣillū either remained in isolated obscurity or were absorbed into the networks of other uymāqs or household structures.

The progressive loss of territory was clearly a factor in the declining power of the Mauṣillū and manifested the crisis of power they were experiencing. Once the Mauṣillū rebelled, their enemies on the local level immediately moved to absorb the revenues that had been due them in anticipation of grants to be made by the shah (as in the case of Amīra Sīyāvash, discussed above in chapter 5). The instant crippling of the Mauṣillū fiscal system made it impossible to put up an effective resistance against both the external enemies—the shāh and the greater uymāqs—as well as the internal enemies—the smaller uymāqs and other bands of individuals that had only localized powers. These two problems brought about military and political collapse in the Mauṣillū system and the Turkamān uymāq in general and at the beginning of 'Abbās I's reign left the survivors with increasingly less territory, wealth, and power.

NOTES

[1] "PSI", 1044*a*.

[2] The term "sulṭān" also held a religious significance for Ṣafavīyya mūrīds. The exact meaning of the word in the Ṣafavīyya context is not clear, but it was probably close to the Bektashi understanding of the term, that is, "one who is subject to divine power and authority" and who has contemplated the Divine Reality. The Ṣafavīyya term was probably given stronger Shī'a connotations. *BOD*, p. 269.

[3] "PSI", 1046*a*.

[4] *AQ*, p. 172.

[5] Ibid., pp. 160-162.

[6] Ibid., pp. 175-177. Also see Appendix B.

[7] Other Mauṣillū descendants went into Ottoman or Üzbek service, but they did not form significant political factions in the service of either and soon disappeared.

[8] *AT*, p. 41; *HS*, pp. 91, 204; *TM*, p. 192.

[9] *AT*, p. 53; "PO" (1), 91; *SN*, I, p. 448; MD, p. 17.

[10] Shah Qulī Sulṭān b. Ghulābī (I) Mauṣillū, the brother of Amīr Beg, was the governor of an ūlkā in Azerbaijan. *TAAA*, p. 227, there is no mention of him in *AQ* at all.

[11] Qāyitmas Beg b. Ghulābī (I) was killed by Khān Muḥammad in 913/1507 (*AT*, pp. 41-42; *TAAA*, p. 32). Amīr Beg was evidently transferred to Khorāsān almost immediately after the conquest and placed in a position of power.

[12] *ASh*, p. 58.

[13] The 'Abdillū were classified as Shāmlū. The Chāūshlū were considered Ustājlū.

[14] *TAAA*, pp. 150, 223, 258-260; *MK*, p. 65; *ASh*, pp. 58-60.

[15] *TAAA*, pp. 322-329; *DJ*, pp. 175-176, 183-184.

[16] Ibid., pp. 139, 227, 258, 262, 296, 301.

[17] Ibid., pp. 301, 306, 322-325.

[18] Ibid., pp. 322, 336; *DJ*, p. 194. The shah, Muḥammad Khudābanda, was away from Qazvīn, supervising the siege of Ottoman-held Tabrīz.

[19] Ibid., pp. 337-341; *DJ*, pp. 194-201.

[20] *TAAA*, p. 380. His son, Bektash Sulṭān, had regained the shāh's favor by 1607 and was enrolled in the qūrchīs. The rest of the family remained in an isolated, extremely remote domain.

[21] Ibid., pp. 336, 340.

[22] *MK*, pp. 60, 118-119.

[23] *KhT*, pp. 34-35.

7

Assimilation of Timurid Elements into the Uymāqs

The preceding chapter emphasized the importance of the entrance of Āq Quyūnlū chiefs into the early sixteenth-century Safavid uymāq system. The changes these chieftains brought about in the system were undoubtedly significant. But because they were the most powerful element in the nascent Safavid uymāq structure (and probably in Iran), it has been assumed that they and their Anatolian or Syrian Türkmen supporters were the only elements backing the Safavids. Minorsky goes so far as to conclude that the earliest phase of Safavid history was little more than the last stage of Turkamān tribal control over Iran and that the leading elements in this phase of the development were survivors from both the Āq Quyūnlū and Qarā Quyūnlū ruling elites.[1] The conclusion that has been drawn from Minorsky's statement in more recent scholarship is that the Safavid uymāqs consisted only of elements that survived from the Āq Quyūnlū and/or Qarā Quyūnlū power structures.[2] This reasoning has been carried so far that Shāh Ismā'īl is depicted by some scholars as considering himself to be the legal heir of the Āq Quyūnlū Sulṭān, or the Mahdī of the Anatolian Türkmen.[3]

In the early sixteenth century the chieftains who had served the Āq Quyūnlū Sultāns were the single most important ruling elite in the Safavid uymāq system. While the uymāq names did reflect the importance of Anatolia (Rūmlū) and North Syrian (Shāmlū) Türkmen in the Safavid system between 1500 and 1510, their predominance in the early period has been overemphasized, particularly after 1510, when greater numbers of new elements began to enter the uymāq system in Khorāsān under the patronage of the greater uymāq amirs. Uymāqs and their chieftains that had served Ḥusain Baiqarā or any of his Timurid successors in Khorāsān were adopted into the Safavid system in a more or less complete condition despite the amazing social, economic, and political fragmentation of Khorāsān in this period. The assimilation of some of these Timurid remnants in Khorāsān was not solely a matter of conquest by force of arms. Followers of the Safavid shaikhs had been present in Khorāsān since the last half of the fifteenth century and perhaps even earlier. Minorsky seems to recognize this fact when he points out that Chaghatāī Turkish had already begun to influence the language spoken or used by Shāh Ismā'īl.[4] There were even some Khorāsānī Türkmen who came to live in or around the Ardabīl shrine at some point in the late fourteenth century. They and their descendants preserved the memory of their Central Asian or Khorāsānī origins by giving themselves such names as Tarkhān or Uīghūr-oğlū. The meanings of these names and the role of these groups in the Safavid system will be discussed at greater length later.

THE TIMURID STRUGGLE TO RETAIN KHORĀSĀN

By the end of the fifteenth century the very extensive realm Timūr-i Lang had carved out in Central Asia and Iran had shrunk considerably. Most of Iran had been swallowed up by the Āq Quyūnlū, while to the north, the Üzbeks and others were beginning to nip at the heels of Timūr's successors. The process of shrinkage was accelerated by the continual division and redivision of the realm among the children, descendants, and relatives of Timūr and his clan. Every city and town gave support to a Timurid prince or princess so that power was effectively dispersed among many individuals. As the dispersal of power increased, the ability of the Timurids to resist attacks by internal rebels or neighbors declined, a phenomenon not foreign to the qizilbāsh uymāqs.[5] Even with their ability to resist impaired by such internal divisions, the Timurids were able to retain control in northeastern Iran, parts of present day Afghanistan, and Central Asia. Even this region was diminished further with the coming of the sixteenth century as the Safavids expanded from the south and the Üzbeks from the north. Timurid princes continued to rule in various cities or towns, but quite often they were subjected to either Safavid or Üzbek rule for short periods, and their effective spheres of influence did not go beyond the walls of their respective cities or towns (or their citadels). By the second decade of the sixteenth century even these princes had been eliminated except in the domain of Bābur. The leaders of the greatest Timurid uymāqs, the Birlās and the Mīrānshāhī (the major Birlās subtribe) went mostly into the service of Bābur. The Oghuz, Turkish, and Mongol tribes or segments of tribes that they had ruled remained partly under the rule of the Safavids, partly under the control of the Üzbeks, and partly in the service of Bābur. Those tribal leaders who had impressive enough credentials or family backgrounds were taken into the lower levels of either the Safavid ruling elite or the Üzbek political and military elite. Some, such as the Yaḳa, Ukhlū, or Yomut remained entirely unassimilated and continued to cause problems along the Üzbek-Safavid border until well into Safavid times. The fragmentation and fractionalization of these groups that had once served the Timurids was eloquent testimony to the cataclysmic events that brought about the end of the Timurid state in Iran.

The Timurids had been pushed out of their holdings in Khorāsān by both the Safavids and the Üzbeks. By 930/1524, under Bābur they were able to establish a hold over Balkh, Qundūz, Badakhshān, and Qandahār. But in the period between 1506, the year of Ḥusain Baiqarā's death, and 1524 they were pushed out of even these holdings by their aggressively expanding neighbors. During the period of Üzbek-Safavid rivalry for Khorāsān, Bābur was able to reconquer and maintain hold over the northern part of that province by allying himself with Ismā'īl I.

Another Timurid prince, Muḥammad Zamān Mīrzā b. Badī' al-Zamān Mīrzā, was able to maintain a precarious independence over parts of Khorāsān, but he was subjected first to the Üzbeks, then to Ismā'īl I, and finally to Bābur. He revolted from Ismā'īl I's control just before the battle of Chaldiran and became an independent ruler for a short time, sending expeditions into Astarabad, Gharjistān, and even Hirāt. During this revolt the author of *Habīb al-Siyār*, Ghīyās al-Dīn b. Hamām al-Dīn al-Ḥusainī Khāndamīr, was in the service of Muḥammad Zamān Mīrzā and provided an eyewitness account.[6] After two years of precarious independence, Muḥammad Zamān Mīrzā was defeated by Bābur in 922/1516. Bābur appointed him as governor of Balkh and Shiburgān, which Muḥammad had just taken from the Safavids.[7]

Khān Mīrzā (also known as Sulṭān Uvais Mīrzā), Bābur's cousin, took refuge in Badakhshān in 915/1509-1510 when he recognized Üzbek suzerainty, but with the reconquest of Hirāt by Ismā'īl I, he went over to the Safavids. When Bābur reconquered Transoxania, he observed the superiority of his cousin. At his death in 926/1519-1520, Bābur named his own son Humāyūn ḥākim of Badakhshān.[8]

The Arghūn governors of Qandahār, who had held the province under the Timurids, for a time held aloof from Safavid control, despite an expedition sent there by Ismā'īl I in 1513. They came under nominal Safavid control, however, until in 928/1522, after a three-year siege, Bābur forced the city to capitulate to him. Bābur made his son, Kāmrān Mīrzā, the governor of the city in his name.[9]

The reestablishment of a definitive zone of Timurid presence and control led to the assimilation into a domain ruled by Bābur of the greater tribes that had supported the various Timurid houses. The Birlās and their affiliated tribes, along with the great notables like the Arghūn chieftains, had all returned to Timurid service by 1522. These great chiefs groaned under the onerous rule of potential competitors who had preceded them into the service of the Safavids from their support of the Āq Quyūnlū. Their fortunes as great chieftains rested with allegiance to the Timurid prince Bābur, not in the service of the Safavids, where they would be subjected to the authority of chiefs they considered their equals.

The Assimilation of "Chaghatāī" Elements into Safavid Uymāqs

The fact that most of the greater chiefs found the Safavid uymāq structure inflexible in regard to them, does not mean that many of the lower-level chieftains were unwilling to come to terms with the Safavids or the qizilbāsh chieftains. In fact the Qarā Bayāt, one of the sub-uymāqs listed as "Chaghatāī" by Iskandar Beg, was from a very early date loyal to the Safavid family. The Qarā Bayāt chiefs under Ilyās Beg Uighūr-oğlū had fought in the armies of Ismā'īl's brother (Shaikh Sulṭān 'Alī) and father (Shaikh Ḥaidar). Ilyās Beg and his sons (see Appendix C) also seem to have been among the chiefs whose tribesmen pastured their animals around Ardabīl in summer quarters or at least in the coastal plains of Gīlān, though they probably had lands, pastures, or both in Khorāsān around Mashhad as well.[10] This chief was among the first of the so-called Chaghatāī Turks and Turkified Mongols to join the Safavid movement. It is not known whether his ancestors served the Safavid family, though this seems possible. The Qarā Bayāt of Khorāsān and the Alburz range were the main element in the Chāūshlū sept of the Ustājlū uymāq. Many, if not most, of the chiefs belonging to the Chāūshlū were of paternal or maternal Qarā Bayāt lineage and were served by Bayāt tribesmen.[11]

Iskandar Beg Munshī did not regard the Chaghatāī as a group of tribes that had been affiliated with the Kipchak Horde ruled by Chaghatāī b. Changīz Khān or his descendants, but as those tribes, whatever their origin, that were ruled by the descendants of Timūr-i Lang. Many of these tribes ultimately did trace their origins back to service in the Chaghatāī horde, and the descendants of Chaghatāī still ruled as khāns of the ūlūs Chaghatāī in the early sixteenth century. This category was extended by the Iskandar Beg to cover many Central Asian tribes not of this origin that had come under the rule of Bābur, the Üzbeks, and others (including the Hizāra tribes), as well as numbers of former Timurid subtribes that entered Safavid service.[12]

Such labelling by Iskandar Beg was not whimsy. He was drawing from a long tradition regarding the family of Timūr-i Lang. Timūr claimed maternal descent from Changīz Khān through his son Chaghatāī. He himself belonged to the Birlās tribe, which had long served the descendants of Chaghatāī in Central Asia. As a result of this long service, Timur, his descendants, and their retainers, whatever tribe they actually belonged to, were designated as members of the ūlūs Chaghatāī.[13] Those tribes that were either eventually taken into Safavid domion or that had been subjected to Safavid service by force, or that had previously belonged to the ūlūs Chaghatāī, or that served individuals who had claimed affiliation with that ūlūs, retained the title Chaghatāī or a name that indicated origins in Central Asia outside the pale of Āq Quyūnlū influence.

Two other *nisbas* (names) in addition to Chaghatāī implied origins in a group of people either living in Central Asia or ruled by Timūr. The term "Uīghūr-oğlū" refers to one such group, the family of Bābā Ilyās Qarā Bayāt. It is often cited as "Anghūt-ughlī," "An'ūt-ughlī," or "Aighūt-ughlī," but the actual term was "Uighūr-oğlū." Ghīyās al-Dīn Khāndamīr, who was an administrator in the service of Muḥammad Zamān Mīrzā and was presumably more familiar with Central Asian names, cites the name of Ilyās Beg Qarā Bayāt as "Uighūr-oğlū" consistently throughout his chronicle. In fact, this was the only tribal name he gave this individual.[14] The origin of the term is obscure, but several possibilities might be mentioned. The first is that this family represented descendants of Uighūrs or Sinicized Uighūrs transferred from the Uighūr steppe or China at some point during the thirteenth century, when such transfers were common.[15] It is more likely that this family was descended from Uīghūrs, who, in the late fourteenth century, had been imported from the Uighūr steppe and Besh Baligh into the realm of Timūr-i Lang as administrators.[16] But in the long run, none of these explanations can be totally satisfying, since a number of other explanations for the term can be given. The name may refer merely to "ally" as Rashīd al-Dīn would have it,[17] or it may merely be a corruption of Oghuz (since the Bayāt are normally listed as one of the Oghuz tribes). There can be no doubt, however, that the term refers to an origin in the Timurid principality.

Another term that may or may not refer to Timurid origins was the nisba "Tarkhān," which was given to a branch of the Turkamān uymāq. The first individuals to appear in this branch were actually amīrs subject to the Āq Quyūnlū.[18] This reference to chieftains in the Āq Quyūnlū realm does not mean that these individuals served or were descendants of those who served the Timurids. The term "Tarkhān" appeared most commonly in Timurid administrative practice and referred to those chiefs who were exempt from certain levies, exactions, or services.[19] This practice was in turn a survival of the Mongol and Turkic practice described by Juvainī as follows:

Tarkhān are those who are exempt from compulsory contributions, and to whom the booty taken on every campaign is surrendered: whenever they so wish they may enter the royal presence without leave or permission. He [Changiz Khan] also gave them troops and slaves and of cattle, horses, and accoutrement more than could be counted or computed; and commanded that whatever offence they might commit they should not be called to account therefor; and that this order should be observed with their posterity also down to the ninth generation.[20]

"Tarkhān" as a status was extremely common among the followers of Bābur, but was extremely rare, both in Āq Quyūnlū and Safavid Iran. It is highly possible that some of the individuals listed as Tarkhān were in reality descendants of individuals who for a number of generations had been granted certain privileges by a Mongol successor chieftain who recognized the *Yasa* (*jasak*) (code of laws uttered by Changīz Khān).

The list in Iskandar Beg's history of Chaghatāī tribal groups that had attained qizilbāsh status at certain junctures provides a clear message—the Chaghatāī tribes under Safavid rule were admitted to qizilbāsh status only gradually. The earliest mention of any Chaghatāī chiefs following the Safavids has already been alluded to. The Qarā Bayāt tribe was the original Chaghatāī uymāq to accept Safavid leadership. The relationship between the Bayāt and the Safavids dates back to a distant point in the history of the Safavid Order. How far back is not exactly known. This tribe became part of the Chāūshlū sept of the Ustājlū uymāq and was the first Chaghatāī tribe to achieve uymāq status in the Safavid state. By the end of Ṭahmāsp I's reign in 1576, only a few other tribes were enrolled as uymāqs or affiliates of greater uymāqs. These included the Geraīlī, the Fīrūz-i Jang (probably an affiliate of the Qarā Bayāt), plus the leader of a tribe who was merely designated "Chaghatāī."[21] By 1629 the number of Chaghatāī tribes with qizilbash status had further increased. There were the Qarā Bayāt, located between Nishapur and Mashhad in summer quarters (the traditional homeground of the tribe from at least the early Safavid period; the Geraīlī located on the borders of Astarabad; the Michkī (Michingī?) of Turshīz; the Firūz-i Jang near Turbat-i Ḥaidarīya; the Tuvakilī, located in the *vilāyat* ("province") of Jām, the Jalāyir, the Qamarī near Jahān-Irghān; the Qarā-bāsh; the Ghūrī in the hinterland of Hirāt; and the Jamshīdī around Karkh near Hirāt. Even the troublesome Yaka received status at qizilbāsh.[22] This trend demonstrates that at least two processes were occurring. First, between 1500 and 1629 the number of Chaghatāī tribes with qizilbāsh status was on the increase partly as the result of the influx of some tribes, such as the Yaḳa, from across the Üzbek/Safavid border. Others may only have been splinters off larger groups like the Qarā Bayāt. But by and large most of the tribes, like the Jalāyir, Geraīlī, Ghūrī, and others had existed in Khorāsān at an earlier date. Most had existed in a limbo, at least as far as their leaders were concerned, before they became qizilbāsh, and were subservient to the greater uymāqs, most probably the Qarā Bayāt (and the Ustājlū) as well as the Shāmlū 'Abdillū, who normally held Hirāt. The sudden growth between 1576 and 1629 in the number of Chaghatāī uymāqs with qizilbāsh status is illustrative of a second set of processes—the decrease in power and authority of the greater uymāqs and the parcelling out of their wealth, holdings, and military power to smaller elements that were formerly constituent members of the greater uymāqs, or that were little more than servile dependent groups. Their sudden independence in growing numbers was eloquent testimony to the disruptive internal influences and the debilitating external pressures that were causing the greater uymāqs to break up.

NOTES

[1] *TM*, pp. 17-32; "PSI", p. 1007*a*.

[2] A most notable example is the approach of the Turkish nationalists, especially Faruk Sümer, *Safevi Devletinin Anadolu Türkerleri Rolü* (Ankara: Ankara Üniversitesi Basimevi, 1977).

[3] *AQ*, pp. 180-181; E. Glassen, "Schah Ismā'īl, ein Mahdi der anatolischen Turkmenen?" *ZDMG*, 221 (1971), 61-69.

[4] "PSI", 1010a does not consider the possibility that scholars trained in Chaghatāī in Khorāsān were already serving the Safavids and that imitation alone would not suffice to influence their language.

[5] Wilhelm Barthold, *Herat unter Husein Baiqara dem Timuriden* (Leipzig: Deutsche Morgenlandischen Gesellschaft, Brockhaus Verlag, 1938) p. 15.

[6] *HS*, IV, pp. 394-404.

[7] A. S. Beveridge, *The Bābūrnāma in English* (London: Luzac and Co., Ltd., 1969) pp. 365, 385, 402, 427, 428; *HS*, IV, p. 404.

[8] Ibid., pp. 516, 524-525; *AT*, p. 127; Beveridge, *Bābūrnāma*, p. 257.

[9] *HS*, IV, pp. 572-573, 578-579, 585-591; *AT*, pp. 169-170, 174-175; Beveridge, *Bābūrnāma*, pp. 330-339.

[10] Sarwar, pp. 28, 33.

[11] The Chāūshlū and the Bayāt will be discussed at greater length in the next chapter about the Ustājlū.

[12] *TAAA*, pp. 99, 141, 295, 389.

[13] *TJA*, pp. 225-226, 239-241, 252; Beveridge, *Bābūrnāma*, p. 320.

[14] *HS*, IV, pp. 454, 460, 473, 475.

[15] Ch'en Yüan, *Western and Central Asians in China under the Mongols* (Berkeley and Los Angeles: University of California Press, 1966) passim.; *TJG*, pp. 607 ff.

[16] Sharaf al-Dīn 'Alī Yazdī, *Zafar-Nāma* (Tashkent: Academy of Sciences of the Üzbek SSR, 1972) fol. 220b.

[17] Rashīd al-Dīn, *Jāma' al-Tavārīkh* (Tehrān: Iqbāl, 1338) p. 33.

[18] *AQ*, pp. 86-87, 89-90, 95, 97, 105, 205 (Rustam Tarkhānī); *AT*, pp. 6-7 (Ḥusain 'Alī Tarkhānī).

[19] Beveridge, *Bābūrnāma*, p. 31.

[20] *TJG*, pp. 37-38.

[21] *TAAA*, p. 141.

[22] Ibid., p. 1087.

8

Crisis and Conflict in a Greater Uymāq
The Ustājlū

The social and economic organization of the Safavid uymāq system did not permit the development of a sound political system in the Iranian Empire. The uymāq system was a society that fed off the existence of crisis and in which the strong leader always felt compelled to achieve success at the expense of the misery and misfortune of others. He applied all his economic might and all the political and military weapons in his personal arsenal to achieving his ends. The grimness of this chauvinism cannot be exaggerated, though it was not constantly at a high pitch.

Of the fifty-two years of Ṭahmāsp I's reign almost the first ten were marred by interfactional strife. The other forty-two were relatively peaceful because of the great chiefs' ability to cooperate with one another. Beneath this peace at the upper levels of society, was a boiling, seething mass of troubles nagging away at the qizilbāsh and imperial institutions within Safavid society. Pastoralists unable to find pasture, impoverished or displaced peasants, disgruntled artisans and laborers in the cities and towns, and the dissatisfied members of the reputable and not-so-reputable religious groups all bore witness to the social problems confronting the qizilbāsh masters of society in the "peaceful" years of Ṭahmāsp I's reign.[1] There must have been many more troubles than received notice in the chronicles, for the chroniclers usually noted only the gravest. Problems at the lower levels managed to find their way into the upper levels of Safavid society with the death of Ṭahmāsp, when the bickering of the uymāqs for the spoils of empire sent a paroxysm of darting pain throughout the entire state and set off a series of spastic convulsions that set the Safavid system to shaking for three decades. It was this competition between flabby and oversized uymāqs stuffed with ill-gotten nourishment that comprised the essence of the crisis of the Safavid state in the late sixteenth century.

Certainly it is possible, on the basis of international economic and social trends, to draw parallels between the crisis in Iran and other parts of the world, to note that trends toward inflation or regression in the Mediterranean world or in China also had their effects upon Iran. But to tie Iran into one or the other of these economic "world systems" is not entirely possible since Iran could not at one time be fully dependent upon one system and then later withdraw and enter more fully into another. Before the great Ottoman-Safavid conflicts of the sixteenth century, silk from Persia and China found its way to Mediterranean sea ports. But after 1514, silk and other trade items were increasingly exported through the Eurasian steppe zone via Astrakhan on the Caspian Sea.[2] Trade links with China and India were also increased over contacts with the Ottoman mercantile community. If there were links with international problems, they were minimal and originated from many directions. The international trends had less to do with Iran's problems than with problems in Western Europe or even India. This root of the social issues contronting Safavid society must be found mainly in the dysfunction of a system that had harmed itself by allowing the growth of cancerous "states within states" which expanded to the point where conflict between them was inevitable. The explosion within society at large, as seen in the inter-uymāq conflicts, was accompanied by implosions within the several great tribal substates of the Safavid Empire. As uymāqs grew large through the ravenous ingestion of large chunks of territory, they sometimes developed acute cases of indigestion, and the processes of aging and disintegration began, leading at times to death. The Ustājlū uymāq was such an organism. The history of its rise and then rapid deterioration is indeed fascinating.

The Growth and Expansion of the Ustājlū, 1500–1576

The crises experienced by the Ustājlū uymāq can, strangely enough, be attributed to its growth. It was the growth of the uymāq and the inability of its leading families to adapt to its new size that brought the uymāq organism to an untimely end.

The origin of the uymāq is difficult to trace. It was evidently formed out of the leading tribal families that supported the Safavids early in the existence of the Ṣafavīyya order. The uymāq included at least part of the Ṭālish, who were examined earlier and who sought to break away from the Ustājlū. There were other groups in the uymāq as well. The earliest and most important was the Qarā Bayāt, out of which came the most prestigous family in the uymāq: the Chāūshlū. Finally, the uymāq confederates were numerous, but consisted of many minor families with little or no relationship to the Chāūshlū. The greatest of these were the Qich-oğlū (also known as Fatḥ-oğlū), located at Alamut from the early Safavid period to the beginning of 'Abbās I's reign, and the Kungurlū, composed of the Ṭālish and other independent families located mainly in Azerbaijan. The history of the uymāq's early expansion is interesting to follow. One might almost posit that the failure of the uymāq to take control of the Safavid Empire in the mid-sixteenth century was the result of shifting economic trends. The territory it came to include was located along the old silk route, but the sudden drop in the silk trade affected the commerce that flowed along the old highway. The result is that the expansion was limited in terms of economic growth, but extensive in terms of territory controlled. Had the Ustājlū chiefs gained a grasp on the very vital international trade, they might have retained a more unified and powerful organization. As it was, the various chiefs sank their roots into localized "dispersed" economies. This state of affairs led to the gradual development of a crisis within the uymāq itself.

The expansion of the Ustājlū uymāq began from Gīlān and went to the east, west, and north in the mountains bordering the Caspian Sea and into Azerbaijan. The core area of early Ustājlū economic power was located in Gīlān within close proximity to the Safavid center at Ardabīl. With Safavid successes, the personal and collective domains of the Ustājlū grew by leaps and bounds. While in Safavid service, Khān Muḥammad Ustājlū and his brother Qarā Khān made sweeping territorial gains first in Kermān and then in Dīyārbakr, which eventually became their personal domain separate from the properties of their Chāūshlū kinsmen. Other Chāūshlū and Ustājlū chiefs made personal gains as well in areas outside of northwestern Iran.[3] These gains may have aided Ustājlū prestige abroad, but they did not necessarily help expand the Ustājlū realm in northern Iran where it grew mainly as the result of the natural increase in the members of the ruling families. It was not possible to maintain a familial domain within limited boundaries as long as the number of family members continued to rise. As long as the subject populace increased and their economic productivity kept pace with the growing needs of the ruling families, there was a state of equilibrium. But the ruling families increased in size far more rapidly than those of their subjects owing to the practice of polygamy and the maintenance of numerous concubines whose children all had equal rights to the family wealth. Even when a few male siblings were eliminated in the stiff competition for power, the result was still negative since there were too many hands seeking a share of the proverbial pie. It was this circumstance that propelled Ustājlū expansion, and also caused the numerous problems that the tribe began to face. For the time being, however, the Ustājlū obtained power and prestige through a gradual expansion into the relatively little controlled Alburz range and into the more-hotly contested plains and mountains of Azerbaijan and northwest Iran.

The internal crisis fostered a movement away from the centers of Ustājlū power. After the initial setback of the late 1520s and early 1530s, the Ustājlū began to increase rapidly in number and moved into new lands at an almost undiminished pace.[4] The Fatḥ-oğlū set themselves up in Alamut at about this time, and other young Ustājlū princes received new holdings in areas scattered throughout the Alburz.[5] By the 1570s, Murshid Qulī Khān and his family were establishing themselves in Khorāsān, thus completing a chain of

Ustājlū command throughout northern Iran. With them these chiefs brought portions of the Qarā Bayāt subtribe—the major link in the Ustājlū chain of power in north Iran. Expansion also proceeded in a westerly direction. Badr Khān Ustājlū and the amīrs who survived the qizilbāsh civil wars initiated a movement into Azerbaijan as well as into the Alburz range and Khorāsān. Badr Khān himself held Sulṭānīya and Ṭārum. This westward expansion never seems to have had any strength, and the Azerbaijānī Ustājlū were never deeply involved in the affairs of the uymāq's inner circle. The Kungurlū, for instance, were quite ready to fight other portions of the uymāq and indeed did so in a hair-raising little episode in Qazvīn during the reign of Muḥammad Khudābanda.[6] The Ṭālish, too, were only nominally under Ustājlū control and always maintained an existence independent of the main Ustājlū organization.

The ventures of the Ustājlū chiefs brought on serious problems within the uymāq. The most serious was the loss of control. As the sons and other relatives of great chiefs became eligible for qizilbāsh status, they were established within their own little realms in new territory where a portion of the subtribe(s) owing allegiance to the Ustājlū were assigned to serve them. A whole complex of problems resulted. First, even if this new chief never rose to a higher status, his independence made him difficult to keep in tow. Large numbers of such small independents (like the Ṭālish and Kungurlū) constituted as serious a problem as non-confederates since they were always prone to overtures from outside powers.[7] Secondly, the continual division and redivision of tribal resources sapped the strength of the uymāq leader(s). The apportioning of manpower and armies meant that economic, military, and political power was divided into smaller and smaller units that were gradually coming into competition with one another or forming sectional interests that contravened uymāq solidarity. During the reign of Muḥammad Khudābanda, for instance, Silmān Khān Chāūshlū who headed the Ustājlū of Gīlan, was at odds with Murshid Qulī Khān, his kinsman who headed the Ustājlū of Khorāsān.[8] Third, when Ustājlū colonization reached the outermost limits and came up against similar efforts by other tribes like the Shāmlu and Mauṣillū, the principle of dividing the tribal realm among all possible male heirs of qizilbāsh status meant trouble for the internal security of even the sectional portions of the uymāq. Many new qizilbāsh chiefs among the Ustājlū failed to obtain new holdings when they advanced to their new status. This, in essence, was what had propelled the drive for colonization in the first place. It also led to the system established by Ṭahmāsp I in which the different uymāqs cooperated with one another in finding places for new amīrs. But the burden became too much, especially as the limits of expansion were reached, and new posts became scarcer and scarcer as time passed. Many chiefs were thrown on the mercy of the courts of the greater chiefs and became their dependents, and, if these unenfranchised were forced to grovel or were overly ambitious, they might easily have become an enemy of their own uymāq chieftains. Nothing quite so dastardly as the killing of Mehdī Qulī Khān Dhu'l-Qadr by his nephew Ya'qūb Khān seems to have taken place among the Ustājlū though there was plenty of dissension and bitterness between the haves and have-nots. There was probably as much fratricide and advancement through the killing of relatives on the lower levels of Ustājlū society as there was among other tribes.[9]

Disintegration and Crisis in the Ustājlū Uymāq

The problem of too many amīrs capable of holding portions of the patrimony was the most serious of the uymāq's troubles and inspired all the other difficulties that faced the qizilbāsh leaders of the Ustājlū uymāq. Growing size meant a growing diversity of interests within the uymāq itself. Colonization within Iran and wars with foreign powers were one manifestation of the diversifying impulses within the tribe while increases in inter-uymāq disputes on all levels also demonstrated that impulses of separatism were tearing away at the tribe. The Ustājlū, even if they had been diversified in the beginning, were of a single purpose under the leadership of the young Ismā'īl I. There had been few, if any, problems in maintaining a unified front against the enemies of the uymāq: first the Āq Quyūnlū, later the Dhu'l-Qadr. Brother cooperated with brother, cousin did not seek to kill cousin.[10] There was a recognizable enemy in those times, and the frustrations of overpopulation could be vented upon them with far less anxiety than later. But as the Safavid war machine lost most of its external targets (except for the Üzbeks), the greater uymāqs, like the Ustājlū, fought among themselves, first in civil wars that began in 1524 and continued to the mid-1530s[11] and after 1576 both among and within themselves. The internationalization of the uymāq conflicts was clearly the result of the problems discussed at the end of the previous section and constituted the breakup of the regional empire that the Ustājlū had built. The crisis of the Ustājlū uymāq had been caused by its own imperialistic urges. Too many factions and factions within factions existed for a unified and healthy uymāq to survive.

At the upper levels of the tribe there were rifts between the Kungurlū, Chāūshlū, and the irrepressible Ṭālish. Within the Chāūshlū, the largest and most powerful of the three, were the Fatḥ-oğlu; the Gīlān Chāūshlū, led by Silmān Khān; and the Chāūshlū of Khorāsān, led by Murshid Qulī Khān. In addition there were class antagonisms between the Qarā Bayāt chiefs of lesser status like Ḥājjī Uvais Beg, and the upper level Chāūshlū chiefs who had to contend with several revolts by the Qarā Bayāt.[12] The imperialist ventures of the Ustājlū led to the formation of individual and unrelated social and economic enclaves that might appear unified on paper but in reality were nothing but a great tangled mess of antagonisms and conflicting interests.

The more the uymāq expanded, the less viable it became as a unit of decisive control and government. Revolts increased among Iranian subject peoples, reaching a high point in the reign of 'Abbās I. The Ustājlū, like other qizilbāsh tribes, were no longer able to govern effectively since they had expanded their own individual interests in a highly disorganized fashion and were no longer capable of keeping their own houses in order, much less of managing to rule the various provinces and governmental districts left in their charge. If, for instance, the Ustājlū had been able to keep a handle on the silk trade, they might have been able to develop a stronger central institution, but, as it was, any silk producing ventures that they may have held before 'Abbās I were parcelled out among the Gīlānī and Lāhijānī chiefs. Other economic formations were treated in the same fashion so that each chief had just enough wealth to maintain himself in a small court, but no single chief could become more powerful than another. The formation of the factions was inevitable, therefore, since there was no concerted or well-directed plan of expansion other than the movements required by the exigencies of the biological emergencies nipping at the heels of the ever-larger qizilbāsh families.

The crisis of the qizilbāsh system among the Ustājlū had severe repercussions in the reign of 'Abbās I. The Ustājlū, torn apart from within by internal dissensions and divested of most of its lower-level tribes (like the Qarā Bayāt), was by 1606 left in only a "bastardized" and disenfranchised form. The lines of uymāq authority had been totally disrupted by internal rebellion, civil war, and the policies of 'Abbās I, leaving a truncated, almost totally disabled uymāq structure. In 1609 the most significant Ustājlū holding was not even in the old Ustājlū homeland around the shores of the Caspian Sea. Ḥasan Khān Ustājlū was the beglārbegī of Hamadān. None of his retinue were from any of the old Ustājlū confederate or subordinate tribes. His functionaries included Iskandar (chief of the Muqaddam tribe), Ni'matullāh Sulṭān (*mīr-i Ṣūfī* ['chief of Sufis']), Khusrau Sulṭān (chief of the Pāzūkī tribe), Qabān Sulṭān Begdīllū Shāmlū, Sārū Qurghān, Khalīl Khān Sīl Süpür, and Qubād Khān Mukrī–a very motley crew of Kurds, local (non-Ustājlū) qizilbāsh, and other nondescript elements.[13] These chiefs were mainly from Kurdish and lower level Turkish tribes. Most never had any affiliation with the Ustājlū, and none of their tribes had ever had any connection with the Ustājlū. Such isolation in the provinces represented the final blow to the Ustājlū and left the remaining chiefs in a pitiable state and in psychological shock. No longer would the Ustājlū uymāq be a commanding force in Iran. Of the whole Ustājlū superstructure in northern Iran, only the liberated elements of the lower-level tribes such as the Qarā Bayāt remained.

CONCLUSIONS

This study of the Ustājlū uymāq and its chiefs, together with the other examples of uymāqs, is an attempt to reveal the dynamics of a complex society. Until now works on Iranian tribalism have focused on a single tribal group (Tapper on the Shāh-savan, Barth on the Basseri, Irons on the Yomut Turkmen) and, in nearly every case (except for Tapper), limited themselves to the nineteenth century. Worse, no historical perspective has been developed for Iranian social and economic history before the nineteenth century. Even more troubling, the cultural history that has been written has focused on the religious conflicts that have torn Iran apart from the seventh century on. Almost nothing has been done in the fertile fields of social, economic, and cultural history.

This work has attempted to seek solutions to the problems and prejudices created by the examination of single units of a much broader society by examining a much broader cross-section of that same community than has usually been considered. By perceiving the multiple and interdependent relations of several societies in an earlier period, it has attempted to remold the conceptions of society and thereby lead the way to a new vision of Iranian history and its role in South Asian history—a vision not dependent upon any ideology, only upon historical fact. It should be realized, however, that even historicity is difficult to prove, and historical fact, insofar as it has survived the vagaries of time, the lapses of human memories, or the slips of the hands of scribes, can only be impartial and unfixed in nature. The indefinite nature of the past, in many ways as intriguing and uncertain as the future, has been well demonstrated by the lacunae in the structure of the uymāqs depicted here. If the upper levels of society can be seen only indeterminately, the state of knowledge as regards the lower levels of that society can well be imagined. No *polyptiques* or *praktika* (registers of property belonging to certain institutions) as exist for ninth-century France or fourteenth-century Byzantium have survived. This has left the state of knowledge as rigid and severely restricted as the Romanesque statues that grace the portals of European churches and give but a poor glimpse of the god they sought to depict. The description of the Ustājlū uymāq presented in this book therefore contains many errors and many lacunae that were impossible to contradict or fill due to the state of the sources. By searching out local archives and probing in their documents, by studying archaeologically the places where Ustājlū tribes and subtribes maintained their summer and winter camp grounds it might be possible to uncover some bit of the past and to add to our present, inadequate knowledge of tribalism and pastoralism in Iranian history.

NOTES

[1] The popular revolt in Tabrīz (*AT*, p. 198), the movements of the Yaḳa Turkmen into Khorāsān, and the rebellions of Gīlānī Iranian amīrs are all examples of these troubles.

[2] Halil Inalcik, "The Ottoman Mind and Aspects of the Ottoman Economy, *Studies in the Economic History of the Middle East*, ed. M. A. Cook (London: Oxford University Press, 1970) pp. 207-218.
[3] Sarwar, pp. 44-47, 53-54.
[4] The civil war between the Ustājlū and the Rūmlū/Takalū in 1526 and later is best described in *AT*, pp. 95 ff. Despite the grim circumstances, the Ustājlū emerged from the struggle triumphant.
[5] For the Fatḥ-oğlu (also called or written as the Qūchilū or Qizillū) see *KhT*, p. 32; *TAAA*, pp. 196, 365. Badr Khān became the ḥākim of Astarabad for instance, see: *TAAA*, pp. 108-109; *TJA*, p. 303.
[6] Muḥammad Khudābanda fought for days against warring Ustājlū factions (the Fatḥ-oğlu and Sharaflū) who tore Qazvīn apart in their insatiable lust to exterminate one another. The shah was in his armor for fourteen days, attempting to end the lunacy that was affecting even the chieftains in his own capital. *TAAA*, p. 316.
[7] The rebellion of the Ustājlū under Kūpūk Sulṭān Chāūshlū in the 1520s was not accompanied by inner uymāq disturbances. The revolt of Murshid Qulī Khān in 1589 saw the entire uymāq desert the cause of tribal solidarity.
[8] *TAAA*, pp. 262-264, the split between Silmān Khān and Murshid Qulī Khān. This division was reflected as early as 1576 when the Gīlān chieftain Pīra Muḥammad Khān, the Ustājlū rīsh sifīd, could not obtain the backing of the majority of the uymāq.
[9] For the Dhu'l-Qadr incident see *KhT*, pp. 39-40. Ya'qūb became a khan, the governor of Shīrāz, and the chief male in Mehdī Qulī Khān's ḥaram and household by the simple act of killing his uncle in the act of rebellion.
[10] Khān Muḥammad and his brother Qarā Khān cooperated well in their campaigns in Dīyārbakr. Sarwar, pp. 44-47.
[11] *AT*, pp. 95 ff. describes the qizilbāsh civil wars after the death of Ismā'īl I.
[12] *TAAA*, pp. 196, 201, 205; *AT*, pp. 202-205. The revolt of Ḥājjī Uvais Beg Qarā Bayāt against his Ustājlū overlords.
[13] *TAAA*, p. 853.

9

Crisis of the Qizilbāsh Uymāqs

Was There a Crisis?

A perusal of both the primary and secondary sources dealing with the Safavid period indicates that by the end of the sixteenth century, the large, secular institutions set up by the uymāqs were breaking down. Shāh 'Abbās I repressed the most prestigious and most powerful uymāq chieftains because they were rivals for his sovereignty or at least for parts of his domains. Lower grade military chieftains began to compete with their superiors, fighting them, as well as others of their own station, for more property. It must also be assumed that the entire uymāq social structure was in convulsions and that even independent flockowners and flockless laborers were scrambling to raise their stations, though there is little documentary evidence for this last contention.

The breakdown of the uymāqs is explained away in a very unsatisfactory fashion by most historians, who are unable to establish the criteria for examining the issue. Obviously the breakdown of the uymāq system cannot be characterized in the same terms as the crises of western European aristocracies facing the encroachments of a developing capitalism. Taken in this sense, there was only a minor crisis within the Safavid Empire in the time of 'Abbās I. A far more severe crisis existed at that time: the dismemberment or total destruction of some uymāq networks. Portions of the uymāqs survived the crises of the Safavid period in altered form. The breakdown of the uymāqs has already been called a crisis (or crises), but was the decline of the uymāqs between 1576 and 1629 a crisis in any sense of the word? Is it possible to apply criteria that have been employed to measure crises in other societies to a similar phenomenon in Iran? The answer to both questions is yes, but with reservations. Quite frequently those who attempt comparative evaluations ignore the individuality of the civilizations or cultures they are comparing. The myopic analysis that results places everything on a one-dimensional plane. The present anlysis will establish those factors of crisis which may be found in other civilizations at the time of the Safavids and use them to measure a crisis within Iranian society under the Safavids. Only those factors that prove relevant to an analysis of Iranian conditions will be used. In addition, several factors unique to the Iranian area will be added to the list.

The literature concerning "crisis" is extensive for seventeenth-century Western Europe. The most appealing works are by Lawrence Stone and E. J. Hobsbawm.[1] Other studies while good for describing crises in particular regions, contribute little to a comparative understanding of the problems. It should also be noted that the article by Hobsbawm is concerned primarily with the ultimate development of capitalist econmic formations in west Europe, an issue which concerned Iran only in a peripheral way in the seventeenth century. Lawrence Stone does not perceive the emergence of capitalist economic formations as the ultimate result of the crises of the seventeenth century. However much this may underrate the problems facing Europe at this time, it does examine an issue which is more comparable to the present study–the partial collapse of a ruling elite in sixteenth and seventeenth century Western Europe. Stone's work is also useful because it provides a core of analytical principles for evaluating a preindustrial ruling elite at the moment it begins to experience changes in its traditional organization.[2]

The Criteria for Crisis

The essence of the crisis among the ruling elite perceived by Stone was multidirectional. He reduced the number of criteria for crisis to ten:

1. Decline of the wealth of the ruling elite in relation to members of lower hierarchical positions
2. Shrinkage in the holdings of the great families
3. The decay of the military power of the ruling elite
4. Venality of rank or office in large numbers
5. Changes in attitudes toward the village [and pastoral] populations
6. The undermining of the influence of the ruling elite in religious and political matters
7. Conspicuous consumption
8. An increase in nonmilitary and nonreligious education among members of the ruling elite
9. A rise in individualism and the establishment of a religious doctrine in which a rigid or elaborate spiritual hierarchy was worked out
10. A breach between the central government and the provincial ruling elite

Not all these factors are applicable to Safavid society in the seventeenth century. The nature of the crisis in the Safavid Empire was unique, bearing resemblance to few other regions in the world. Nonetheless, there was a crisis in the Safavid ruling elite, and, that being the case, a social, scientific scale must be devised to measure it. On the basis of Stone's criteria, and by eliminating the less applicable factors and adding several new ones that reflect the uniqueness of Iran, such a scale is formulated here.[3]

The qizilbāsh uymāq organization can be characterized as a system continually faced with the possibility of crisis. The lack of internal constraints and regulations in regard to the allotment of property was responsible for the continual threat of dysfunction within each uymāq. Perpetual crisis was the product of the remolding of steppe economic traditions to fit an Iranian environment.[4] Islamic law alleviated the difficulties inherent in multiple inheritance of private property, even up to the level of the uymāq households. Central Asian steppe perceptions of domain nonetheless weakened the structure rendered by Islamic law to such an extent that most qizilbāsh domains were frequently subject to complex struggles for the succession. The disputes were more than mere competitions for property. They were another phase in the assimilation of steppe practice to a nonsteppe region. Unlike the contemporary struggles in the expanding Muscovite state, the internal disruptions in the Safavid Empire did not culminate in the almost total rejection of pastoral organization or steppe traditions.[5] On the contrary, pastoralism survived these struggles in a relatively strong position. In western Europe the decline in the prestige of the ruling elite was accompanied by a definite downgrading in their legal status. That was not the case among the qizilbāsh, whose status was obscured in the early sixteenth century by the victory of Safavid ideology and polity. The qizilbāsh certainly had a distinct place in the old Safavid religious hierarchy, but since the religious status of the chieftains did not match their secular rankings (and since a wide cross section of Turkic society in Iran was considered qizilbāsh), it was not possible with any accuracy to pinpoint a definite shift in the legal position of the qizilbāsh. From these reservations it is evident that some of the criteria for crisis given above will be inappropriate as discussed below.

1. THE DECLINE OF THE WEALTH OF THE QIZILBĀSH ELITE IN RELATION TO MEMBERS OF LOWER HIERARCHICAL POSITIONS

The qizilbāsh chieftains of the highest ranks experienced a perceptible reversal in the fortunes of their great households and began to lose the revenue sources that had been attached to their households. The loss of wealth and power began to occur in the third quarter of the sixteenth century. Lesser uymāqs and households began to supplant the immense holdings that had formerly belonged to the qizilbāsh chiefs of the highest status. The wealth that had heretofore been the patrimonial inheritance of many qizilbāsh chiefs, was now passing into the hands of qizilbāsh and non-qizilbāsh leaders of lesser status or to royal slaves. The major provinces of the Safavid state were all scenes of devastation as far as the qizilbāsh were concerned. Azerbaijan had been wrested from the control of the Mauṣillū and turned over to the maintenance of their former subordinates, the Qarāmānlū.[6] Southwestern Iran fell from the hands of the Dhu'l-Qadr and the Afshār into the hands of lesser Shāmlū lineages in the region, to Lurs, Kurds, and Arabs who had all ruled areas of southwestern Iran as subordinates of the great qizilbāsh houses of Mansūr Beg Afshār and Ilyās Beg Dhu'l-Qadr. 'Alī Qulī 'Abdillū Shāmlū's control of Khorāsān was dealt a severe blow by the ravages of war with the Üzbeks and by the stern policies of 'Abbās I. New groups, such as the Yaḳa and groups of deported qizilbāsh from other parts of Iran, began to establish independent enclaves within the Khorāsān of the Shāmlū. The Īnāllū dynasty of Kermānī governors was also pushed out of power and replaced by Baluchi chieftains who had formerly been their subjects.[7] Greater numbers of chieftains were now absorbing the same amount of revenues but, in areas like Khorāsān, they absorbed smaller amounts of revenues.

The decay of the holdings of the great amīrs resulted in a severe decline in their wealth. The wealth was redistributed among many chieftains, some of whom belonged to lesser uymāqs, some of whom were revolting against their families. Royal slaves now controlled major incomes and outfought the great amīrs for high positions and wealth. The conscious policy of the Safavid government under Shāh 'Abbās was partly responsible for this reversal in the fortunes of the magnates, but their losses were also due to the innumerable usurpations in holdings under their control as well as to the large number of squabbles for succession and disputes with other uymāqs. In the period before 1576 the smaller uymāqs listed in Minorsky's commentary to the *Tadhkirat al-Mulūk*[8] and in other sources were dependent upon the greater uymāqs. Ḥasan-i Rūmlū, for instance, does not mention a single one of these smaller uymāqs. Over time, however, they were able to shake off their ties to the great chiefs and establish a more independent hold over the territories they considered their own possessions. Many less powerful qizilbāsh and other families continued to hold ūlkās in their hereditary possession, but by the time Iskandar Beg Munshī had written his history, many of these smaller chieftains had been freed of their obligations to more powerful overlords and could form independent uymāqs.[9] With the fuller absorption of revenues at levels closer to the production base, the greater chiefs were unable to control revenues to their own end. This was nowhere so evident as in the beglārbegī of Hirāt, which over two centuries sank from the most to the least remunerative of revenue districts.

There were larger numbers of these smaller hierarchical units developing a stronger foothold within the Iranian economy, nibbling away at the revenue base that had formerly been the prerogative of greater chieftains. The Qarāmānlū family was a case in point. Before the reign of 'Abbās I, the Qarāmānlū clan was almost nonexistent, but 'Abbās I gave control of expansive territories to Dhu'l-Fiqār Khān and the generalship of the Safavid army to Dhu'l-Fiqār's brother Farhād Khān. The lists Minorsky provides indicate that Kurdish and Lurī chiefs became independent of their qizilbāsh overlords and established themselves as qizilbāsh chieftains in their own right. Even Jalālī refugees, who were mostly Kurds, were able to set up independent regimes in the Mughān steppe, Chukhur-i Sa'd, Qarā Bagh, and 'Urūmīya. Shūshtar and Dizful were lost to Khalīl Khān Afshār during the revolt of Qalandar (Kalandar-oğlū), the great Syrian Jalālī. As late as the 1820s the khanate of Yerevan had remnants of these refugee bands, still called Jalalī, which had settled into a particular economic relationship with other peoples in the steppe there.[10]

In addition to the influx of smaller tribal units from Anatolia, the great uymāqs also began to degenerate into smaller tribal units that competed ever more fiercely for the dwindling rewards of position and wealth. While the position of rīsh sifīd had held some importance among the major uymāqs in the first three quarters of the sixteenth century, early in the reign of 'Abbās I it began to decline, as did most other "central" offices or roles in the uymāqs. Competition for control of provincial holdings and positions in the Safavid government (like the *īshīk-āqāsī-bāshī, yasāvul-i ṣuḥbat* (or *yasāvul-bāshī* 'court master of ceremonies'), *qūrchī-bāshī*, and other offices) erased all the old interrelationships and led to fierce contests for power even between father and son as well as among other sets of close relatives.[11] Once great uymāqs such as the Arashlū, Īnāllū, Gündüzlü Afshār tribes, the Shīrāzaī Dhu'l-Qadr, and other uymāqs to a lesser degree, fell victim to their own self-destructive tendencies as early as the reign of Ismā'īl II.[12] The wealth belonging to these groups was divided and subdivided again and again. Chieftains belonging to the same tribe eradicated one another in a fury of destruction that was just as violent as struggles between opposing factions. Where there was a survivor in these wars, he was destroyed or exiled to a distant post by the shah, who could now deal effectively with the debilitated survivor.

The evidence of Safavid chronicles clearly indicates that this category would definitely be a factor in any scientific measurement of the breakup of the Safavid uymāq system after 1576.

2. SHRINKAGE IN THE HOLDINGS OF THE GREAT FAMILIES

A comparative evaluation between western Europe and Iran in this category would be difficult to make. More fruitful parallel studies could be made in the study of Muscovite Russia in the sixteenth and early seventeenth centuries and with Ottoman-dominated Anatolia in the same period.[13]

The main factors in the breakup of the large estates of the English peers was due mainly to sterility and incompetence, for which Stone provides statistics.[14] Similar statistical evidence is lacking for Iran. What little information the chronicles give is not usable for delineating the causes for the breakup of the qizilbāsh holdings. It is only possible to say that the mighty institutions that once belonged to the patrimony of the great chieftains were gradually divided up among a larger number of competing chieftains (qizilbāsh and non-qizilbāsh).

Another dimension to the problem was that in the late sixteenth century, even before these properties were divided, the Iranian revenue and patrimonial systems had generally been in a state of dispersal. The blocks of revenue shown in the *Tadhkirat al-Mulūk*, for instance, were never regarded as whole or undivided revenues as in the English and other European examples of the same period.[15] Patrimonial inheritances were the property not of an individual, but of a nuclear or extended family. This dispersal of holdings among several individuals was made in the official holdings of the qizilbāsh governors as well as in the private domains of the great qizilbāsh houses. The usufruct of certain properties was distributed among subordinates of the great chieftains in a manner similar to that of the rīsh sifīds of obas, though pasture lands were only part of the allocations made. In fact some of the greatest families held more than one provincial or governmental post and these were distributed among the members of the family by the main chieftain almost as if they were part of the family's personal property. When Mehdī Qulī Sulṭān Arashlū revolted against Safavid control in the 1530s, seizing control of Dizful and Shūshtar, it was his relative, Sıvındık Beg Arashlū qūrchībashī, not the Safavid shah, who commanded the rebel to be subdued. 'Alī Qulī Beg 'Abdillū; the Īnāllū chieftains of Hamadān; Muḥammad Khān Ustājlū, Murshid Qulī Khān Ustājlū, Musayyib Khān Takalū; the Dhu' l-Qadr chiefs of Shīrāz; Muḥammad Khān Sharaf al-Dīn-oğlū, Amīr Khān Mauṣillū; and the Purnāk governors of Tabrīz, among others,[16] divided private possessions and public positions in the same way—as family possessions, not individual inheritances.

Even if statistics were available, it would not be possible to use them with any accuracy because individual increments or income figures would represent only the official figure before partitioning. The only truly accurate statistics would be those that would describe the finances of the family estates of the qizilbāsh (as well as other) chiefs. Even then a large block of the items would be income in kind which had relative, not absolute cash values.[17] Continual allocation and reallocation of incomes in kind and cash was not only the central mechanism of households and empires built up by the Turkic ruling elite in Iran (and elsewhere), but it represented the main force that crippled these households. On paper, for instance, 'Alī Qulī 'Abdillū Shāmlū was the overlord and the beglārbegī of Hirāt. In reality he had to contend with competitors outside his household institution, mainly the Ustājlū, Īnāllū, and Mauṣillū/Purnāk, who wanted to take control of his holdings. Within his household he continually had to deal with the threat of being abandoned by one or more of his retainers or kinsmen.[18] These perpetual tensions so weakened the northeastern provinces of Iran that they frequently fell prey to Üzbek invasions.

In the late sixteenth and early seventeenth century a cycle of regression similar to that noted by Stone and in a broader context by Braudel was evident among the qizilbāsh ruling elite. It may in fact be regarded as the catalytic agent in the dissemination of steppe social and economic practices among local Iranian populations. Whether some international forces were responsible for such a regression is unclear. Certainly Muscovite expansionism in the sixteenth and seventeenth centuries was laying the foundation for the eventual breakdown of the vigorous traditions of steppe life. For the immediate purpose at hand, however, the Muscovites were pushing various Turkic peoples into Central Asia. Most were Üzbeks, whose migration back into the steppes ended north of Khorāsān. Their continual attacks represented a mini-crisis for the marches of Khorāsān. But to place the decline of the financial and economic power of the qizilbāsh into the context of a similar, worldwide crisis is not possible. Even those who attempted to do so recognized that Iran and certain other areas, including Russia, were outside the scope of the developing European imperialism and less subject to the vacillations of Eurocentric economic systems.[19] The economic reasons for the breakup of the large qizilbāsh estates were not the same as those for the disruption of aristocratic estates in European regions. The problems of the qizilbāsh cannot even be put on the same economic scale, since the European aristocracies were almost wholly dependent upon agricultural economic systems while the qizilbāsh households were formed out of the alliance between agriculture and pastoralism.

The dynamics of decline is another story. The basic trends Stone and others note may also be traced in the Safavid Empire. The processes that brought about the dissolution of the economic power of the ruling elites in western Europe, the Ottoman Empire, and Iran, as well as elsewhere, are comparable. There was a dramatic shift in the wealth controlled by the qizilbāsh chiefs and their families, just as there was a similar shift in the destinies of the European and Muscovite elites. Midway through the reign of ʿAbbās I chieftains who would have received powerful public offices or who would have commanded vast resources of private and public wealth controlled only restricted holdings. At nearly the same time and in the same manner, but for radically different reasons, the European nobilities began their own cycles of impoverished existence. The positions of the European and the Iranian ruling elites, when compared at this level, are not so radically different, however, as some Marxist scholars would argue. West European mercantilism was barely mature enough to present an overwhelming threat to the old ruling elites. The disruption of the wealth held by the old ruling elites in Iran and in Europe[20] as well as in the Mediterranean Basin, was part and parcel of the economic cycles that propelled the circumstances of economic decline. Certain local variations were, of course, unique, due to particular local conditions. Iran and the qizilbāsh households did not decline because of any great worldwide trend, but because the situation at the top was getting out of hand. Too many chieftains were attempting to control too few holdings. The result was economic disintegration. The same conditions were afflicting most of Europe (except England, where primogeniture was the rule), but here there was an added force: a nascent capitalism that began to detract, though minimally, from the power of the nobility.

Despite the radically different economic spheres under question, it is possible to use this criteria as an evaluative factor in the discussion of the dynamics of social and economic disruption.

3. THE DECAY OF THE MILITARY POWER OF THE RULING ELITE

Very little needs to be said here other than to note that too much has been made of the relative decline of the military technology that supported the qizilbāsh institutions. Unconscious or conscious comparison with western Europe may be at fault. The main Persian secondary source on Safavid military organization asserts that the qūrchīs, and the qizilbāsh in general, used only swords, maces, bows and arrows, and lassos, and wore only chain mail corselets with spiked helmets. "They rejected the use of firearms as unmanly."[21] The chief western source on this subject, Minorsky, makes the same claim, that the qizilbāsh used only outmoded weapons. He implies further that the *qullar* (slave troops of the shah) were the only members of the Safavid army to use firearms.[22] The evidence, even that presented by Minorsky himself,[23] shows that exactly the opposite was true. In many respects the uymāqs in times past did not hesitate to adopt technological advances that would enable them to improve their living conditions and to protect their way of life. The qizilbāsh may have scorned the muskets and harquebuses for their ineffectiveness at long ranges, but they realized their value in massed battle conditions at short range.[24] The old arguments that qizilbāsh military strength declined in relation to the growth of slave units or musket-wielding peasants are totally out of character. The sources mention that qizilbāsh chieftains supported large households of slaves. Shāhvirdī Khān Zīyād-oğlū Qājār captured thousands of slaves on a raid into Georgia. Most of them presumably entered his service, either as household servants or as guards.[25]

The main problem confronting the chieftains was not technology but rather how to obtain sufficient troops. The continuous division of larger spheres of control into smaller ones suited to members of the families often meant that less and less troops were available to the chieftains. To compensate, qūrchī troops, nominally in the service of the central government, were often put at their service. Special units of retainers or auxiliaries composed of Pāzūkī, Kalhur, or other Kurdish soldiers were also allotted to them.[26] After 1610 refugees from the unsuccessful rebellion of Kalendar-oğlū, a Kurdish Jalālī, poured into Safavid territory. They entered the service of several qizilbāsh chiefs in turn but were so unmanageable that they eventually came into conflict with their new overlords.[27] This shortage of good troops weakened the chieftains militarily in relation to the central government, which possessed not only slave troops in its direct service alongside qūrchīs but the collective forces of all the uymāqs. Under such circumstances it was difficult, if not impossible, for qizilbāsh chiefs to remain independent for long.

4. VENALITY OF RANK OR OFFICE IN LARGE NUMBERS

This factor was not a feature of the general crisis of the ruling elite in Iran. The decreasing value of the status of qizilbāsh from the time of Ismā'īl I signified the existence of the same problem that led to the increasing sales of office in western European regimes. The preconditions to venality of office or rank existed in Iran and the Safavid state. The status of qizilbāsh had begun to lose much of its intrinsic value. Someone bearing the title of "qizilbāsh" was no longer a religious devotee in the purest sense of the word as early as the time of Shaikh Junaid Ṣafavī, though, by the end of Ismā'īl I's reign, the term qizilbāsh was applied to (*a*) any of the uymāq households (Īnāllū, Bayāt, Ustājlū, Afshār, Qājār, 'Abdillū, Dhu'l-Qadr, and so on), (*b*) and sometimes, though more and more infrequently, to the pastoral and agricultural units beneath them. This change represented an objectification of the status allotted to the qizilbāsh. The chieftain and those of his followers who still called themselves qizilbāsh were only mūrīds in a strictly formal, extrinsic sense. The real role of the qizilbāsh in Safavid society had become less religious and more political, military, and administrative. The familial structure of the qizilbāsh system and the traditions of the Turco-Mongol ruling elite of Safavid Iran did not permit the expansion of the hierarchical order to reach the degree it did in western Europe and the Ottoman Empire.

5. CHANGES IN ATTITUDE TOWARD THE VILLAGE [AND PASTORAL] POPULATIONS

The transformation of feudal relationships is explicable only in west European terms. The conditions that prevailed in western Europe during the period when classical feudalism developed also existed in other areas. But these conditions long outlived the feudal institutions in western Europe.[28] The most important of these conditions was a poor system of communications and transportation. As a result societal interrelationships were forced into a more localized scheme. The need arose for individuals who could assume the burden of controlling the affairs of a locality either for themselves or in the name of someone else and who did not need to rely too heavily on instruction from a superior. In Iran and the Central Asian steppes, pastoralism and the steppe pattern of organization served rulers well. Even after these rulers ceased to be pastoralists themselves they continued to practice the itinerary of pastoralist societies in order to ensure proper control of their domains.[29] The travels of the ruler, as well as those of a khan or chieftain of pastoralists, were complex and far more extensive than those of their subjects. The most successful rulers and chieftains countered the communication/transportation problem by traveling continually. In western Europe the aristocracy became a less and less significant factor in local affairs, while in Iran the local notables and chiefs continued to play an important role in the life of the communities they controlled. Qizilbāsh chiefs were just as harsh and ruthless in making exactions from the agriculturalists and pastoralists beneath them as were the Turco-Mongol chiefs who had been their predecessors, and in some cases, ancestors.

6. THE UNDERMINING OF THE INFLUENCE OF THE RULING ELITE IN RELIGIOUS AND POLITICAL MATTERS

The most extensive work has been done on this aspect of the qizilbāsh. The writings of R. M. Savory effectively cover the history of the Safavid political system and provide an excellent insight into its problems. The undermining of the religious influence of the qizilbāsh in the Safavid religious structure has been examined in greater depth than any other aspect of qizilbāsh history. Unfortunately this overemphasis on the religious aspect of the qizilbāsh has led to countless repetitions of distorted and hackneyed concepts of the role of the qizilbāsh. The best, and most realistic work on the subject has been done by Erika Glassen and R. M. Savory.

The rapid militarization of the Safavid religious order in the second half of the fifteenth century, combined with the conversion of many members and families of the old Turco-Mongol military elite, signified the politicization and militarization of the order itself. Most, if not all, of these military chieftains had little liking for theological matters, and their lack of understanding was responsible for the development of a more authoritarian chain of command, such as that worked out in Shī'a theology regarding the hierarchy of the imāms. At the same time, these military chiefs patronized scholarship and especially the plastic arts, that dealt with secular subjects and matters that they could understand more easily. The boom in miniature painting in the Safavid period may be attributable in part to the penchant of great qizilbāsh patrons for works of visible aesthetic qualities. Many qizilbāsh chiefs or descendants of great qizilbāsh houses turned to the arts—perhaps more than can now be known, since many of them may have lost their uymāq *nisbas*.[30] A few qizilbāsh religious scholars existed by the end of the sixteenth century, but their works were neither prodigious nor great. The greatest contributors were in the arts, literature, and the sciences. Ṣādiqī Beg Afshār was a poet and an artist as well as the librarian of 'Abbās I. Iskandar Beg Munshī was a scribe and an historian. Ḥasan-i Rūmlū was an historian. The list could continue for pages, but it is evident that by the mid-sixteenth century the major contribution of the qizilbāsh was in both producing and patronizing secular works.

7. CONSPICUOUS CONSUMPTION

Evidence for extravagant and lavish living among the qizilbāsh chiefs or their subordinates is extremely weak. The fact that increasing numbers of the qizilbāsh turned away from military service or performed only the minimum required of them must not be considered an indication of overly sumptuous and lavish life-styles. The few examples of qizilbāsh who did engage in such life-styles were probably the exception rather than the rule. Ṣādiqī Beg has left a notice of one Ṣūsenī Beg Mauṣillū, who was forced to sell his services as a soldier to high amīrs of his own status because he overindulged in opium-smoking, drinking, and gambling.[31] Another piece of evidence that is almost certainly a caricature, not a reflection of reality, is the painting by Riḍā-yi 'Abbāsī entitled "Nashmī the Archer." The subject, a qizilbāsh warrior, is quite clearly shown as slovenly.[32] A more straightforward representation of a qizilbāsh chieftain was executed by Ṣādiqī Beg of his former patron, Tīmūr Khān Ustājlū. Tīmur Khan is depicted not as either decadent, like Nashmī, or a hero, as was common in the Turkamān and early Safavid styles of painting, but as an educated, refined patron of the arts with a slightly martial bearing despite his obesity. There is only a hint of the satirical in this depiction.[33] These few pieces of evidence, along with some other isolated cases, have been blown out of all proportion, and, as in the case of religion, an unconscious comparison with the European example has prejudiced the approach to the qizilbāsh and other ruling elites in the Middle East.[34]

8. AN INCREASE IN NONMILITARY AND NONRELIGIOUS EDUCATION AMONG MEMBERS OF THE RULING ELITE

This section of analysis is a corollary to section 6 and must be examined in connection with the premises put forward there. As noted in section 6, there had developed a trend away from religious learning that was noticeable in many ways before Ismā'īl I's defeat at the battle of Chaldiran. Administrative skills and learning had suddenly become an urgent prerequisite for the operation of the Safavid state. Scholars such as Iskandar Beg Munshī and a few other qizilbāsh leaders entered the scribal and administrative institution of the Safavid state in later times along with a host of Tājīk bureaucrats. In fact the *Tārīkh-i 'Ālam Ārā-yi 'Abbāsī* might be regarded as a highly literate administrative manual that is especially useful for the qizilbāsh, but for other groups in Safavid society as well. This need for administrators left the door open to other forms of secular education and artistic production and resulted in the development of a society that was less oriented toward religion. The new secularizing thrust was the means of blunting the sharp and unified purpose that the qizilbāsh had formerly possessed.

9. A RISE IN INDIVIDUALISM

The hierarchization of society by the Safavid religious order, particularly under the influence of Shī'ism, was a significant element in early Safavid propaganda. The world community was ideally a place or a society in which everyone possessed a distinct status or position. This ideal community was to be the transplantation of the heavenly kingdom onto earth. The Safavid world order was to be nothing more than a microcosm of the great chain of being as it existed in the greater cosmos. The poetry of Ismā'īl I represents an extremely degenerate form of this hieratic conceptualization. The scientific, Neoplatonic, and astrological perceptions of previous metaphysical doctrines were not very well understood by Ismā'īl or his chieftains. All that remained were the devotion to the belief that they were the instrument of God's will on earth and the military hierarchy that grew out of this belief. As mentioned earlier, however, most of the qizilbāsh took the preaching of the young Ismā'īl with a grain of salt. The result of this was an increased propensity toward individualism almost from the moment of Ismā'īl's triumphs. By 1576 the particularist tendencies of the uymāqs and the individualistic motives of their chieftains burst into a phantasmagoria of nightmarish struggles for power. Amazingly, the peoples belonging to the median groups of Safavid uymāq society were able to remain in their particular family groupings, although individualism had torn away at the lowest and highest levels of the various communities. Rebels and adventurers disrupted the order of the old, established uymāqs, often leaving the leaders without a following or without property. Khalīl Khān Afshār was forced to abandon the homeland of his ancestors to the rebel Qalandar, who seems to have created the circumstances that weakened the Afshār hold over Kūh-Gīlūya and led to their ouster from Shūshtar and Dizful a decade later.[35] The Īnāllū chieftains of Kermān were likewise replaced by chieftains who had been their underlings in the reign of 'Abbās I.[36] Personal individualism was minimal, however, except at the upper levels of the uymāq hierarchies.

The tendency at the lower levels of Safavid society was toward the formation of smaller tribal or other social units. The Afshār, for instance, lost their power in Kūh-Gīlūya and were gradually subjected to the rule of Shāmlū and then Lūrī chiefs. The Īnāllū tribe, which had shared in the control of Kūh-Gīlūya, was dislodged from its holdings there and ended up in widely scattered places throughout western Iran. After the late 1570s, the Īnāllū were gradually broken down. Some were placed under the control of the Shāmlū. Others appeared in the north in the reign of 'Abbās I among the newly organized Shāh-savan groups there. Still others like the descendants of Qāsim Khān, remained in isolated pockets independent from anyone's control. Groups that had formerly been subject to Afshār rule in Kuh-Gīlūya and Ināllū rule in Hamadān eventually broke free from the control of their overlords and in some cases managed to take the position formerly held by the tribe(s) of their former chieftain. The Lurs, for example, gradually replaced the Afshār as the pastoral element in Kūh-Gīlūya.[37] Individualism of this sort was more of the group than of the person. Even the rebels against local authority who joined in with groups where the individuals were not genealogically related eventually became organized into tribalized units—notably the Shāh-savan groups.

Personal individualism was the priority of the great chieftains. Individuals belonging to the greatest uymāq families broke away from the old, accepted genealogical units and established their own power bases. Amīrs often surrendered their rights in an older uymāq power structure for smaller, but independent holdings elsewhere. Government policy forced other chieftains to migrate to distant regions. The majority of occurrences began in the 1570s and extended into the 1620s, aquiring more and more the countenance of forced movements propagated by the shah. Lineage names that were standard among the Qājār of Astarabad in the nineteenth century are only hinted at in some of the names of Qājār tribes in sixteenth century Georgia. While 'Abbās I was the first person to set the Qājār up in Astarabad through his policy of *sörgün* (deportation), it was also evident that the deported Qājār amīrs probably welcomed the chance to establish an independent domain far removed from the bickering and chauvinism of relatives who considered themselves superior.[38] Amīr Khān b. Ghulābī (II) Mauṣillū was another example of the individualism that was disrupting the uymāq system in the 1580s. His willful and chauvinistic control of the Turkamān uymāq gained him many enemies within the uymāq and even among the members of his own family. His own brothers and children plotted against his life. When he was taken prisoner by Safavid representatives, they refused to rebel or to intercede on his behalf.[39] The gradual split-up of the great uymāqs led to the eventual extinction of some and the crippling of others.[40]

10. A BREACH BETWEEN THE CENTRAL GOVERNMENT AND THE PROVINCIAL RULING ELITE

The break between the Safavid central government and the qizilbāsh seems to have been a factor almost from the beginning of Ismā'īl I's reign. The greatest qizilbāsh families had a stake in the operation of the state and considered themselves viable alternatives to the rule of the Safavid family. From a very early date, at least from the 1520s, uymāq chiefs sought either to control the Safavid shah or to replace the Safavid rulers with their own families. In the reign of Ismā'īl I, the Ustājlū held supreme power within the Safavid state but when they were pushed out of their primary position in the 1530s, they skulked in remote corners of Iran, awaiting a chance to return into imperial favor and overthrow the uymāqs with whom they competed for power. During those years of exile they held their possessions in Gīlān without royal approval and were a hostile element in the very midst of the Safavid Empire. The Ustājlū did regain power after a time, but they were merely one of several uymāqs competing for the primary position. By the 1580s, the Chāūshlū Ustājlū of the Bayāt tribe gained a strong foothold in Khorāsān. They supported 'Abbās I for the throne, but once they succeeded in putting him at the head of the Safavid state, they lost this power when their leader, Murshid Qulī Khān, who was the vakīl, attempted to absorb revenues belonging to the royal family into his own treasury. This act was tantamount to rebellion and a sure sign that Murshid Qulī Khān intended to establish himself as sole ruler of Iran. 'Abbās I cut Murshid Qulī Khān off from his ambitions, executed him, and put an end to Ustājlū control over himself.[41] Such incidents were common in Safavid Iran. These revolts demonstrated the continuous tension between the great amīrs and the shah. That none of them fully achieved their goals until the end of the seventeenth century was a tribute to the ability of the Safavid ruling princes to manipulate even the most impossible political circumstances to their own benefit. The lion's share of the tribute must be given to 'Abbās I, who was able to weaken the uymāqs sufficiently to maintain his own power and to cause them to break up into increasingly smaller units that were at cross-purposes with one another.[42] Without denigrating his role in the process, it must be added that, down to the middle of the seventeenth century the other Safavid shahs, with the possible exception of Muḥammad Khudābanda, maintained themselves well. The very fact that tensions existed between the different uymāqs made the task of the shahs easier.

Crossed Patterns of Power and Authority

In the previous section, ten items used to describe the "crises" of a ruling elite similar to the qizilbāsh but in another area were analyzed for their relevance to the qizilbāsh. It was not intended to imply that the problems the qizilbāsh faced were qualitatively or quantitatively like those of a western European aristocracy at or near the same period of time. The aim of the analytical framework established above was much more modest: only to provide a scientific apparatus for measuring the problems encountered by a certain segment of the Safavid ruling elite. The blind adaptation of phenomena used to measure the distress of another society in another place will inevitably lead to mistaken conclusions. In order to study Safavid society effectively, therefore, it is necessary to determine the unique element or elements that propelled Safavid society into the course that it ultimately followed. The forces that led to the paralysis of the Safavid society and economy cannot be characterized in the same terms as the Hegelian dialectic or its Marxist reinterpretation. Still less can these crises be perceived as the working out of some vague divine or imperial will, as the Safavid chroniclers would have their readers believe. The ultimate and more or less continuous debilitation of the uymāq system in Safavid Iran was the result of innumerable causes, some of which have been pointed out above. More than anything else, however, multiple (not dialectical) forces tore the qizilbāsh system apart. The Marxist theory of precapitalist economic formations cannot explain the coexistence of slavery with what it calls feudalism in the Middle East.[43] One major array of symptoms that was irrelevant to the west European crises was the multiple nature of each Safavid uymāq system. Each uymāq was a political, economic, social, and military unit in and of itself. The greater household within each uymāq was not the sole unit, but merely the predominant family among a number of other families, each with its own household organizations. Divisions within the uymāqs were not limited to distinct kinship groupings, but extended into the families themselves. As sons received a share of the patrimony from their father, they became independent rulers in their own domains, even though in theory they were subject to the family's authority. In most cases this independence was necessary since each son required assistance in operating his domain (or his proportion of the family domain) and developed the financial, familial, economic, and social establishments of a distinct or a separate organization. Naturally, conflicts over the sources of wealth developed, there was an increase in the division of the holdings within each domain, and the wealth that once supported one or more chiefs gradually came to support even more. The spiralling increases in the holdings of wealth led to the development of competitive cultures seeking to derive a living off the same limited base. The producing units, the obas and villages, that supported this ever more elaborate system of benefices were divided into counters of wealth that returned less and less supportive wealth to the uymāqs as the number of amīrs increased who desired to develop their own household structures. At the height of the inflation of these holdings, the competitive households were forced to extract wealth from the domains of their neighbors or fail to survive as an entity. These "crossed patterns of economic, political, and social power," as they shall be called here, led ultimately to the total paralysis of the uymāq at large and of the different households under its aegis. Increasing individualism, the breakup of the uymāqs, the shrinkage of the holdings of the great families, and the other relevant factors discussed in the foregoing section may all be perceived in the light of these developing crossed patterns of power. The crises of the Safavid state in the early part of Ṭahmāsp I's reign and between 1576 and the early part of the seventeenth century were also the result of the paralytic effects of the crossed patterns syndrome.

What needs to be stressed at this point is the nonwestern dimension of the social organization that produced such patterns of life. Steppe societies and societies derived from steppe-type social and economic organizations perceived the patrimonial domain in a manner similar to that of the pastoralist. Land was not to be measured out in exact increments and utilized according to legally established practices as in agriculturally based societies. Pastoral societies perceived land as the element upon which the fodder for their animals grew. Wealth was not measured in amounts of land, but in terms of animals and the amount of fodder needed to feed one animal or a group of animals. Larger units of measurement were the houses or households (*khāna* or *ujāq*) which included not only the amount needed to support humans, but the necessities required for the maintenance of animals.[44] The same principles of management followed by "houses" that actually looked after livestock were transferred to the greater households of the Turco-Mongol magnates (both in the Central Asian steppe and in Iran), only on a broader and more complex level. Outside the steppe, the households of the magnates formed combinations with other social and administrative forms, so that in Iran part of the administrative staffs of these magnates was composed of Iranians who oversaw the administration of the agricultural wealth belonging to the chieftains. The groupings controlled by the chieftains were not considered to be immovably attached to any certain region, unless, of course, they were agriculturalists, which a part of them were, even in the massive steppe zones. The main structural element of the pastoral communities was their movability and, therefore, their assignability to different pasture areas over time. Newly formed groups might be assigned to the same pasture land where an older group traditionally maintained itself. It would share the pasture rights with the older members if there was enough pasture land for both groups. The new head of a family might likewise start his life as the head of a house by being assigned to a totally different camp group from the one in which he was raised as a boy. In his new environment the young man might begin a new flock or herd and share the pastureland of his new companions.[45] Such sharing out and repartitioning would only cause grave problems in an agricultural society, where the product being raised cannot be moved so easily once crowding occurred.

The task of allotting pasturage from season to season belonged to the chieftain. He also assigned the supervision of several camp groups to each adult male in his family. Each man was allowed to obtain revenues for himself in kind (wool, hair, butter, cheese, milk, transport animals, and war animals) and in services (military service and herdsmen's duties).[46] In Iran the chieftains also controlled a more extensive agricultural sector, from which they derived dues in cash, kind, or services.[47] Each member of the chiefly family was entitled to these services and became the head of his own micro-household consisting of administrative, military, and economic or smaller household units. As in the obas, a capable young man was set up in his own independent household and given the means to begin an independent existence as the head of his own familial organization. The independent status of the household organizations subject to the chieftain's male relatives was often the basis of tension and conflict within each uymāq. The qizilbāsh version of this system was much more complicated than the organizations found in the steppes since it involved a parallel operation of pastoral and agricultural societies, both of which, by the sixteenth century, had been fully incorporated into an Iranian bureaucratic structure. The crossing patterns of possession rights, power, and authority were also more complicated. The multiplicity of minor, chiefly households within the uymāq framework became a crushing burden to a society that was partially immovable due to the nature of its economic organization. Both pastoralists and agriculturalists could manipulate such an overabundance of chiefly authorities to their own advantage by playing the competing elements off against one another. Their shifting from one chief to another constituted the core of the crossed pattern syndrome. When the situation became grave fratricidal wars or territorial civil wars broke out.[48]

NOTES

[1] *CA*; E. J. Hobsbawm, "The Crisis of the Seventeenth Century," *Crisis in Europe, 1560-1660*, Trevor Aston, ed. (Garden City, New York: Doubleday and Co., Inc., 1967) pp. 5-62.

[2] *CA*, p. 4. The work by Stone takes a non-Marxist approach to the issue and is a useful counterpoise to the views of Hobsbawm.

[3] Ibid., pp. 350-351.

[4] The subjection of an agricultural economy to control by an elite organized according to the rules of a pastoral economy frequently resulted in a more or less continual struggle among the members of the pastoral-based elite.

[5] *RR*, pp. 1-7. Only a mutant form of pastoralism was retained among Slavic Cossacks.

[6] *TM*, p. 18 (breakdown of control over lesser households); *AQ*, pp. 210-211; *TAAA*, pp. 442-443, 491-492, 756-757, and the appropriate passages in *KhT* record the rise of the Qarāmānlū in the provinces of Azerbaijan and Gīlān.

[7] *TA*, pp. 17-18, Kasravī, pp. 68 ff. (the Afshār); *TAAA*, pp. 381-388 (the Shāmlū); *TK*, pp. 265 ff. (the Kermān Īnāllū).

[8] *TM*, pp. 17-19; *PZP*, pp. 30-32.

[9] Perhaps Iskandar Beg was more methodical in laying out the details of tribal organization than the other chroniclers, so that many independents, especially Kurds, were not discussed by other chroniclers.

[10] *SN*, passim; "SSE"; *TAAA*, pp. 280 for qalandar, and pp. 780 ff.

[11] *KhT*, p. 72.

[12] *TAAA*, pp. 138-650, is filled with seemingly endless narratives of these internal wars. See Appendixes for their disastrous effects. See also *KhT*, paṣsim, for an in-depth description of the years just after the accession of ʻAbbās I.

[13] S. F. Platonov, *The Time of Troubles* (Lawrence: University Press of Kansas, 1970) pp. 164 f. and passim; *RR*, pp. 10 ff. 49; Mustafa Akdağ, *Celâli Isyanları, 1550-1603* (Ankara: 1963); Shaw, *Ottoman Empire and Modern Turkey*, Vol. I, 185-186.

[14] The conditions outlined in Stone, pp. 76-88, 93-94, are placed in greater perspective in Braudel, *Mediterranean*, II, pp. 706-709.

[15] *TM*, pp. 100-105.

[16] See Appendixes A-C.

[17]The socioeconomic approach of Henri Pirenne (*Medieval Cities* [Garden City, N.Y.: Doubleday and Co., Inc., 1956, pp. 1-34 and passim]) has been responsible for many misconceptions about preindustrial and nonwestern economies. According to him, all economies having a low cash flow (as in ninth-century western Europe) are "non-market" economies. Such reasoning is nonsensical, of course. The inability to measure an economic phenomenon in recognizable western (or modern) equivalents does not mean that the phenomenon did not exist.

[18] *TAAA*, pp. 230, 243-247; *KhT*, pp. 42-44.

[19] Immanuel Wallerstein, *The Modern World System* (New York: Academic Press, 1974) pp. 301-302.

[20] The limits of the author's expertise will not allow him to make comparative comments about China, Japan, or Southeast Asia. See Wallerstein, *Modern World System*, p. 286.

[21] Khānbābā Bayānī, *Tārīkh-i Nizāmī-yi Īrān: Daura-yi Safavīya*, (Tehran: Artishtaran, 1353) pp. 54, 72-74.

[22] *TM*, pp. 32-34.

[23] Ibid., p. 31, the report of d'Alessandri and the evidence of *AT*.

[24] Gad Rausing, *The Bow* (Lund: Lunds Universitets, 1967) pp. 119-128.

[25] *TAAA*, pp. 70-73; *AT*, pp. 143-144.

[26] *TM*, p. 107; *TAAA*, p. 466.

[27] *TAAA*, pp. 773-774.

[28] Compare: Bloch, *Feudal Society*, I, pp. 60-65, with Braudel, *Mediterranean*, I, pp. 355-394.

[29] The same comment could be made about early medieval Europe, where many of the Germanic tribes were pastoralists who were able to establish more efficient or more effective control over Roman imperial territories than the imperial authorities.

[30] Two or three scholars cited by Ṣādiqī Beg had no tribal name, for instance: *MK*, pp. 112-113, Maulānā Shānī, whose tribal affiliation would otherwise be unknown except for a mention by Ṣādiqī Beg.

[31] *MK*, pp. 118-119.

[32] *SAAI*, fig. 12, p. 65.

[33] *ASh*, fig. 11, p. 63.

[34] Walter Minchinton, "Patterns and Structure of Demand," *The Fontana Economic History of Europe*, Vol. II, *The Sixteenth and Seventeenth Centuries*, C. Cipolla, ed., (Glasgow: Collins, 1974) pp. 83-84, 108-110, 111-115, 130-143.

[35] *TAAA*, p. 503.

[36] *TK*, pp. 266 ff.

[37] *TAAA*, pp. 500 ff.; Kasravī, pp. 68 ff.; *BK* pp. 58 ff.

[38] F. Sumer, "Kadjar," EI^2, p. 387; *SN*, pp. 186-187; *TAAA*, pp. 385, 657, 671, 740, 1025; Fasā'ī, pp. 1-2.

[39] *TAAA*, p. 322.

[40] See chapter 6 for further analysis.

[41] See chapter 8 for fuller details.

[42] R. M. Savory, "The Safavid State and Polity," *Iranian Studies*, 7, 1-2 (1974), 179-212; H. Roemer, "Comments (on R. M. Savory, 'The Safavid State and Polity')," *Iranian Studies*, 7, 1-2 (1974), 213-216.

[43] Note the criticisms of Eric Hobsbawm in his introduction to: Karl Marx, *Pre-Capitalist Economic Formations* (New York: International Publishers, 1977) pp. 22 f., 27.

[44] F. Barth, *The Nomads of South Persia* (Boston: Little, Brown and Co., 1961) p. 11.

[45] Barth, *The Nomads of South Persia*, pp. 11 ff.

[46] Variant forms of this social organization existed from tribe to tribe and from region to region, but some of its characteristics can be found in most Turco-Mongol tribes, as well as in Iranian tribes heavily influenced by Turco-Mongol practices. For an example of this organization among the Mongols, see: Kuo Yi Pao, *Studies on the Secret History of the Mongols* (Bloomington: Indiana University Press, 1965) pp. 32-42. For the qizilbāsh, see *TM*, pp. 32, 100-109.
[47] Martin, "Seven Safawid Documents," Document VI.
[48] See chapter 7 below for an example of this in regard to the Mauṣillū.

10

Tenor of Life
The Course of Rebellion

Coercion and Violence as Preconditions to Rebellion

Violence was one of the most common aspects of life in Safavid Iran. Society seems to have been embroiled in one long war of competition for wealth and power.[1] Accounts detailing the assassinations of members of one's own family and other competitors for power filled the chronicles year after year with a macabre monotony. If it was not possible or practical to subordinate a rebel or an independent chief, it became necessary to destroy him or the forces that supported him. Subjects of all degrees were not immune to the threats of death and destruction. If the chieftain who governed the area where they lived rebelled against either the Safavid state or the uymāq rīsh sifīd, the subjects were invariably drawn into the ensuing conflict. If they were not threatened with death or the pilfering of their property, the subjects suffered from the effects of prolonged sieges whether they were inside or outside the walls of the city being besieged.[2] The rural populations were brutalized mainly by the exactions of armies constantly on the move.[3] In the western border areas of the Safavid Empire, the agriculturalists, who possessed mainly immovable belongings, suffered from the constant warring between the Ottomans and the Safavids, while the same problems existed along the border with the Üzbeks.[4] Pastoralists were no less fortunate, since, even though their herds or flocks were movable, the loss of human and animal life during a forced movement could have been high, particularly if they were forced to move rapidly. Economic losses must have been phenomenal to both agriculturalists and pastoralists. The farming population was forced to leave behind destroyed villages and charred fields, while the pastoralists were not always able to carry their heavy tents, carpets, and other heavy utensils (tools, plows, looms, and cooking utensils).

Violence and coercive measures were frequent occurrences within the interior of the Safavid Empire as well. During the Üzbek invasion of Kermān in 1510, the Kermān Īnāllū subtribes were rooted out of their yailāqs and made prisoners by the Üzbek chiefs. A giant swath of destruction, death, and burned fields and pastures remained. The anonymous chronicler telling of the scene describes long queues of refugees descending upon Kermān City, many of whom were members of Īnāllū families.[5] The war with the Üzbeks must have disrupted the economic life and the social organization of the migrating Īnāllū families considerably, as well as the life of the villagers in Kermān. Similar disruptions, probably on a smaller scale, accompanied the wars between qizilbāsh chieftains seeking control of the economic resources they needed to support themselves. The devastation that accompanied these wars between members of the qizilbāsh ruling elite is not recorded in most cases since it was not the place of the chronicler to record the wrongdoings of chieftains who could easily take revenge upon him. The documentary evidence that survives shows that chieftains most commonly made illegal exactions of produce, property, or cash from the dominions of their enemies and even from the communities exempted by the Safavid shah in the cases of rebels bucking the royal authority.[6] The same principle was observed on the upper levels of the qizilbāsh elite. When ʻAlī Qulī Khān Shāmlū took control of Khorāsān-i Mashhad in places, he reallocated governorships to his own protégés. With the accession of ʻAbbās I, chieftains who were opposed to his rule were eliminated, while governorships were taken from some chiefs and given to others.[7] Seizure of property, legally or illegally, was at the base of the competitive forces in the Safavid uymāq system. Those chieftains with the best survival instincts were able to build their wealth at the expense of their competitors' property, and in between both or all the various households struggling to retain or obtain wealth were the people who actually produced the economic "surplus" that made the exactions possible. The only means of subjecting an independent or equal force was through the effective absorption of the opponents' revenues and incomes into one's own treasury or larder, thereby limiting that enemy's ability to resist subjection.

The preexistence of these violent acts and the coercive forces that implemented the rule of one or several men was an aspect of society that not only led to the breakdown of the Safavid state in the late seventeenth century but also allowed the continual existence of independent enclaves of resistance at all levels of Safavid society. These blocks of social resistance to central authority, or to subordinating authority, represented every state of social organization possible at that time, from genealogical or semi-genealogical tribes, to religious orders, guilds, and associations of the Safavid netherworld, where the ability to fight or perform some function was more of a qualification for entry than links of blood. Such organizations definitely existed in Tabrīz, but probably in the other great cities as well.[8] The rural areas of Iran also possessed a large number of bandit organizations that were neither tribal nor entirely associative groupings like the guilds or religious orders. These bands were best represented by the Köroğlu stories that first appeared in Safavid popular literature in the seventeenth century.[9] The widespread nature of this folk epic in later times implies that a great deal of latent hostility toward the controlling uymāqs existed among the local populations, pastoral and agricultural. Occasional glimpses of this netherworld in the Safavid chronicles do not provide a very clear picture of these independent, nontribal, or semi-tribal, enclaves at the lower levels of society. The qazāqlar certainly represented this phenomenon, as did the refugee Jalālīs who fled from the Ottoman Empire. There were probably many other groupings of this nature that the sources fail to mention since, in all likelihood, these groups did not fit into any perceivable structure or organization.[10]

The widespread nature of these lower-level social movements must not be overemphasized, however, since on many occasions these bands either eventually became tribalized or actually formed part of a tribe to begin with.[11] Their existence was nonetheless a fact, whatever societal form they eventually evolved into. The Shāh-savan tribe in Azerbaijan probably began as such a lower-level organization, or at least incorporated elements of such groups into itself over a long period of time.[12] The processes of disruption on the lower levels of society certainly resembled class struggle, though in fact these processes were not. Upon reaching the threshold of success, groups formed themselves into the same tribal system they had displaced and even allowed some of their former enemies to join them (among the Shāh-savan, for instance, were the Īnāllū [or Īnānlū], Takalū, Begdīllū, and even the Ṭālish groups that had formerly been qizilbāsh). There must not have been a great deal of unity among them at the outset, but they had one thing in common with each other and with the shāh—they opposed domination by greater qizilbāsh chieftains.[13] In the time of Shāh ʻAbbās the qizilbāsh were so divided among themselves that the shah could not establish effective control over them. He sought to wipe out these internal divisions at the highest levels of society. He overthrew big uymāqs by fostering the agitation of those groups subjected to control by greater qizilbāsh households and by breaking up the qizilbāsh units into smaller segments that would present a less serious threat to the state.

Violence and coercion were the compulsions that brought about these agitations within the Safavid Empire at the time of ʻAbbās I. The elements of society most concerned with the coercion and subordination of others beneath them, that is, the qizilbāsh, bred within their domains and the domains of their neighbors and relatives, a force to resist at the greatest extreme, and an impulse to abandon the land at the least. The chieftains did not act consciously, of course, but over time they presented such a harsh burden to those beneath them (for a variety of reasons), that if any paternal or patrimonial links had ever existed between them and their subordinates, they were gradually dissolved, and the resultant social backlash almost produced what Norman Cohn has called "egalitarian millenarianism."[14] Like the premillenarian movements described by E. J. Hobsbawm, rebellions in

Safavid Iran were the vortexes of innumerable social tendencies within the communities where they spread. They did not go beyond this stage because the rebelling groups could not agree upon the composition and organization of a new society to replace the old. The very fact that many of the qizilbāsh had joined in to protect their privileges against the impositions of elder members of their tribes or clans was an indication that if an egalitarian ideology or program did exist, it was doomed to failure from the start.[15]

THE GROWTH OF REALISM AND THE BREAKDOWN OF UYMĀQ LIFE

The early Safavid movement had bred a certain amount of real or imagined idealism among those who accepted the message of Ismā'īl I and his predecessors. It was indeed the only identifiable millennial movement in Iran between the end of the fourteenth century and the early nineteenth. It promised not only a new worldly order that would reflect the heavenly hierarchy worked out by Shī'a theology and cosmogony and placed beneath God, it even produced a leader, Ismā'īl I, who claimed to be the Mahdī and the incarnation of God in human form. The acceptance of a logically false belief such as this required a rigid adherence to an ideal. The religious emotions expressed by the Safavid message became transmuted into tangible expressions, graspable mysteries, and visible shapes and figures. The symbols in Shāh Ismā'īl's poetry represented a potent phantasmagoria of varied beliefs, customs, and popular myths concerning the end of the world. Ismā'īlī and Ithnā 'Asharī religious dogma were mixed with archaic, shamanistic practices and unrefined mysticisms of various brands to produce a panacea. This clutter of contradictory ideas or pseudoideas, when placed side by side, produced beliefs that were conceived as physical absolutes and could range themselves before the very eyes of Shāh Ismā'īl's followers.[16]

The formation of such a rigid theology by the Safavid murshid and the advent of its triumph bred a fanatical adherence to extremes within certain levels of society in late fifteenth-century Iran. Social and religious stereotypes abounded to an unprecedented degree. The ethical works of Jalāl al-Dīn Davvānī, for instance, represented little more than a restatement, in partially orthodoxized form, of the *Akhlāq-i Nāṣirī*.[17] It reduced the ethical and logical studies of Nāṣir al-Dīn Ṭūṣī to a more substantive and florid prose that emphasized style rather than logical merit. Even those who supposedly belonged to a more educated element of society reacted vehemently—fanatically—to the growth of the Safavid movement which represented the ultimate in rigidification.[18] The establishment of such corporeal sets of ideals brought a clear-sighted, absolute vision of society that lingered on even after the drastic reversals suffered by the religious dogma of the Safavids early in the sixteenth century. The religious ideal had become preposterous when transformed into a social reality. All that remained of it in the sixteenth century was a profound awareness of reality and realism. The great surge in the plastic arts, notably miniature painting, and what art historians call the minor arts, was one aspect of this trend. The production of finely bedecked literary works that had little to recommend them was another aspect of the phenomenon. It was the intention of the artists to produce works (paintings or literature) pleasing to the eye and to the ear. These productions were themselves physical aspects of the environment in which they were produced and therefore represented aesthetic realities, not imaginative aesthetics. The rigidity and the substantivity that had so permeated Safavid preachings continued to form a significant aspect of social as well as aesthetic life in the sixteenth and seventeenth centuries. The uymāqs and the qizilbāsh superstructure participated in the trend no less than any other segment of society.

Considered within the framework of this social and intellectual trend, the splintering of the great qizilbāsh uymāqs during the course of the sixteenth and early seventeenth centuries looms prominently on the horizon of Safavid history. Just as the great chieftains probably accepted more or less reluctantly Ismā'īl's message, and the movement it inspired, as a political expedient to save themselves, so too did the corporality of the message force the uymāqs to form into deceptively solid social units. Even down to the present day it is accepted that only seven uymāqs followed Ismā'īl. The propensity to categorize into absolute blocks is highly evident in the sources of the period. The embodiment of conceptualizations of society into more rigid and hierarchical formulae in Safavid theology and social theory during the course of the fifteenth century led to a rigidification of the tribal systems supporting the Safavids as well. While membership in any uymāq was never really closed, the formation of new uymāqs was extremely rare before the 1570s. New leadership elites came into the Safavid, qizilbāsh hierarchy through the existent uymāq system, rather than by forming a new uymāq, although in fact the new elite did represent a distinct household organization possessing a separate social and economic base from those groups already in the uymāq. The result of this grafting operation was that the uymāq system became too fixed as an institution and was no longer able to provide enough viable alternatives to suit all members. Consequently the uymāqs fell into disarray when the uymāq leadership–the rīsh sifīd and his allies–was no longer capable of providing sufficiently for the needs and defense of subordinates to the central household.

In addition to the case studies and the problems discussed in earlier chapters, it is important to take a stance independent of the circumstances revealed in the case studies. The particular circumstances of any one tribal group can be very misleading. A case in point was the Īnāllū clan, which served the Shāmlū as well as the Afshār during the early Safavid period and only later entered the Shāh-savan confederation. Depending upon the point in time or the vantage point from which the Īnāllū clan is studied, it could appear to belong to only one of these larger groupings. The prejudices created by staying behind only one vantage could result in a whole array of serious errors. The discussion that follows is therefore gauged to complete the requirements of an independent, scientific analysis of the phenomenon of tribal systems in Safavid Iran.

The Independence/Subordination Syndrome: The Dynamics of Society

The world of Safavid Persia abounded in tensions that ultimately weakened the society.[19] Paramount among these internal, disruptive forces was the syndrome that has been called the independence/subordination syndrome. The independence element served as a disruptive factor, while problematical cohesion was brought about by the subordination of formerly independent leadership elites. The early Safavid movement was itself the product of the breakup of Iranian society into a number of self-contained, internalized societal units. Originally the core of local self-defense in northwest Iran as early as the time of Ṣafī al-Dīn himself, the Safavid family protected the region against raids by the Georgian princes.[20] With the collapse of Īl-khān rule in the early fourteenth century, associations or alliances of the type formed by the Safavids became extremely important, acting as a containment to voracious ruling elites. Though in theory subjected to the will of the ruling elites, the Safavid murshid gradually worked himself into a position of secular power and supported himself in his claims to secular dominion with an ever-waxing military strength. Once the Safavids became real contenders for royal power, the internal force of the message that had brought them a large following became diluted. The Safavids themselves then became the subjectors of people with a horrible force that surpassed even the greatest atrocities perpetrated by the warring members of the Āq Quyūnlū dynasty. They were transmuted from the bulwark of independent resistance against both rulers and foes to a social force backed by a religious dogma that demanded absolute obedience and self-abnegation before the Safavid leader. The force of the impulse to subject people to a rigid, hierarchical organization did not abate once the religious dogma, or its most distinctive elements—for instance, that Shāh Ismā'īl was the mahdī—lost their credence. The individual no longer lived independently within such an unyielding schema and was firmly incorporated as an immovable part in the cadre of tribe or family.

The major feature of the higher universal order the Safavid murshid preached was the crystallic consolidation of the hierarchical, socioreligious doctrine formulated by Shī'a theologians, including the Hillī family and

Nāṣir al-Dīn Ṭūṣī. Persian secular conceptions of hierarchy had received currency in the Islamic Middle East since early 'Abbāsid times and had been given their freshest literary and ideological expression in the *Shāhnāma* by the poet Firdausī and the "mirror for princes" literature. The highly dogmatic nature of early Safavid theological approaches largely precluded any clear restatement of Persian secular conceptions of world order since the organization of society was best laid forth in the religious law and in the decrees issued by the representative of the heavenly order upon earth—the shah/murshid. The main literary achievements of Islamic society in Persia were deemed to have been completed, and in the sixteenth century, literature was treated as an extension of the administrative function. Painting and the plastic arts were far more in accord with the temperament of the times and replaced literature as the finest, most cultivated art form in Safavid Iran. Pictorial representations expressed eloquently and sublimely the life of the times in which they were produced, while literature, including history, was stifled in its growth and prevented from a fuller development by the exile, in the early sixteenth century, of the greatest literati from Iran. Literature was by no means dead, it merely survived best in a combination of literary and artistic talents, such as may be perceived in the celebrated work of Ṣādiqī Beg Afshār, a writer as well as a painter of miniatures. The craft of librarian provided the best medium for uniting the artistic and literary abilities of a leading scholar. The household of the shahs possessed a chief librarian, as did the most important qizilbāsh households.[21] In such an environment the greatest creative tendencies were exercised in enhancing already existing works through the skills of bookbinders, illustrators, and calligraphers, all of whom were given the task of preparing and reediting older works in a finer, more eye-pleasing form. The plastic arts were the highest mode of expression, therefore, and possessed the most insightful expression of society's attitude toward itself.

The hierarchical conceptualization of social order was fully expressed in the miniatures of the Safavid period. Throne groups were a product of Persian miniature painting from its inception in Iran late in the thirteenth century. The early miniatures show a ruler, seated on an enclosed and raised throne (or a carpet) surrounded by his courtiers.[22] Only on extremely rare occasions do the courtiers show subservience toward their ruler and patron in either their facial expressions or bearing. Later, in Safavid miniatures, subservience before rulers took on subtly new dimensions. The painting depicting the court of Gayūmars is the most elaborate expression of the new hierarchical conceptions of society imposed by the Safavids. This piece from the Houghton *Shāhnāma* shows Gayūmars enthroned as the master of both the human and the natural world. Sulṭān Muḥammad thus struck a balance between naturalism and formalism that closely paralleled the politicization of the theological formulae relative to the Shī'a perception of mahdī as perceived by the late Safavid murshids, especially by Ismā'īl I. The various elements in the painting have organic and autonomous life but are nonetheless placed into a formal, even hierarchical arrangement beneath Gayūmars. The natural elements recede into the symmetrical equilibrium of the two rows of courtiers, formed in a circular, descending pattern beneath the shah.[23] Three other miniatures from the Houghton *Shāhnāma* depict the increasing tendency to illustrate the self-effacement of even great heroes like Rustam before the awe and majesty of a royal patron, who in earlier miniatures would only have appeared as one of the characters in many passages of the epic.[24] In each case, the abasement of self and personal dignity, actual or posed, represented the ideal of subjecting even the proud, perhaps ungovernable amīr to the will of the shah. Reticence and the concern for proper behavior can be read in the faces of each of the three figures—all amīrs. They are standing as if in obeisance to one greater than themselves. This was the motif that Ṭahmāsp I and his successors desired to promote most within society at large.

The miniature paintings where the symmetrical relationships between ruler and ruled broke down paved the way for the more individualistic style that became current under Shāh 'Abbās I. In these works the tension between controlled individualism and independent status bursts forth in a mélee of activity that was often used to express irony or satirical situations: The prince is surrounded by an orderless hubbub and, on occasion, sinks into obscurity. The courtiers or soldiers show very little deference to the ruler.[25] The miniature depicting the assassination of Khusrau Parvīz in the Houghton *Shāhnāma* portrays graphically a scene that on several occasions was nearly acted out upon Ṭahmāsp I. The lackadaisical mien of even the guard at the entrace to the palace woefully explains the end to which an unjust or incompetent ruler must come.[26]

The violent scene in which the Iranian army is attacked by a Turanian force also displays unrestrained confusion. The status of the different figures in the scene cannot easily be determined. The miniaturist may have intended a jibe at the ineptness of the qizilbāsh as a military force, since the foes of the Iranians are wearing the uniforms of the Ottoman Turks. The satire was probably intended to communicate that the qizilbāsh were not attentive to military affairs—the function that had been allotted to them in the Safavid system along with military government. Utter confusion and desperation can be read on the faces of the trapped amīrs who are seeking ways out of a desperate situation. The satirical intentions of the painter further communicate the inability of the qizilbāsh to remain permanently fixed in one power superstructure, or why else, the artist seems to be questioning, would similar expeditions led by qizilbāsh chiefs fall prey not only to the enemy, but to the poor organization and leadership of the chieftains?[27] The eventual result of this attempt to satirize the military institution was the work of Riḍā-yi

'Abbāsi. In it, in the finest individual style, he portrays one Nashmi the archer, who appears totally hapless and incompetent as a soldier. His lack of discipline is clearly evident, and beneath the complacence of his countenance lurks a vicious resentment for authority.[28]

Pictorial evidence therefore provides a fresh insight into the dynamics of Safavid society that is sometimes lost in the chronicles. Of all the sources, the miniatures best document the independence/subordination syndrome, though even this is haphazard, at best, due to the very imprecise nature of the works involved. Nonetheless, the vibrant individualism of style that marked the miniatures of the sixteenth and seventeenth centuries permits a glimpse at the personal mores of the society that produced the artists, at the ideal that the Safavid shahs attempted to institute–hierarchicalization of society–, and at the ultimate rejection of this ideal by those who served them, the qizilbāsh. The scribes and/or historians who recorded the incidence of rebellion were frequently too formal in their presentations to be able to present the emotions involved in the spiralling, vertigo-inspiring whirlwind that fragmented society into unmanageable social units. The bits of information that the historians and writers tucked away in scattered corners of their chronicles only remain obscure, even obsolescent, in the places where they occur, speaking no truths and providing no systematic means of analyzing the independent organizations that lay beneath the Safavid state. Only when all the isolated fragments of information have been collated and formed into a cohesive whole can a more precise picture of the compulsions toward independence be obtained.

Revolutionary Change within Safavid Society

The foregoing sections of this chapter have noted literary and artistic survivals of the Safavid period and employed them together as tools for examining the cultural explosion that marked the zenith of social development in Safavid Iran. The validity of artistic sources, particularly the Persian miniatures, may be doubted since they do not represent the ultimate historical absolute–the fact. On the other hand, the miniatures do provide an illusory insight into the quality of life that historical absolutes, wherever these might be accepted without question,[29] can only formulate in a most implacable form. The need to rely upon such sources to explicate historical processes was indicative of the revolution itself. In the long run neither the historians nor the artists ever provided a clear picture of the revolution: they were too close to the events to provide accurate evaluations.[30] Archives, even if they existed, could only shed a partial, quantitative view of the revolutionary change in Safavid Iran. After taking the limitations of the various sources into consideration and ruling out the novelties and the mutations arising from the progression of time, it is evident that there was a conscious effort, a will, to change the organization of society in the second half of the sixteenth and the early part of the seventeenth centuries. The specter of change peered into the very souls of the great chieftains and left them with a repository of experience and a harrowing fear that was not soon forgotten. The rebellion of Qalandar (Kalendar-oğlū) deprived Khalīl Khān Afshār of his revenues, his domain in Kūh-Gīlūya, and most of all, his powerful position in the Safavid court. Never again would a Kūh-Gīlūya chieftain from an Afshār (or Īnāllū) family be powerful.[31]

Qualitative social changes occurred when the social awareness of surviving lineages of the qizilbāsh elite became more apparent as in the case of Khalīl Khān Afshār mentioned above. "New blood" worked its way into positions of greater power, establishing itself in the places formerly held by their defeated or extinguished masters. The alteration of the values inherent in the social and economic life of the steppe systems brought to Iran from Eurasia was set in motion during this era, particularly in the reign of Shāh 'Abbās I. The steppe tradition was temporarily submerged beneath the veneer of a polished court tradition that glibly emphasized individual performance in a highly developed, cosmopolitan community. The austere, dispassionate paintings that portrayed court scenes, epic battles, and hunting scenes with passionless élan were transformed into livelier, more colorful depictions crowded with scenes from daily life. Emotions that could be encountered in actual life were taken from the realm of the poet's pen and given over to that of the artist's brush. This revolution in the arts paralleled the social rebellion that is disguised to the modern person in thousands of isolated and obscure references throughout the chronicles and that is lost or scattered about in irreplaceable documents belonging to the now defunct Safavid archives.[32] The steppe tradition, so remarkably idealized and romanticized in some of the early miniatures, temporarily gave way to a resurgence of non-Turkic, nonsteppe economic and social traditions. Everywhere in the Iran of Shāh 'Abbās, the grip of the chieftains whose families operated on the plan of an Iranized steppe economy (and government) was loosened and in some cases broken off completely. The Lurs in Khūzistān and Kūh-Gīlūya, the Kurds in Azerbaijan and Khorāsān, the Baluchis in Kermān, the Shāh-savan in Azerbaijan and numerous other areas and other Persian and Arab tribes formed households that filled the vacuum left by the defeat of great qizilbāsh families.[33]

The steppe tradition was not dead once the social transformations occurred. Survivals of the uymāq system remained everywhere in the Safavid Empire, inhabiting the Iranian plateau to the nineteenth century (and many even to the present day). The Īnāllū, Qājār, and Afshār uymāqs outlasted the scramble for power and wealth and in the seventeenth, eighteenth, and nineteenth centuries proliferated alongside the "newer" uymāqs (the Yomut Turkmen, the Shāh-savan, the smaller Lurī and Kurdī uymāqs, and in later times, the Khamsa and Qashqāī). The conscious attribution of uymāq origins to practices first developed in the Eurasian steppes was no longer clear. The economic organization of the uymāqs in the seventeenth century bore a ragged, depleted semblance to the economic organization imported from the steppes. Once restored to health, the survivors were the bearers of a tradition that had been metamorphosed into a new condition. The relations between pastoralists and agriculturalists still remained in balance, with the chieftains of the pastoral groups establishing households that exploited both economic systems, but the intrinsic existence of the relationship was altered. First, Turks no longer predominated over the hierarchical order. In many places Turks and Tājīks switched roles–the Tājīks (or subjects) becoming pastoralists, the Turks, agriculturalists. Secondly, the uymāq households continued to expropriate the wealth and the labor of the peoples they ruled, but these appropriations no longer bore the clear impression of the steppes. Agricultural and pastoral systems had intermingled, adjusted to one another, evolved to heights of balance and internal cooperation, and were suddenly jolted loose from one another at the end of the sixteenth century. By the end of the seventeenth century, the process reintegrating the agricultural and pastoral systems of Iran was again under way, culminating in the downfall of the Safavid dynasty and the rise of a rapid succession of new "uymāq" dynasties–the Afshārs, the Zands, and the Qājārs. The revolutionary processes involved were not dialectical but, as in other societies, multilinear transmutations caused by the political antagonisms of the uymāqs and the social and economic changes within diverse regions of Iran over the course of one-and-one-half centuries.[34] External influences also played a frequent and devastating role in the changes that resurrected the uymāq system at the end of the seventeenth century. The ineptness of both Iranian and Ottoman governmental institutions left the border zone open to the existence of independent social and economic units. The drastic decline in the political well-being of the Safavid dynasty further enabled most regions of the Iranian Empire to become retribalized. Even as early as the end of 'Abbās I's reign, the slaves serving the dynasty were forced to seek out revenues in the same manner as the uymāq chieftains had done and in many cases began to compete with qizilbāsh chiefs for the wealth produced by the subject peoples. The fact that even slaves could become external, independent powers in and of themselves was an indication that the uymāq system was well on its way to being reestablished in peripheral areas such as Qarā Bāgh, northern Khorāsān, and Afghanistan and that almost as soon as it broke apart was on its way back to restoration in a rearranged form.

NOTES

[1] Miniature paintings featured mainly scenes of battle, of combat between champions or between a champion and a monster or a dīv, and of the hunt, which symbolized warfare. A full discussion of such motifs would only produce insipid results, and will not be examined here.

[2] In the Üzbek siege of Hirāt in 1588, 'Alī Qulī Khān 'Abdillū distributed remaining food supplies to the defenders of the city, leaving the populace to fend for itself, *KhT*, pp. 34 ff.

[3] See Chs. 2 and 3 where the Iranian text structure is discussed.

[4] Shaw, *Ottoman Empire and Modern Turkey*, Vol. I, 81, 95, the "scorched earth" policy of Ismā'īl I and Ṭahmāsp I.

[5] *Ismā'īl*, pp. 326-327.

[6] Martin, "Seven Safawid Documents," pp. 198-201, the exactions from Khalkhālī villagers by a Ṭālish subchief.

[7] *TAAA*, pp. 377 ff.

[8] *AT*, pp. 95 ff. The artisans' revolt in Tabrīz, for instance.

[9] *OECA*, pp. 300-304.

[10] *PR*, pp. 1-56 provides an incomplete spectrum for the scientific analysis of premodern social movements.

[11] "NRPMI", passim., fails to recognize the importance of these lower level movements in Iran.

[12] "SSE", pp. 321-331; idem., "Black Sheep, White Sheep and Red-Heads, A Historical Sketch of the Shāhsavan of Āzarbāijān," *Iran*, 4 (1966), 61-84.

[13] This does not mean that everyone involved in these movements was anti-qizilbāsh. In fact many were probably lower-level qizilbāsh amīrs who for one reason or another had no patrimony. But most Shāh-savan leaders were probably not from the qizilbāsh elite as Tapper ("SSE", pp. 326-327) indicates. They were originally non-qizilbāsh as Shāh-savan traditions themselves relate (ibid., pp. 331-340).

[14] Norman Cohn, *The Pursuit of the Millennium* (New York: Harper and Row Publishers, 1964), pp. 209 f.

[15] *PR*, pp. 30-32; *FS*, I, 244-254, and especially pp. 255-260 for a comparative analysis of a similar institution of coercion in medieval Europe.

[16] *AQ*, pp. 2-7.

[17] *LHP*, III, pp. 442-444.

[18] Ibid., IV, pp. 78-80; *Aminī*, pp. 65-81.

[19] Amin Banani, "The Structure of the Persian Empire in Its Heyday," *State and Society in Iran*, A. Banani, ed. *Iranian Studies*, 11 (1979), 83-116.

[20] *LHP*, IV, 36-45.

[21] *MK*, passim; *ASh*, passim.

[22] See, for instance, D. T. Rice, *The Illustrations to the World History of Rashid al-Din* (Edinburgh: Edinburgh University Press, 1976) nos. 4, 5, 6, 8, 14, 16, 18, 20, 21, 26, 27, 28, 45, 47, 50, 65, 66, 67, 68, 70; the only exception to the rule was no. 69. This motif was very popular in later miniature styles as well. See for example, L. Binyon, J. Wilkinson, B. Gray, *Persian Miniature Painting* (New York: Dover, 1971) plates 38, 47, 49 A-B.

[23] Stuart Cary Welch, *Persian Painting, Five Royal Safavid Manuscripts of the Sixteenth Century* (New York: George Braziller, 1976) plates 2-3; item., *A King's Book of Kings, The Shāh-Nāma of Shāh Tahmāsp (the Houghton Shāhnāma)*, (New York: Metropolitan Museum of Art, 1972) pp. 88 ff. Many other scenes in this *Shāhnāma* portray elements of the symmetrical array portrayed here. See also: P. Pal, *Islamic Art* (Los Angeles: Los Angeles County Museum of Art) plate 208.

[24] S. C. Welch, *A King's Book of Kings*, pp. 128-131 (Mihrab paying homage to Zal), pp. 144-147 (Rustam before Kay Qubad), pp. 152-155 (the most striking example, Bizhan before Kay Khusrau).

[25] The ruler or hero was normally given an obvious place in the war scenes of all the different styles of painting.

[26] Welch, *A King's Book of Kings*, pp. 184-187.

[27] Ibid., pp. 156-159.

[28] *SAAI*, pp. 29, 65.

[29] And this state of being is indeed rare.

[30] Later generations of historians, Persian and western, made the history of this period into a myth. Even in this study it is often difficult to differentiate myth from reality since the primary sources are limited.

[31] *TAAA*, pp. 503, 769-772 for Qalandar.

[32] Banani, "Structure," notes that documentary evidence may still survive among the families which have preserved records of their holdings.

[33] *TAAA*, p. 1106; *PZP*, pp. 50-53; J. Perry, "Forced Migration," *Iranian Studies*, **8**, 4 (1975), 199-208.

[34] *RC*, pp. 1-14.

Appendix

A. Ṭālish Chieftains

1. Dede Beg or Abdāl 'Alī Beg (fl. 897/1493-918/1512). A retainer of Shaikh Sulṭān 'Alī and Ismā'īl I. He was involved in every major campaign of Ismā'īl I until he was disgraced in 918/1512. From an early date in the rise of Shāh Ismā'īl I to 915/1509 he was the qūrchībāshī and held Qazvīn, Sāvuj Bulāgh, Rayy, and Khār as his domain. In 915/1509 he was deposed from all of them, but in the following year he became the ḥākim of Marv. *Ismā'īl*, pp. 30, 33; *AT*, pp. 26, 29, 50, 54, 55, 65; *TAAA*, pp. 24, 41; *TM*, p. 191.
2. Khādim Beg (d. 920/1514). A retainer of Shaikh Sulṭān 'Alī and Ismā'īl I. He served in many of the campaigns of Ismā'īl and especially in the one against Iraq. He became ḥākim of Baghdād in 913/1507-1508 and, within a few months, beglārbegī of the province of Arabian Iraq. He also received the position of khalīfat al-khulafā that same year and presumably was the guardian of the shrine at Karbalā. He died at the battle of Chaldiran in 1514. *AT*, pp. 46-49; *TAAA*, pp. 24, 25, 31, 34; Sarwar, pp. 27, 31, 33, 38, 52, 54-55, 80.
3. Ḥamza Beg Ṭālish (fl. ca. 905/1500). He plotted to assassinate Ismā'īl after the latter returned from exile at Lāhijān in 906/1500, in conjunction with the Āq Quyūnlū ḥākim of Ardabīl, Sulṭān 'Alī Beg Chāgirlū. His plan was foiled by his son Muḥammad Beg. He may previously have been ḥākim of Āstārā, but no mention is made of this. His son is called Mīrzā Muḥammad Beg, implying that he came from a long line of rulers. *AT*, p. 13.
4. (Mīrzā) Muḥammad Beg b. Ḥamza Beg (ḥākim of Āstārā in 906/1500). He rebuked his father for attempting to assassinate Ismā'īl but soon weakened in his own support of the Safavid murshid. He was intending to betray Ismā'īl but was dissuaded by another follower of Ismā'īl. He was a very active campaigner for the new Safavid shah and participated in numerous expeditions. It is not clear whether he remained the governor of Āstārā since he appeared in command of qūrchī troops during these campaigns (*Ismā'īl*, pp. 174-175). These were most certainly Ṭālish qūrchīs who served permanently in the army (*Ismā'īl*, p. 352). *AT*, pp. 13, 51 ff.; *Ismā'īl*, pp. 124, 174, 175, 317, 339-341, 342, 345, 352, 354, 357-358, 360, 376-381, 385-387, 464; Sarwar, pp. 33, 61-62.

5. Shīr Bakht. Nothing is known of this individual, whose name appears only as part of a title (Shīrbakhtoğlū).
6. Muḥammad Beg Shīrbakhtoğlū (fl. ca. 945/1538-1539). He was a minor chief, perhaps a retainer of the ḥākim of Āstārā, who went on campaign against the ruler of Shirvan in 945/1538-1539. *AT*, p. 130.
7. Nushīr Beg (fl. ca. 905/1500). The Ṭālish governor of the Mughān steppe. *AT*, p. 14.
8. Pīr Ghaib Beg (probable date of death, 920/1514). Ḥākim of Astarabad until he was deposed by an Üzbek invasion. *AT*, p. 71.
9. Ibrāhīm Khalīfa (fl. 984/1576). He was ḥākim of an area in Chukhur-i Sa'd at the death of Ṭahmāsp I. *TAAA*, p. 141.
10. Qarā Khān (fl. 984/1576). He was governor of Shūra Gīl in Chukhur-i Sa'd at the death of Ṭahmāsp I. *TAAA*, p. 141.
11. Alpāvūt Beg (fl. 984/1576). He was ḥākim of a region in Chukhur-i Sa'd at the end of Ṭahmāsp I's reign. *TAAA*, p. 141.
12. Ḥājjī Uvais Sulṭān (fl. 984/1576). Iskandar Beg simply lists him as a "great amir." *TAAA*, p. 141.
13. Ḥamza Sulṭān (d. 984/1576). His genealogy is not given in the sources, but he may have been a descendant of Mīrzā Muḥammad Beg b. Ḥamza Beg. (The name "Ḥamza" was common among Ṭālish chiefs, though the key to the naming pattern is not evident in the sources.) He was designated one of the amīrs of the court in 984/1576. He opposed the accession of Ismā'īl (II) Mīrzā to the throne. As a result, his household compound was attacked, its treasury plundered, and he himself put to death. *AT*, pp. 202-205; *TAAA*, pp. 141, 193, 198.
14. Bāyandur Khān (fl. 946/1539-1540 to the 1580s). He was named ḥākim of Āstārā in 946/1539-1540, after the rebellion of the previous governor. Between 1568 and 1580 he actively participated in a number of campaigns against the rebellious governors of Gīlan—Sulṭān Maḥmūd Khān and Khān Aḥmad. Sometime in the 1580s his son Amīr Ḥamza Khān succeeded him to the *ḥukūmat* ('governorate') of Āstārā. *AT*, pp. 133, 190; *TAAA*, pp. 112, 141, 267, 269, 441, 1086; *TG*, pp. 34, 41.
15. Amīr Ḥamza Khān b. Bāyandur Khān (d. 1001/1592-1593). In the 1580's he succeeded his father as governor of the fortress at Shīndān and the area around Āstārā. He rebelled against the Safavid state early in the 1590s, after which he died as the result of a plot by the Qarāmānlū amīrs. See pp. 90-94.
16. Clients of Amīr Ḥamza Khān. Only four of Amīr Ḥamza's clients are mentioned. Two of them (*b, c*) were responsible for assassinating Amīr Ḥamza, while a third (*a*) was only tenuously loyal.
    a. Amīra Sīyāvash Khān (fl. from 986/1578 to the beginning of the seventeenth century). He came from a long-established Iranian

family that had traditionally ruled Gaskar in the name of the Ṭālish chiefs. He was a protégé of Amīr Ḥamza Khān and, in fact, his uterine brother. He was responsible for the death of Shīrzād Beg, another retainer of Amīr Ḥamza Khān. After a period out of Amīr Ḥamza's favor for this act, he became more powerful again and was restored to a favorable position. He participated in the rebellion of Amīr Ḥamza Khān in 1592 but refused to flee with him. He remained as ḥākim of Gaskar, though he lost Khalkhāl, which had been given to him earlier. *TAAA*, pp. 267, 269, 449-451, 460, 494, 878, 893, 955; *TG*, pp. 93, 98-102, 105, 106, 110, 119-112, 132-133, 135, 137, 152-155, 156, 248; Chapt. 6 above.

b. Muḥammad Bāqir (d. late 1590s). A Persian protégé of Amīr Ḥamza. He was responsible for murdering his master while the two were in exile at the Ottoman outpost in Shirvan. *TG* depicts him as a thoroughly corrupt individual and notes that he was later executed later by his new master, Dhu' l-Fiqār Khān Qarāmānlū, for committing murder. He had been in the employ of Dhu' l-Fiqār Khān when he assassinated Amīr Ḥamza. *TG*, pp. 237-239.

c. Mullā Fāḍil (d. late 1590s). The second assassin of Amīr Ḥamza Khān. After his role in the assassination, he rose to the command of an ūlkā in Qarāmānlū service, though according to *TG* he was never deemed trustworthy by anyone. He was later ordered to be put to death by the ulama for his part in the death of Amīr Ḥamza Khān. *TG*, pp. 237-239.

d. Shīrzād Beg (d. 1580s). One of the great notables of Gīlān Bīya Pas, who served Amīr Ḥamza Khān as vazīr and *īlchī* ('herald'). He was a rival of Amīra Sīyāvash who eventually killed him. He participated in many campaigns against Lāhijān that were staged by the rulers of the Ṭālish. *TG*, pp. 76, 77, 87, 89, 90, 95-97, 99-101, 104-112, 114, 115, 117-125, 239.

17. Bāyandur (or Pāyandur) Khān b. Amīr Ḥamza b. Bāyandur (fl. 1580s-1590s). He was the eldest son of Amīr Ḥamza. Upon his father's flight to Shirvan, he was appointed ḥākim of Āstārā in his place. Shāh 'Abbās I made the appointment personally, also giving the daughter of Ḥusain Khān 'Abdillū (ḥākim of Hirāt) to Bāyandur Khān as his wife. The significance of this marriage alliance was not made clear, though the Ṭālish were evidently placed under the protection (and surveillance ?) of the 'Abdillū Shāmlū. He ruled Āstārā for seventeen years until his death. *TG*, p. 240.

18. Qilīch Khān b. Amīr Ḥamza b. Bāyandur (fl. 1580s-1590s). He participated in the attack staged on Gīlān Bīya Pīsh (Lāhijān, governed by

Khān Aḥmad Khān), along with other brothers. He fled with Īraj, two other unnamed brothers, and his father to Shirvan. *TG*, pp, 119, 239.

19. Īraj Khān b. Amīr Ḥamza b. Bāyandur (fl. 1580s–1590s). He was with the force that attacked Gīlan Bīya Pīsh. He fled with his father to Shirvan. *TG*, pp. 119, 239.
20. Sārū Khān b. Amīr Ḥamza b. Bāyandur (fl. end of the sixteenth century to the mid-1630s). 'Abbās I appointed him ḥākim of Āstārā at the death of his elder brother Bāyandur. He was given in marriage to another daughter of Ḥusain Khān Shāmlū. He ruled until his death in the 1630s. *TG*, p. 240; *TAAA*, p. 1086; *Dhail-i TAAA*, pp. 16–17, 188, 215, 220, 222, 223, 225, 231.
21. Sārū Khān b. ? b. Sārū Khān b. Amīr Ḥamza (fl. end of the seventeenth century). He was the commander of the Safavid army in Khorāsān in the reign of 'Abbās II (1641–1666). *'Abbās-Nāma*, pp. 82, 108, 118, 136.
22. Ḥamza Khalīfa. A chieftain of the Ṭālish whose exact role is unknown, except that he was the father of Mehdī Qulī Sulṭān.
23. Mehdī Qulī Sulṭān b. Ḥamza Khalīfa (fl. 1580s). After the rebellion of Amīr Khān Mauṣillū, he joined in with the Turkamān and Takalū chiefs who rebelled against Muḥammad Khudābanda. His revolt was unsuccessful, however, and he rejoined the forces of Muḥammad Khudābanda. When the army of 'Abbās I approached the royal camp in 996/1587, the chiefs supporting Muḥammad Khudābanda made a pact to protect one another, but Mehdī Qulī Khān and the Ustājlū chiefs fled the royal camp shortly thereafter. Chapter 8; *TAAA*, pp. 340, 367, 368.
24. Allāh Qulī Sulṭān b. Ja'far Sulṭān Ṭālish-i Kungurlū (fl. in the 1580s). He was involved in the operations against the last Turkamān stronghold to resist the forces of Muḥammad Khudābanda.
25. Yādigār 'Alī Sulṭān (Khulafā) (fl. 1012/1609–1032/1628). He was a descendant of Dede Beg Ṭālish (and probably Amīr Ḥamza Khān as well). He ruled several places in the Ṭālish, but his chief distinction is that he served in the ambassadorial corps of the shah. He patronized the building of a number of monuments in Ardabīl, including a madrasa and some mosques. *TAAA*, pp. 1070, 1086.
26. Ḥusain Qulī Beg b. Yādigār 'Alī (fl. 1024/1616). He was yüzbāshī in the Ṭālish qūrchīs. *TAAA*, p. 893.
27. Badr Khān (Khulafā) b. Yādigār 'Alī. He was ruler of some places in the Ṭavālish, replacing his father in 1628. *TAAA*, p. 1086.

B. Mauṣillū Chieftains

A full genealogical table of the early Mauṣillū can be obtained from *AQ*, p. 208, where there is a description of their role in the Āq Quyūnlū system. The emphasis here will be upon the role of the Mauṣillū in the Safavid system.

A. Descendants of Bakr b. Bektāsh Mauṣillū in Safavid service
   1. Mūsā Beg b. 'Īsā b. Bakr b. Bektāsh (fl. in the first half of the sixteenth century). After the revolt of Alma (Ulāma or Ulma) Sulṭān Takalū, he was awarded the beglārbegī of Azerbaijan and the ḥukūmat of Tabrīz by Ṭahmāsp I in 937/1530-1531. *AT*, p. 113.
   2. Tājlū, the daughter of 'Īsā b. Bakr was given as a wife to Ismā'īl I. *AQ*, p. 208.
   3. Sulṭānum, the daughter of Mūsā b. 'Īsā, was given as a wife to Ṭahmāsp I. *AQ*, p. 208.
   4. 'Alī Khān Beg b. Mūsā or 'Īsā. The nephew of Muḥammad Khudābanda. He was the retainer of Pīra Muḥammad Khān Ustājlū. *TAAA*, pp. 200, 220.

B. Descendants of Ṣūfī Khalīl Beg b. Bektāsh in Safavid service
   1. Aḥmad Beg b. Bektāsh b. Ṣūfī Khalīl b. Bektāsh. He was in command of the army sent by Ismā'īl I to the aid of Bābur, the Mughal ruler, in 917. The following year, he helped to organize the defense of Hirāt against an Üzbek attack. *AT*, pp. 58 (note 8), 106.
   2. 'Alī Beg b. Bektāsh b. Ṣūfī Khalīl b. Bektāsh (fl. in the early part of the sixteenth century). He and his brother Aḥmad had originally been the retainers of an amīr called Dhu' l-Fiqār.

C. Descendants of 'Umar Beg (Amīr-i Tuqmāq) b. Bektāsh in Safavid service
   1. Qayitmas Beg b. Ghulābī (I) (d. 913/1507). He was the Āq Quyūnlū governor of Dīyārbakr in 1507. He refused to surrender to Khān Muḥammad Ustājlū, and when Safavid forces occupied 'Āmid, he was killed. He was the only one of Ghulābī (I)'s sons to refuse service to the Safavids. *AQ*, pp. 207-208; *AT*, pp. 42-42; *TAAA*, p. 32.
   2. Amīr Beg b. Ghulābī (I) (d. 928/1522-1523). This chieftain led a very colorful life. At various times, he submitted to the Āq Quyūnlū and the Safavid states. He was an independent ruler of Mauṣil before the Safavid conquest. At the end of his life, he rebelled against Safavid authority in Khorāsān. He submitted to Ismā'īl I in 913/1507-1508. He was appointed muhr-dār the same year by Ismā'īl I. Before becoming the lala of Ṭahmāsp I, he governed Qā'īn in Khorāsān, where he commanded an army that was sent against the Üzbeks, defeating them at Marv in

1510. He was obviously an astute politician and was able to increase his own power rapidly at the expense of other chiefs (like Dede Beg Ṭālish) who could not really compete against him. In 916/1510-1511 he was given the beglārbegī of Khorāsān and ruled from Hirāt. He was an oppressive ruler and an opportunist. He possessed an extremely large train of dependents and clients upon his entry into Safavid service, and these increased with his rapid rise in the Safavid system. Later the lala of Ṭahmāsp (I) Mīrzā, he became the governor of Khār and Rayy, which he seems to have ruled in his capacity as the Mīrzā's tutor. *HS*, pp. 511, 513; *Ismā'īl*, pp. 191-197, 365, 366, 403, 411-417; *AAS*, pp. 121-123, 310, 311, 483, 582, 589-594; *SN*, I, p. 448; *TAAA*, pp. 44, 139; *AT*, pp. 41 (note 1), 53, 74, 84, 86-87; *TM*, p. 192; MD, p. 17; *AQ*, pp. 177, 207-209; Sarwar, pp. 8, 52-53, 61-62, 70-71, 79-80, 90, 91-93; "PO" (1), p. 91.

3. Shāh Qulī Sulṭān b. Ghulābī (I). He is not mentioned in *AQ*. Iskandar Beg states that he was a brother of Amīr Beg, and that he was given an ūlkā in Azerbaijan with the rank of khān. *TAAA*, p. 227.
4. Sulṭān Murād Khān b. Shāh Qulī b. Ghulābī (I) (fl. 986/1578). He was also given an ūlkā in Azerbaijan in 1578, like his father. He received this ūlkā as a donative from Muḥammad Khudābanda.
5. Ibrāhīm Beg b. Ghulābī (I) (d. 934/1528). He was active in the campaigning against the Üzbeks from 924/1517-1518. He later became the ḥākim of Baghdad and obtained the rank of sulṭān. *AT*, pp. 81, 82-83, 101-102; *AQ*, p. 208; Sarwar, pp. 91-93.
    a. Malik Qāsim Beg (d. 934/1528). A son of Ibrāhīm, about whom little is known. *AQ*, p. 208.
    b. Muḥammadī Khān b. Malik Qāsim. He was the foster brother of Ṭahmāsp I. *TAAA*, p. 76.
6. 'Alī b. Ghulābī (I). Also called Nukhud Sulṭān?
7. Nukhud Sulṭān b. Ghulābī (I). Probably the same individual as the Nakhwud Beg of Sarwar (p. 92). He was active in the affairs of Khorāsān in the 1520s. *AT*, pp. 101-102.
8. Dhu' l-Fiqār Khān b. 'Alī b. Ghulābī (I) (d. 935/1529). Ḥākim of the Kalhur Lurs. He rebelled against Safavid rule in 934-935/1527-1529, and he seized Baghdad. His own kinsmen put him to death, however. *AT*, pp. 101-102, 106; *AQ*, p. 208.

D. Descendants of Amīr Beg b. Ghulābī (I) in Safavid service

1. Marjumak Beg b. Amīr Beg b. Ghulābī (I) (d. 934/1528). He belonged to the administrative cadre serving his father in Khorāsān, but his position is not clear. He was present at the first

Üzbek siege of Hirāt in 1521. *HS*, p. 579; Sarwar, p. 92; *AQ*, p. 208.

2. Ma'ṣūm Beg b. Amīr Beg b. Ghulābī (I) (d. 934/1528). Very little is known of him.
3. Ghulābī Beg (II) b. Amīr Beg b. Ghulābī (I) (d. 1528). His descendants became extremely important in Safavid political affairs. His son, Amīr Khān, became the rīsh sifīd of the Turkamān uymāq. Very little is known of him. *AQ*, p. 208.
4. Ismā'īl Sulṭān b. Ghulābī (II) (d. early 1000/1592). He participated in a Mauṣillū rebellion in 1000/1591-1592. This rebellion occurred after the deposition of Muḥammad Khān Mauṣillū in 1587 and involved remnants of Mauṣillū power remaining in western Iran. He fled to the Ottomans along with his coconspirators after suffering a defeat at the hands of an Afshār army. *TAAA*, pp. 336, 339-340; *KhT*, p. 98.
5. Pīr Aḥmad b. ? . A kinsman of Ismā'īl Sulṭān (D. 4). He attempted to save his kinsman, Ismā'īl, by taking him to the sanctuary of the Imāmzāda Ḥusain. Both were taken by the shah's forces while fleeing from the court at Iṣfahān and were killed. His exact relationship to Ismā'īl is not known. *KhT*, p. 98.
6. Saqali Sulṭān ? (d. 1585). The name Saqali is a corrupted form of another name which cannot be determined from this present form. This individual was either a relative, retainer, or slave of Amīr Khān. He was actively involved in the Mauṣillū rebellion of the mid-1580's. *DJ*, pp. 196, 200.

E. Amīr Khān b. Ghulābī (II) and his descendants.

1. Amīr Khān b. Ghulābī (II) (d. 994/1585). He was one of the most powerful amīrs of Safavid Iran. He gained such an extensive network of adherents that he was capable of considering himself a successor to Safavid rule. He represented such a great social and economic enclave in the Safavid realm that he was considered a desirable husband for Muṣṭafā Mīrzā's sister (a Safavid princess). He was active in Safavid politics and administrative life at some point prior to 972/1565-1566. At this time, he led several military expeditions into Gīlān and elsewhere. He was ḥākim of Tabrīz during the reign of Ṭahmāsp I. By the time Ismā'īl II took the throne, he was in a position of supreme power in the Turkamān uymāq. During a dispute he led the other uymāq chieftains in opposing the Takalū chiefs. He supported Muḥammad Khudābanda for the shāhanshāhī, and when Muḥammad Khudābanda became shah, he rewarded Amīr Khān by creating the position of rīsh sīfidī in the Turkamān uymāq and appointing him to it. This position was created in recognition of the

nearly monarchical powers held by Amīr Khān and was also an official recognition of his authority. He was also appointed beglārbegī of Khorāsān in 986/1578. In this capacity, he led or authorized several expeditions against Ottoman forces in the Caucasus. He soon became involved in an extensive struggle for the control of southern Khorāsān with the 'Abdillū Shāmlū and the Chāūshlū Ustājlū. He marshalled all the forces of the Mauṣillū against these new enemies and fostered his relationship with the other elements in the Turkamān uymāq (like the Purnāk). He also established friendly relations with old enemies like the Takalū. Muḥammad Khudābanda remained neutral during the course of this long civil war, realizing that the victor in the struggle might overshadow the Safavid house and come to control more than half of Iran. Both Amīr Khān and 'Alī Qulī Khān Shāmlū seem to have had ambitions of replacing the Safavid dynasty with their own dynasties. As soon as the Ustājlū withdrew from their alliance with the Shāmlū, Muḥammad Khudābanda was able to take sides with the weaker member in the dispute (the Shāmlū). Amīr Khān fell out of his graces at this time, because it was the politically opportune moment for the shah to do away with the Mauṣillū threat to his throne. Amīr Khān revolted, threw up barricades around Tabrīz, and prepared for a siege, but his brothers and sons abandoned him. He was forced to surrender to the shah's forces and was later put to death. During his early career, he had been the ḥākim of Hamadān, and had been a great patron of the arts. He had been the patron of Ṣādiqī Beg Afshār, the author of the *Majma' al-Khavāṣṣ*. *TAAA*, p. 112, 150, 216, 218-220, 223-225, 231, 234, 235, 252-253, 258-263, 276, 293, 296-301, 307, 320, 322-329, 336-337, 340, 401, 440; *AT*, pp. 184, 202; *MK*, p. 65; *KhT*, pp. 27, 41, 98; *ASh*, pp. 58-60; *DJ*, pp. 132, 165, 175-176, 183-184.

2. Protégés of Amīr Khān

This miniscule listing does not even begin to exhaust the number of individuals who served Amīr Khān. Undoubtedly a fuller study of the Tājīk administrative corps in Safavid service would provide a great deal of information concerning the administration of Amīr Khān (as well as other great qizilbāsh chiefs).

a. Qāsim Beg. The Vazīr of Amīr Khān. There were other vazīrs serving Amīr Khān, but Qāsim Beg seems to have been the most important. *TAAA*, p. 296.

b. Mīrzā 'Abd al-Ḥusain. He served under Amīr Khān as kalāntar of Tabrīz, while Amīr Khān was ḥākim of the city (and before he received promotion to the beglār-begī).

c. Bisṭām Āqā (d. after 1013/1604-1605). He began his career in the service of Amīr Khān. What function he performed in the household of Amīr Khān is not disclosed. Later he held high positions in the Safavid central government. *KhT*, p. 27; *TAAA*, pp. 443, 459, 604, 638, 643, 653.

3. Muḥammad Khān b. ? (d. 997/1589). He was probably a brother or son of Amīr Khān. In the great civil war between the Shāmlū and the Turkamān, he and Ismā'īl Qulī Khān Īnāllū were sent to protect Murtizā Qulī Khān Purnāk (ḥākim of Mashhad). He was to prevent Mashhad from being absorbed by the Shāmlū. He received Kāshān as his ūlkā early in the reign of Muḥammad Khudābanda and became the center of resistance to the growing power of Amīr Khān. He was the leader of the plot by Amīr Khān's relatives to depose the rīsh sifīd. Eventually he took control of the greater portion of the Turkamān uymāq, or at least those remnants that survived the civil wars. He lost Azerbaijan because of the debilitating influences of the civil wars of the 1580s. He concentrated the remaining economic, military, and administrative power of the Turkamān in the region of Kāshān-Qum-Sāva. Between 1585 and 1587 the strength of the uymāq was further wasted by a civil war fought with the Takalū (for control of the vikālat) and by wars with both the Shāmlū and the Ustājlū (who were backing 'Abbās I for the throne). The economic power of the Turkamān chief and his family was totally stripped during this period. The pastoralist groups that supported him were transported by force to Rayy and Dāmghān. He and his sons remained in precarious control of Kāshān until 'Abbās I took Kāshān away from them and degraded them. *TAAA*, pp. 258, 262, 276-280, 296, 301, 302, 306, 322-325, 329, 330, 336, 337-341, 353, 380, 401-402; *DJ*, pp. 194-201.

4. Yūsuf Beg b. Muḥammad Khān (d. 995/1586 or 1587). He was left to guard Kāshān against attack while his father and brothers were on campaign. Shāhvirdī Khalīfa Shāmlū attacked and captured the citadel of the town. Yūsuf was captured and killed. *TAAA*, pp. 301.

5. Valī Khān Sulṭān b. Muḥammad Khān. He and his father were sent into exile from their lands at Kāshān. They had some

minor holdings around Ardabīl and a few places at Isfahān. *KhT*, pp. 34, 35, 83; *TAAA*, pp. 241, 301, 353-354, 359-360, 363-364; *DJ*, pp. 195-200.

6. Bektash Sulṭān b. Muḥammad Khān. He was one of the few Mauṣillū amīrs to regain the favor of 'Abbās I. He was promoted from Beg to Sulṭān for his conduct in the campaign of 1607–1608 against the Ottomans. He was also given more lands to administer in Shirvan. He was fluent in Georgian. He became the yüz-bāshī of the Turkamān qurchīs serving at the royal court. *TAAA*, pp. 364, 671, 679, 878.
7. Mauṣillū chiefs or retainers whose identity is not precisely known. These individuals were related to Muḥammad Khān some way.
   a. Valī (or 'Alī) Khalīfa b. ? (d. 994/1586). This individual was not the same person as Valī Khān Sulṭān, since he died much earlier than Valī Khān. He was among the forces of Muḥammad Khān that invested and took Qazvīn in 994/1585. He was killed when one of his servants, who had been marching in front of him, accidently discharged a gun he had been carrying on his shoulder. *DJ*, pp. 195-200.
   b. 'Alī Pigmān (d. 994/1585). A Mauṣillū chieftain who died in the rebellion of that year.
   c. 'Alī Khān b. Muḥammad Khān. Probably a son of Muḥammad Khān. He was sent to retake Kāshān from Shāhvirdī Khalīfa Shāmlū. He besieged the town and siezed the citadel. The town was fortified by his forces and attacked again unsuccessfully by a royal army. Eventually, the domain of Kāshān was removed from Mauṣillū control during the course of 1587. *DJ*, p. 206.
8. Ghulābī (III) Khān b. Amīr Khān b. Ghulābī (II). He was a co-conspirator of Isma'il Sulṭan b. Ghulābī (II) in the rebellion of 1000/1591–1592. When the rebellion was crushed, he fled to the court of his sister's husband, Sharaf al-Dīn Khān Rūzagī-yi Bidlīsī. *TAAA*, pp. 336, 340.
9. Sulṭān Murād Khān b. Amīr Khān b. Ghulābī (II). He was the ḥākim of Sāva in 997/1588, a position which he probably held until the rebellion of 995/1585–1586, which the royal army defeated. He began to flee to Anatolia, but returned to Safavid service before he reached there. *KhT*, p. 441; *TAAA*, p. 340.
10. 'Ufat Qabāb Jān-Āqā Khānum (d. 1033/1623-1624). She was the daughter of Murād Khān (b. Amīr Khān ?) and the wife of

'Abbās I. 'Alī Qulī Khān Shāmlū had been her tutor early in her life. *TAAA*, p. 1009.

11. Sulṭān Maḥmūd Khān b. Amīr Khān b. Ghulābī (II). The eldest son of Amīr Khān, he had priority over his other brothers and half brothers to the rīsh sifīdī. "Because of several unfortunate occurrences, he speaks crazily between the passages of his poetry." *MK*, p. 60.
12. Süsenī Beg b. ? He was a distant relative to Sulṭān Maḥmūd Khān, served in the qurchīs, and was known to be a brave soldier. As a result of the "persistent use of wine, opium, and much gambling he had to sell his services to other begs, and his life was spent in this manner." His poetic abilities were renowned, Ṣādiqī Beg considered his poetry to be in the same style as that of Mīr 'Alī Shīr Navā'ī. Süsenī evidently had connections with Amīr Khān while the latter was ḥākim of Hamadān, since Amīr Khān commanded Ṣādiqī Beg to go to Hamadān to obtain Süsenī Beg's unfinished dīvān. *MK*, pp. 118-119.
13. Shāh Būdāq Beg b. ? Amīr Khān. He was the governor of Āva in 1588. He participated in the rebellion of 1000/1591-1592 (see above: D. #4; E. #s 8 and 9). Like Sulṭān Murād Khān (E. 9), he began to flee to Anatolia but changed his mind, returned to Iran, and submitted to the Safavids. Later he held Ṭūn as ḥākim but was deposed by a coalition of Ustajlū amīrs who feared his power. He was involved in border skirmishes with the Üzbeks in 1002/1593-1594. *TAAA*, p. 403, states he was of the sept of Amīr Khān but does not show the exact relationship. *KhT*, pp. 41, 78-79; *TAAA*, pp. 340, 403, 489.
14. Shāṭir 'Abdullāh Beg b. ? . A retainer of Amīr Beg and probably a very close relative. He became dārūgha of the Turkamān tribe and was killed fighting the Üzbeks. *AT*, p. 84, *TAAA*, p. 107.

F. Miscellaneous

1. Sulṭānūm. The daughter of Mūsā b. 'Īsā. She became the wife of Ṭahmāsp I and the mother of Muḥammad Mīrzā. *TAAA*, pp. 125, 132, 150, 201, 211, 224, 250, 327, 372.
2. Khadam-'Alī Sulṭān Khānūm (d. 1002/1593-1594). She was the sister of Mūsā Khān Mauṣillū and a member of Ṭahmāsp I's ḥaram. *TAAA*, p. 490.
3. Tājlū. Sister of Mūsā Khān Mauṣillū and wife of Ismā'īl I. *AQ*, p. 208.
4. Imām Qulī Mīrzā ? . *TAAA*, p. 250.
5. Ṭahmāsp Qulī Beg. He was the yüzbāshī of the Turkamān qūrchīs early in the reign of Muḥammad Khudābanda. His exact relationship with the Mauṣillū is not known.

C. Ustājlū Chieftains

CONTENTS

A. Unidentified Ustājlū Chiefs

1. Ḥasan Āqā (fl. ca. 893/1488). He was one of the earliest supporters of the Ṣafavīya from the uymāq with this name. He served as a retainer of Ḥaidar and was the standard-bearer of the uymāq (or a portion thereof). He served in the battle of Zirihgārān in the campaign of 1488 against the Shirvān-shāhs. *Amīnī*, p. 80; *TM*, p. 190.
2. Ḥamza Beg (fl. 906/1500-1501). He was the leader of one thousand Ustājlū families that joined Ismā'īl I in 906. He may have been the same person as a Ṭālish chieftain of the same name (see Appendix A, number 3). *AT*, p. 18.
3. Khizr Āqā. An Ustājlū standard-bearer credited with saving Ismā'īl I at the battle of Chaldiran in 1514. *AT*, p. 70; *TAAA*, p. 43.
4. Ālāsh Sulṭān. He was the governor of Dāmghān in 1527 and an Ustājlū retainer. MD, p. 102.
5. Sardār Beg (d. after 932/1526). Sardār Beg controlled Ganja and Barda'a in 932/1526, though there is some conflicting evidence on this point. A letter of Haidar Chelebī mentioned by Feridun Beg in *Münshe 'āt ül-selātin* (I, 1274/1858, p. 462) notes that he was among the Safavid amīrs killed at Chaldiran in 1514.
6. Khamīs Beg (fl. 930/1526). He served as governor of Qazvīn in 930/1526. Perhaps the same person as 'Abdullāh Khān Ustājlū, though positive identification is impossible. "Une liste", p. 106.
7. Badr Beg (Khān) (d. after 965/1557-1558 AH). He was an extremely influential Ustājlū chieftain, perhaps of the Chāūshlū sept, though his genealogy is not given in the sources. He was a subordinate of Kūpūk

Sulṭān, and joined the other Ustājlū chiefs in the rebellion of 932/1526 against Dīv Sulṭān Rūmlū. He and two other amīrs of the many Ustājlū chiefs who had gone into exile in Gīlān were the only exiles of the era to survive. He later rose to a position of great prominence in the uymāq and in the service of Ṭahmāsp I, living to a senile old age. Under Ṭahmāsp he served in innumerable expeditions against the Üzbeks, becoming ḥākim of Astarabad, a province that had been taken from Üzbek control, as early as 939/1533. His position there seemed to represent the growing influence of the Ustājlū throughout the Alburz range and into the steppe of Astarabad. As governor of the region, he was confronted by the disturbances of the Yaḳa Turkmen and was one of the main officers in the expedition that sought to replace the deposed Mughal emperor. Badr Khān was also active in raising armies that defended against the Ottoman invasions. Toward the end of his career, he gave up the ḥukūmat of Astarabad, entering more fully into his office of *mīr-i dīvān bāshī* (head counselor). He led an extremely disastrous expedition against the Yaḳa Türkmen after 965/1557-1558, during which he died. MD, pp. 239, 245; *AT*, pp. 95, 130; *TAAA*, pp. 61, 70, 71, 76, 83, 86, 98, 108, 109; *THA*, p. 34, *SN*, pp. 11, 171; "Une liste", p. 99 (under Bakr Beg).

8. Imām Qulī Beg Fusūnī b. ?Badr/Nadr Khān. Reign of Ṭahmāsp I. He is a poet mentioned in the catalogue of Ṣādiqī Beg. *MK*, p. 114.
9. Tāj al-Dīn Beg (d. 933/1526-1527). An Ustājlū chief who died supporting the rebellion of Kūpūk Sulṭān at the Battle of Shurūr. *AT*, p. 98.
10. Darvīsh Beg (d. 933/1526-1527). An Ustājlū chief who also died at Shurūr supporting Kūpūk Sulṭān. *AT*, p. 98.
11. Qiyāpāī Beg (d. 933/1526-1527). He was the leader of a unit of scouts (*charkhchī* "skirmishers") in the army of Zainal Khān Shāmlū when he was killed in battle with the Üzbeks. *AT*, p. 98.
12. Jalāl Sulṭān (fl. reign of Ṭahmāsp I). He was an amīr powerful enough to control and maintain two hundred fully armed horsemen. He was in command of a force that hunted down a rebellious Gīlānī chief named Amīra Shāhrukh. *TG*, p. 32.
13. Amīr Ghaib Beg (fl. 957/1550-979/1571-1572). He was one of the Ustājlū subchiefs who established himself in the region of Astarabad in the foothills of the Alburz range. His ancestry is not known, though he may have been a Chāūshlū. He was active against the internal problems that were confronting the Safavid Empire and the qizilbāsh in particular. He fought against the Yaḳa Türkmen and was also instrumental in putting down the revolts of Gīlānī chiefs like Amīra Sāsān. He was the ḥākim of Dāmghān and later entered royal service as a

qūrchī chief. He was also the patron of the Tājīk administrator, Khāja Hidāyatullāh. *AT*, pp. 157, 161-165, 190, 195; *TAAA*, pp. 108, 114, 166.

14. Valī Beg (fl. 969/1562-1563 to 971/1564-1565). He may be the same individual as Valī Khān Sharaflū. He must have served as yasāvul-bāshī of the Safavid court. He was ambassador to the Ottoman court in 969/1562-1563. Two years later he was sent on a diplomatic mission to the Üzbeks. *AT*, pp. 182, 183.
15. Muḥammad Beg "Sārūqchī" (fl. 996/1587). He was one of the three Ustājlū assassins of Murshid Qulī Khān, the Ustājlū rīsh sifīd. *KhT*, p. 49.
16. 'Abd al-Ghānī Beg (fl. 985/1576-1577). He was the dārūgha of the bazar in Qazvīn in 985/1576-1577. His troops were attacked by a group of dissatisfied darvīshes who had located themselves in the bazar, attacked the establishment authority there, and continually made trouble. The troops captured these darvīshes, and 'Abd al-Ghānī Beg ordered them executed. He was obviously a lower-level officer who neveṛ rose to a higher office (unless he is known by a different name in the sources). Nothing is known of his family background. *TAAA*, p. 208.
17. Dede Khulafā (d. ca. 985/1576-1577). The darvīshes causing trouble for 'Abd al-Ghānī Beg were led by the darvīsh head of the Ustājlū chapter of the Ṣafavīya order Dede Khulafā, whose real name is not given. His family links with the Ustājlū are not clear. He may have been related to an Ustājlū family by blood, though it is more likely that he merely came from a district ruled by the Ustājlū. His qizilbāsh status was of a lower degree than that of a military chieftain bearing the same title. He was more like the kızılbāsh alevis of Anatolia, being considered the head of a subsidiary and subservient segment of the qizilbāsh order. His attempts to meddle in affairs of state were viewed dimly by the secular chieftains of the order, and a command was given to exterminate his dissident darvīsh followers. *TAAA*, p. 214.
18. Ḥasan Beg "Ḥalvāchī-oğlū" (d. 984/1576). The nisba "Ḥalvāchī-oğlū" is known only as applied to this individual and may refer to his relationship with a great personage. He was the constant companion of Ismā'īl (II) Mīrzā. Amīr Khān Mauṣillū had him put to death in a dispute over Ismā'īl II's jewels. *TAAA*, pp. 218-219.
19. Aḥmad Sulṭān Ṣūfī-oğlū: (fl. 905/1500-932/1526). Aḥmad Sulṭān fought in Central Asian and Caucasian expeditions. In 1500 he was sent to Shirvan on campaign. In 1511 a troop under his command aided Bābur against the Üzbeks. After participating in the seizure of Samarqand, it returned to the Safavid Empire. Later the minister Najm-i Thānī led him and other Safavid amīrs in an attack on the

Üzbeks at Ghajdavān. In 918/1513 it was recorded that he was ḥākim of Hirāt during the Üzbek siege in that year. By 932/1526 he had become governor of Kermān. *HS* 522, 524, 529, 532; *AT*, p. 133; *T*, p. 579.

20. Sayyid Muḥammad b. Sayyid Nāṣir (fl. 932/1526). He held the governorate of Kermān and Nayrūz until ca. 932/1526, when, as a result of the Ustājlū revolt, he was forced to take refuge with the Ottomans. He may be identical with Aḥmad Sulṭān Ṣūfī-oğlu, though positive identification cannot be made. *T*, p. 579.
21. "Shaikh" Aḥmad Beg (fl. 994/1586-1008/1599). He was the īshīk āqāsī-bāshī of 'Abbās I's household before the latter became shah. He actively supported Murshid Qulī Khān in the Ustājlū inter-uymāq disputes. In 1598-1599 he was the vice-regent of Muḥammad Bāqir Mīrzā in Nishapur, entrusted with the task of preparing the town for an Üzbek attack. *TAAA*, pp. 369, 370, 567.
22. Ummat Beg "Qarkhis." He was a member of the royalist armies that put down the rebellion of the Mauṣillū in 992/1584-1585. His nisba is probably the name of his subtribe, which was obscure. The Qarkhis subtribe was in all likelihood one of the many lower-level tribal groupings that were subjected to the rule of Ustājlū chieftains. It was lower even than the Bayāt or some of the Bayāt subtribes. This individual or his father may have risen through the military ranks to the status of beg. *TAAA*, p. 339.
23. Bāyazīd Beg (fl. 999/1591). Perhaps the same person who was in the service of the Mughal emperors and wrote *Tadhkira-yi Humāyūn va Akbar* (completed in 998/1590). The author of the *Tadhkira*, Bāyazid Bayāt, will be examined more fully in the section on the Bayāt. This beg is mentioned by Iskandar Beg Munshī as the *qāpūchī-bāshī* (captain of the palace guard at a gate or portal) of 'Abbās I. *TAAA*, p. 435.
24. Būdāq Beg Dīn-oğlū (fl. 1002/1594). A member of a darvīsh group that rebelled in 1002/1594, when he and his companions were killed along with their leader. As in the case of Dede Khulafā (#17 above), he belonged to the religious groups that paralleled the qizilbāsh military/political organization. 'Abbās's policy of eliminating these darvīsh enclaves (with the full support of many qizilbāsh chiefs who considered the alevis meddlesome and obstructive) is illustrated in this man's execution. *TAAA*, p. 476.
25. Bairām 'Alī Beg (fl. 1010/1601-1602). He was an īlchī in the royal service. Beyond this, nothing is known of him.
26. Takhta Beg (fl. 1029/1619-1038/1628). He was the yüz-bāshī of the Ustājlū qūrchīs serving 'Abbās I in ca. 1029/1619. He was active in diplomatic missions to the Ottoman court (1031/1621 and

1037/1627-1628) and in fighting the Ottomans and the qizilbāsh exiles who had sought asylum from 'Abbās's rigorous policies (1032/1627). *TAAA*, pp. 948, 957, 1043, 1050, 1066.

27. Naurūz Beg (d. 1035/1625-1626). He served 'Abbās I first as a qūrchī officer, then as qūrchībāshī. He served actively in diplomatic missions to the Ottoman court. He also led expeditions against Abāza Pāshā, the Circassian ally of the Ottomans. Naurūz Beg was captured and beheaded by the Ottomans in ca. 1626. *TAAA*, pp. 1017, 1030, 1063.

B. THE ĀSĀYISH-OĞLŪ

28. Aḥmad Beg (Sulṭān) (d. 995/1587). He was one of a growing number of disenfranchised and dissatisfied Ustājlū chiefs who was without an ūlkā in ca. 989/1581-1582. As a protégé of Silmān Khān Chāūshlū he eventually received a district near Gīlān. When the Ottomans conquered Tabrīz, though, he lost his ūlkā again. With Shāh Qulī Sulṭān Qarāncha he travelled to Khorāsān and attached himself to the royal camp as a dependent. He eventually received an ūlkā in Khorāsān, representing the general Ustājlū movement in that direction up to that time. He was opposed to the ascension to the throne of 'Abbās I in 1587, probably because he had helped to assassinate 'Abbās's brother and feared reprisal. For his enmity toward 'Abbās I he was executed with six other amīrs in 994/1587. *TAAA*, pp. 267, 280, 342, 370, 372; *KhT*, p. 34.

29. 'Alī Qulī Sulṭān (fl. 1003/1594). He was one of the Ustājlū chiefs who had obtained an ūlkā in Khorāsān. In 1594 he was active in campaigning against the Üzbeks. *TAAA*, p. 489.

30. Ḥusain Beg. Ḥākim of Qarā Bāgh in 932/1526. *T*, p. 603; *TAAA*, p. 165.

31. Nazar Beg b. Ḥusain Beg (d. 1570s). He was the lala of Sulṭān Muṣṭafā Mīrzā and the ḥākim of Lūsūya (or Lavasīya) and Ghūrīyān as well as the *yasāq* (district) in Hirāt (in the province of which his ūlkās were located). He was the commander of a large subsection of the Qarā Bayāt (under Ḥājjī Uvais Sulṭān) that rebelled against Ustājlū rule later in the 1580s. Nazar was active in suppressing the rebellions of the Gīlānī rebel Khān Aḥmad in 972/1565-1566. *AT*, pp. 184, 189; *TAAA*, pp. 112, 120-121, 134, 138-139.

32. Ḥasan Beg Yüz-bāshī b. Ḥusain Beg (fl. 961/1554-1555 to 984/1576). The brother of Nazar Beg, he was active in campaigning against the Ottomans as well as in diplomatic relations with them. He was one of the many Ustājlū chiefs who in 984/1576 supported Ḥaidar Mīrzā for the throne over Ismā'īl (II) Mīrzā. His vazīrs were Khāja Qasim 'Alī and his brother 'Ināyat Turka. Both later became the vazīrs of Azerbaijan. *TAAA*, pp. 101, 138, 165.

33. Ḥusain Beg b. Ḥasan b. Ḥusain (d. 986/1578). When his uncle Nazar Beg

died in the mid-1570s, he succeeded to the *lalagī* ('tutorship' or 'guardianship') of Muṣṭafā Mīrzā and the ūlkās of Lūsūya and Ghūrīyān. At the time of his assignment, he was a dependent of the royal court without any particular holdings. Almost immediately after his accession, Ṭahmāsp I died, and Ḥusain Beg's prince fled from him in fear of his life. Muṣṭafā Mīrzā took refuge with Ḥājjī Uvais Sulṭān Qarā Bayāt, who immediately rebelled from Ustājlū control. Evidently Muṣṭafā Mīrzā had promised Ḥājjī Uvais great rewards in order to gain his support. The ease with which the Qarā Bayāt chief was weaned away from his Ustājlū loyalties shows just how fragile the relationship between the subtribe and the Ustājlū ruling families had been and how susceptible the Ustājlū were to a sudden evaporation of support from their subtribes. Muṣṭafā Mīrzā had reason to fear his lala, since Ḥusain came out as the main supporter of Ḥaidar Mīrzā, and his subsequent flight to the Bayāt cost Ḥusain dearly. Deserted in this fashion by the Bayāt, Ḥusain and his Ustājlū supporters were weakened. In the end his faction was defeated by the followers of Ismā'īl II. His house in Qazvīn was ransacked and destroyed, along with the compounds of his other supporters. He died in 1578 from dysentery. Ḥusain had family links with the royal family, perhaps an indication that he was a distant relative of Murshid Qulī Khān. *TAAA*, pp. 119-121, 134, 138, 176, 193-198.

34. Maulānā 'Abd al-Jabbār. A uterine relative of Ḥusain, he was among the highly-placed Tājīks in the Safavid Empire. *TAAA*, pp. 175-176.
35. Ḥasan Khān b. ? (d 1034/1624-1625). A descendant of Ḥusain b. Ḥasan b. Ḥusain, he was in command of the qūrchīs bearing bows and arrows just after the accession of 'Abbās I to the throne. He became the ḥākim of Hamadān and Qalamrau, where he ruled for twenty-five years in a basically non-Ustājlū establishment. Even though he was the beglārbegī of Qalamrau, he was subordinate to the slave chieftain Allāhvirdī Khān, who commanded the armies of Fārs. He was also in charge of a very mixed group of Kurdish and lesser Turkish chiefs, including a survivor of the Īnāllū rebellions. Ḥasan had aided in suppressing a revolt of the Īnāllū chief in Hamadān and his protégés and kinsmen. As a reward, he was given the beglārbegī, but only in an extremely weakened position. He led annual expeditions against the Ottomans and aided in the recapture of Ganja. But as the result of severe hardships encountered in these campaigns and due to the confinement of his authority and powers, in 1017/1609 he rebelled along with his Kurdish and Turkish underlings. This rebellion seems to be part and parcel of the Jalālī revolts occurring in Syria and Anatolia at the same time. In fact, Ḥasan's forces attempted to recruit large numbers of displaced Jalālīs in an effort to defend themselves against

attacks by the central government. His role in these rebellions is extremely important for analyzing the content of the social disturbances of the period and signifies the great transition that was occurring in the tribal societies of Iran. As with the qazāqlār groups that arose in Central Asia and South Russia at the end of the fifteenth century, established tribal authorities were severely shocked by the challenges to their establishments and were forced to take extreme actions to maintain even a semblance of authority. After Ḥasan joined the Jalālīs under the refugee Mehmed Pāshā, his band was attacked, and he himself was captured near Marāgha. When Ḥasan was later set free, he reentered the service of ʻAbbās I. He remained dilatory in his duties, however, and the shah kept one of his sons hostage in an effort to keep him loyal. He also reduced the size of Ḥasan's army. In 1019/1610-1611. Ḥasan was sent against his former companions in rebellion, who were holed up in ʻUrūmīya near Dim-Dim. He was given musketeers from Isfahān to help him carry out his mission. He defeated the rebels and killed their leaders. After this, he retired from active service, went to Sāva, and helped the daughter of Ḥaidar Mīrzā to administer her domains there. This closing chapter in his life provides partially, the scenario for his rebellions. He refused to surrender loyalties his family bore for Ḥaidar Mīrzā, and as late as the early 1620s, maintained a superannuated sense of an Ustājlū uymāq that had long since been in the throes of death. *TAAA*, pp. 457, 458, 649-651, 708, 714, 782, 785, 793-795, 797-800, 808, 810, 811, 823, 824, 1042.

C. BEKTASH KHĀN AND HIS DESCENDANTS. THE DĀMLŪ TRIBE

36. Bektash Khān (d. 1019/1610-1611). In the early 1580's he began his career as the vakīl of Murshid Qulī Khān in Mashhad. After Murshid Qulī Khān became the grand vazīr of ʻAbbās I in 1587, he was appointed dārūgha of Isfahān as a reward for his support. In 1599-1600 he was appointed ḥākim of Marvchāq and Murghāb in Khorāsān, being given control of the fort with the proviso that he establish an agricultural community in the region and reclaim the land from the desert. He was extremely active in wars against the Üzbeks, sometimes defending against, sometimes attacking the enemy. He was aided in his capacity as governor by his sons. When he died, however, he was succeeded by a Qājār chieftain, not by his sons. *TAAA*, pp. 576, 603, 605, 612-613, 620, 627, 628, 630, 745, 746, 804, 1008.

37. Malkish Sulṭān b. Bektash Sulṭān (d. sometime before 1038/1629). He held Marvchāq jointly with his father, but at the latter's death, he was transferred to the ḥukūmat of Nisā, Abīvard, and Bāghbād on the

Üzbek border. He was apparently succeeded there by his brother Maḥab 'Alī. *TAAA*, pp. 605, 630.

38. Maḥab 'Alī Sulṭān b. Bektāsh (fl. 1629). He was the governor of Nisā at the death of 'Abbās I in 1038/1629. *TAAA*, p. 1085.

D. DESCENDANTS OF SĀRŪ PĪRA: THE SHAIKHLŪ TRIBE (*TJA*, P. 283)

39. Sārū Pīra (d. 920/1514). The eldest brother of Mantashā Sulṭān. Very little information is available about him. He was a commander in Ismā'īl I's armies, commanding an expedition against the Üzbeks in 919/1513-1514. He was qūrchībāshī at the battle of Chaldiran, where he was killed. Sarwar, pp. 79, 80, 81; *AT*, pp. 69-70; *TAAA*, pp. 42-43; *Ismā'īl*, pp. 481, 490, 492, 523; *AAS*, pp. 440, 442-443.

40. Delü Mantash or Mathnā or Mantashā Sulṭān Shaikhlū (d. 952/1545-1546). With the name Muṣṭafā Beg, he became a qūrchī before or in 917/1513, when he helped subdue the rebellion of Sayyid Sulaimān. Delü Mantash fought in the Chaldiran campaign. He served in all the Ustājlū operations against the Rūmlū/Takalū federation, being one of the few Ustājlū amīrs to survive these disastrous civil wars. During these wars, he lost the governorate of Akhlāt which he had held in 932/1526. By 935/1529 he had been reconciled with Shāh Ṭahmāsp, and by 936/1530 or 1531 he had received Mashhad as his gubernatorial domain. Subsequently he served in campaigns against the Üzbeks and Shirvan-shāhs. He may have had some affiliation with the Ṭālish amīrs. His older brother was Sārū Pīra. *AT*, pp. 66, 69, 95, 99; *TJA*, p. 283; *TAAA*, pp. 42, 47-48, 59, 61, 80, 119, 138; *SN*, pp. 11, 558; *T*, p. 585; MD, pp. 188-189, 211.

41. Timūr Khān b. Mantashā (fl. 1579). He was the ḥākim of Sistān and the lala of Badī'al-Zamān Mīrzā. His portrait was painted by Ṣādiqī Beg Afshār, whose patron he was. *ASh*, figure 11; *TAAA*, pp. 136, 137, 139. (See cover illustration.)

42. Murād Khān "Sufrachī" b. Timūr Khān (fl. 956/1545 to after 982/1576. He was a poet and a patron of the arts. According to Ṣādiqī Beg he was a good administrator, but he could not control his temper. Because of his temperament, he "committed some improper acts" and was deprived of the shah's favor. His aggressiveness, courage, and prowess eventually led to his blinding. With the other Ustājlū chiefs, he was a supporter of Ḥaidar Mīrzā. For this reason, he lost the backing of his patron and ally Pīra Muḥammad Khān Ustājlū. When Ismā'īl II defeated the faction backing Ḥaidar, he had no protector and was imprisoned. It was at this time that he was blinded. *MK*, pp. 30-31; *AT*, pp. 202-205; *TAAA*, pp. 119, 121, 139, 200, 503; *ASh*, pp. 61, 62.

43. 'Alī Khān b. Timūr Khān (fl. ca. 1579). The younger brother of Murād, he is known only through *MK*, which states that he was a sensitive person who cared so much about cultural attainments that he cared nothing for power and government. He probably lived at the family court in Sīstān, but he and his father and brother apparently retained strong ties with the Ustājlū homeland–Gīlān. Ṣādiqī Beg in fact implies that they were very familiar with Gīlān since on one of his trips there, 'Alī Khān's family "treated me with great humanity and kindness since I was a stranger there." This strong sense of "roots" showed itself especially in Murād Khān's rash pride and impetuous courage and in his unflagging support for the Ustājlū cause over a period of thirty years, despite the fact that he and his family were isolated from the main currents of Ustājlū expansion. *MK*, p. 66.
44. Mantashā Khān b. ? b. Mantashā? (fl. 996-998/1587-1589). The identification with the family of Sārū Pīra is only tentative and based upon the naming pattern, which occurs nowhere else in the uymāq. He was ḥākim of Turshīz in 996/1587 and was active in supporting 'Abbās I's bid for the throne. He was later appointed governor of Darābjird in Khorāsān but was removed from the post in 997/1588-1599 by the Shah. *KhT*, pp. 27, 54.

E. THE CHĀŪSHLŪ TRIBE

45. Īshīk-'Avaz. This is obviously only a title or nickname and may refer to Pīra Muḥammad Khān, though this is far from certain. *TAAA*, p. 261.
46. 'Alī Sulṭān b. Īshīk-'Avaz (d. 988/1581). He was an amīr of Shirvan, where he was given an ūlkā in 988/1581 by Muḥammad Khudābanda. His advancement was sponsored by Silmān Khān. He was killed in an expedition against the Crimean Tātārs. *TAAA*, pp. 261-262.
47. Yūsuf Beg (fl. 981/1573-1574). He was the retainer of Allāh Qulī Khān Ījak-oğlū, the ḥākim (according to *AT*) or the dārūgha (according to *TAAA*) of Tabrīz. He aided in suppressing the artisans' revolt in Tabrīz in 981/1573-1574. He negotiated with the kadkhudās of the quarters and the guild leaders for a cessation to the hostilities. When the revolt came to an end, he was charged with executing the leaders and placing their heads on pikes before the city gate. *AT*, p. 198; *TAAA*, p. 118.
48. Pīr Qulī Sulṭān. All that remains in the sources concerning him is a notice in *MK*: "He is of the relatives of Yūsuf Beg Ustājlū. He was the lala of Sulṭān Ḥusain Mīrzā. He is a very felicitous person and is also a poet who has completed a *dīvān*." (collection of poetry) *MK*, p. 128.
49. Qazāq Sulṭān (fl. 932/1526). He rebelled with Kūpūk Sulṭan, Badr Khān, and Mantashā Sulṭān in the general Ustājlū uprising of 932/1526. He fought through all the campaigns directed against the Rūmlū/

Takalū, but it is not known from the sources whether he survived the conflagration. *AT*, pp. 95, 98; *THA*, p. 31.

50. Elgüs Sulṭān (fl. 984/1576). Ḥakim of Shūshtar at the end of Ṭahmāsp I's reign. *TAAA*, p. 139.

51. Pīra Muḥammad Khān (d. 988/1581). He was the most influential Ustājlū chieftain in the reign of Muhammad Khudābanda. He began his career as an amīr of Gīlān, serving in actions against Gīlānī rebels in 975/1568-1569. His protégé was Murād Khān Shaikhlū (#42), whom he was forced to blind and send to the court of Ismā'īl II as a hostage. Lāhijān was given over to him in 1568, after the deposition of the rebellious governor of the region. He held this post in concordance with his office as the amīr al-umarā of Gīlān Bīya Pīsh. It was to save these positions that he forsook support for Ḥaidar Mīrzā and gave his resources over to Ismā'īl II. This realistic action may have saved the uymāq from utter extermination by Ismā'īl's forces, but it led to the disruption of uymāq solidarity, leaving wounds that never healed and causing the first breach in the growth of a chasmic division within the Ustājlū. Pīra Muḥammad took direct action in the civil wars that surrounded Ismā'īl II's accession to the throne, blinding his friend and ally Murād Khān, but seeing the Takalū and other supporters of Ḥaidar Mīrzā butcher his own sons. With all his potential enemies wiped out in the civil wars (except for a few isolated cases. See #s 31 and 32), he remained the undisputed head of the Ustājlū uymāq, but probably at a severe cost to his own prestige, since he was never able to maintain order in the tribe afterward. His loyalty to Ismā'īl II may have been influenced by the fact that he was married to Ismā'īl's daughter, but this did not prevent him from abandoning the shah later for Muḥammad Khudābanda. For the time being, however, Ismā'īl gave Pīra Muḥammad indirect control over the internal security of the Safavid realm by making 'Alī Khān Beg-i Turkamān, the dārūgha of the *daftar-khāna*, his retainer. After the civil war he became the ward of Sulṭān Muṣṭafā Mīrzā and the commander of the somewhat recalcitrant Ḥājjī Uvais Sultan Bayāt. Orders were then given to him to execute Muṣṭafā and Sulaimān Mīrza. Then a spate of marriage alliances was concluded between himself and others. He gave his daughter in marriage to Ismā'īl II, thereby creating a double alliance with the ruler. Then he entered negotiations for marriage contracts (*khāstīgarī*) with the daughters of Shamkhāl Khān Chirkis (the Circassian) and Ḥusain Khān Sultān-i Khabūshlū. After the death of Ismā'īl, he joined the factional dispute over the succession, opposing Muḥammad Khudābanda and his Turkamān/Takalū backers. He soon abandoned his Shāmlū allies, made amends with Amīr Khān Mauṣillū, and helped to establish Muḥammad Khudābanda on the throne. The

new shah created the position of rīsh sifīd for each uymāq and rewarded Pīra Muḥammad Khān for his support by appointing him to this office. Ṭārum and Khalkhāl were then given over to him as ūlkās in addition to his other holdings. He became active in unseating the Mauṣillū from the position of primacy that they had held, abandoning his alliance with them. In this activity he had joined forces with the Shāmlū, whom he also deserted after the Mauṣillū were disposed of. After this last venture, he became sick during a campaign against the Crimean Tātārs and died. He was soon replaced by Silmān Khān. His career is illustrative of the shift away from familial enterprise that was becoming more and more common in his time. He functioned as an individual who manipulated for his own personal benefit. The fickleness that characterized his relationships with allies and even family members indicated that personal success had become more important to him than the power of the family unit. He survived as long as he did because he had few qualms about sacrificing or doing away with allies, personal friends, and even close relatives. *AT*, pp. 190, 205; *TAAA*, pp. 114, 134, 139, 196, 198, 200, 205-206, 218-220, 223, 224, 227, 237, 241-242, 248, 258-260, 262-264, 343, 503; *KhT*, pp. 39, 99.

52. Pīra Muḥammad Khān b. ? b. Pīra Muḥammad Khān (fl. 996/1587). This individual is on occasion confused with the rīsh sifīd of the same name, but he was more than likely his grandson, since he is mentioned six years after the rīsh sifīd's death. In 996/1587 he possessed a number of household compounds in Qazvīn. Like his grandfather, he may have been governor of Gīlān. He had an alliance with the Dhu'l Qadr against Murshid Qulī Khān, aiding a number of them to escape after they botched an attempt to assassinate Murshid Qulī. Other than these obscure references to him, the sources give no clues about his life or career. *TAAA*, pp. 343, 503; *KhT*, pp. 39, 99.

53. Maḥmūd b. Pīra Muḥammad Khān (I) (fl. 996/1587-1588). He held the rank of khān. His major accomplishment was finally to bring Khān Aḥmad Khān to bay and to subject him to the rule of 'Abbās I and the Ustājlū chiefs of Gīlān. *KhT*, p. 99.

54. 'Alī Khān Beg b. Pīra Muḥammad (I) (d. 984/1576-1577). He was a supporter of Ismā'īl (II) Mīrzā's claim to the throne in 1576, but he and twenty-four other Ustājlū chiefs were killed and their houses sacked by the followers of Ḥaidar Mīrzā. *TAAA*, pp. 196, 198.

55. Pīra Murād Khān b. Pīra Muḥammad (I) (fl. 988/1581). He succeeded his father as Ustājlū rīsh sifīd, becoming the ḥākim of Gīlān and the other possessions held by his father. *TAAA*, p. 263.

56. Abū Muslim Sulṭān (d. 1001/1592). As a retainer of Murshid Qulī Khān, he received Isfarā'īn as an ūlkā and was called upon by Murshid Qulī

for support in his struggle with 'Alī Qulī Khān 'Abdillū for supremacy. By 1001/1592 Sabzavar, Mazīnān, Jājarum, Shaghān, and Jarbud in Khorāsān were given over to his control, and he formed an important element in the defense of the province against Üzbek attack. Like many other chiefs in the Ustājlū uymāq, he was of Qarā Bayāt origin and continued to command large levies of Qarā Bayāt families. In 1001/1592 he and large numbers of his Qarā Bayāt retainers were killed in the fighting around Nishapur with the Üzbeks. *TAAA*, pp. 304, 364, 408, 414, 444, 445, 446; *KhT*, p. 55.

57. (Qarā) Ḥasan Khān (fl. 996-1001/1588-1592). He was the brother of Abū Muslim. In 1588 he was governor of the capital city, Qazvīn. He conspired with two other Ustājlū chiefs to assassinate Murshid Qulī Khān in order to save the uymāq from a protracted civil war with the forces of the central government. In June 1000/1591 the shah sent him to Tabrīz to negotiate a settlement with the Ottomans. His parleys were so successful that by early 1000/1592 he was rewarded with the government of Kermān province. In addition to these posts, he had been the qūrchībāshī of the troops bearing bows. In 1000/1592 in this capacity he was ordered to deal with the Ṭālish rebel, Amīr Ḥamza Khān, who was holed up in the fortress of Shīndān, not far from Āstārā. He drove the rebel chief out of the fortress and forced him into exile. *KhT*, pp. 49, 55, 94; *TAAA*, pp. 400-401, 442-442.

58. Ḥusain Beg (fl. reign of Ṭahmāsp I). He may have been the same person as Qarā Ḥasan, since he was credited with being the qūrchībāshī in charge of qūrchīs bearing bows. He was also a retainer and/or relative of Murshid Qulī Khān. Identification of this individual in more specific terms cannot be made, though, and he may actually be the father or close relative of Qarā Ḥasan. *KhT*, pp. 83, 99.

59. Khalīl Khān b. Ḥusain Beg (fl. reign of Ṭahmāsp I). Ma'sūm Beg Safavī gave his daughter in marriage to Khalīl Khān. The child of this marriage was Muḥammad Sharīf Khān (#60). *TAAA*, p. 418.

60. Muḥammad Sharīf Khān b. Khalīl b. Ḥusain (d. 999/1591). The story of this family becomes even more confused with this individual. He was supposedly the qūrchībāshī in charge of troops bearing bows in 996/1587, at or near the same time as Qarā Ḥasan. Like the latter, he was appointed to the government of Qazvīn. Now the two offices were held on an annually rotating basis or Iskandar Beg has confused these two individuals with one another. The last possibility seems most likely, since neither office had been held on a rotational basis before. In any event, while Qarā Ḥasan enjoyed the favor of 'Abbās I, Muḥammad Sharīf Khān did not, since he reputedly fell into league with Khān Aḥmad, the rebellious governor of Gīlān. He was also

involved in disputes between various qizilbāsh chiefs, which the shah viewed with disdain. As a result, he was taken by the shah's forces and executed in 999/1591. There is a strong possibility that Iskandar Beg had confused the two chiefs with one another, so their stories must be viewed sceptically until other evidence is brought forth proving their identities. *TAAA*, pp. 370, 372, 399, 418, 439-440; *KhT*, pp. 83, 87, 99.

61. Sāmāyūn Sulṭān. Father of Mehdī Qulī Khān (#62), mention only.
62. Mehdī Qulī Khān (d. 1000/1591). This chieftain was a relative of Murshid Qulī Khān and of Muḥammad Sharīf. In 998/1589-1590 he was made ḥākim of Ardabīl and served in a campaign against the Ottomans. He attempted to aid Muḥammad Sharīf, who had fled from 'Abbās I to Gīlān in fear of his life. Even though his help amounted to very little, his correspondence with the doomed chief, probably a very close relative, incriminated him and led to his execution at Qazvīn. *TAAA*, pp. 410, 437, 439, 440.
63. Aḥmad Sulṭān b. Sāmāyūn (d. 999/1591). Like his brothers, he was a supporter and dependent of Muḥammad Sharīf. He was executed with his brother Mehdī Qulī Khān. *TAAA*, p. 440.
64. Murād Beg b. Sāmāyūn (fl. 999/1591). He was the *davātdār*. When his brothers were put to death, he fled to the Ottoman court. His life was endangered when his patron Muḥammad Sharīf was liquidated. *TAAA*, p. 440.

AIGHŪT-OĞLŪ OR UIGHŪR-OĞLŪ CHĀŪSHLŪ THE RELATIONS OF MUḤAMMAD BEG "SUFRACHĪ"

65. (Qarāja) Ilyās Beg (fl. 905/1500-908/1503). The laqab "Baiburtlū" was also given him, though it is not certain that he belonged to the uymāq of that name. He may simply have been the governor of Baiburt. His main contribution was in the field of military affairs, serving as a military commander against the Āq Quyūnlū. *AT*, p. 15 (n. 2); *TAAA*, p. 30; Sarwar, p. 38.
66. Muḥammad Beg (fl. 915/1515). This chieftain served in only one known campaign at the battle of Erzinjan against the Ottomans under Nūr 'Ali Khalīfa Rūmlū. *AT*, p. 74.
67. Ḥamza Sulṭān (fl. 932/1526-936/1530). Brother of Muḥammad Beg Sufrachī. Ḥamza Sulṭān governed the Mughān steppe until 1526. He followed the lead of Kūpūk Sulṭān in rebelling against Dīv Sulṭān Rumlū in 932/1526. In 935/1529 or 1530 Ṭahmāsp I pardoned him along with the few Ustājlū survivors. *AT*, p. 108; *TAAA*, pp. 46, 48, 138; MD, p. 177; "Une liste", p. 103.
68. Kūpūk (or Köpek) Sulṭān (d. 933/1526-1527). Another brother of Muḥammad Beg Sufrachī. Dīv Sulṭān Rūmlū was appointed joint amīr al-umarā with him in 930/1524 at the accession of Ṭahmāsp I.

This joint command was the source of a great deal of friction and eventually led to the outbreak of civil war. Evidently the Rūmlū were in a slightly more powerful position, leaving the Ustājlū in an untenable situation in the government. They were given the task of attacking Georgia, and while the Ustājlū army was away, Dīv Sulṭān gathered another army, pretending to prepare for a campaign against the Üzbeks. Once the army was levied, Dīv Sulṭān moved against the Ustājlū domains in Gīlān and elsewhere, since they were near his holdings and represented a threat. This seizure of Ustājlū territory provoked the revolt of 933/1526, but since the Rūmlū chieftain and later his Takalū ally Chuha Sulṭān controlled all access to the new shah, they were considered the legal regents and were empowered to act in his name in all matters. As a result, the sources call the Ustājlū disagreement with the Rumlū chief a rebellion rather than a civil war. Kūpūk Sulṭān was the commander of the Ustājlū army at the battle of Shurūr, when he was killed. *AT*, pp. 89 (note 3), 95, 98; *TAAA*, pp. 46-48, 138.

69. Aḥmad Āqā. An Ustājlū standard-bearer and a retainer (*qavāchī*) of Kūpūk Sulṭān. He was involved in the defeat of the Rūmlū force of Bādinjān Sulṭān Rumlū, whom he was reputed to have killed. *AT*, p. 98; *TJA*, p. 285.

70. Muḥammad Beg "Sufrachī" (d. sometime after 932/1526). His nickname was "Chāyān Sulṭān" and his grandson was Aighūt Beg (or Uighūr Beg). The title sufrachī attests to his origins as a "keeper of the table" at a provincial court, perhaps that of Ḥusain Baiqarā or some other Timurid prince, since his origins were in Khorāsān. He was most assuredly a Central Asian Turk, probably a Qarā Bayāt, or even the descendant of an Uighūr immigrant. He was active in Shāh Ismā'īl's early campaigns up to Chaldiran. The amīr al-umarā'ī fell to him twice in 914/1509 and again in 920/1514. His son Bāyazīd replaced him in 930/1524. His brother was Kūpūk Sulṭān (#68). He may have served as ḥākim of Marāgha around 932/1526, although some accounts report his death in 1524. His social status to begin with was not very high; he was counted among the lower level functionaries of Chaghatāī origin. Ismā'īl I raised his status in order to curb the growing power of his qizilbāsh chiefs of higher stature, who were waxing too powerful. *AT*, pp. 50, 69, 71, 89; *HS*, p. 460; *TAAA*, p. 138 which barely recognizes his contributions); "PO" (1), p. 100.

71. Bāyazīd Beg b. Muḥammad "Sufrachī" (d. ca. 930/1524). He was appointed amīr al-umarā in his father's place in 929 or 930. He died himself within a short time and was replaced by the co-vakīls Kūpūk Sulṭān and Dīv Sulṭān Rūmlū. *AT*, p. 89 (note 3).

72. Aighūt Sulṭān b. ? b. Muḥammad "Sufrachī" (fl. 933/1526–972/1565).

His first military experience came during the Ustājlū uprising, when he served as a commander of the force that defeated Bādinjān Sulṭān Rūmlū at the battle of Qarā Dara. Nearly forty years later he was the holder of Kalbud-dū, Nishapur, and Isfarā'īn. *AT*, p. 98; *TAAA*, pp. 139, 261, 267, 342; *TJA*, p. 309; *KhT*, p. 59.

73. Abū Tarāb Beg b. Aighūt (fl. 984/1576). He was a commander of the guard battalion in the royal palace at Qazvīn when war broke out between the Afshār and Ustājlū in 1576. *TAAA*, p. 203.

74. Mehdī Qulī Sulṭān b. Aighūt Sulṭān (fl. 988/1580–996/1587). Silmān Khān was his patron. In 998/1580–1581, when the Gīlānī Ustājlū chiefs were supervising the movements of their subtribes into yailāq, Silmān granted him an ūlkā in the same region as the other amīrs where he could establish his subtribes. He must just have received the ranking of imārat in that year. Mehdī Qulī was also given some village areas as part of the ūlkā, but they were located in the plains at an unspecified location. His military unit was denoted as the charkhchī corps in any Ustājlū levy. In 1581 he was active in helping to suppress the rebel Khān Aḥmad. In 1586–1587 he received an ūlkā in a region not named in the sources. *TAAA*, pp. 261, 267, 268, 342; *DJ*, pp. 212, 329; *KhT*, pp. 59, 72, 86.

75. Muḥammad Khān b. Aighūt Sulṭān (fl. 996/1587–1000/1591). Ḥākim of Jām in Khorāsān. His forces gave support to 'Abbās I and Murshid Qulī Khān in their bid for power in 1587. That same year he was deployed against the Üzbeks with Abū Muslim Khān and Būdāq Khān Chignī while 'Abbās moved his army into Iran and attempted to establish full control over the empire in the wake of civil war. The governorship of Sabzavar was given to him in 1589. He was soon deposed, and the city was given over to Budāq Khān Chignī. *TAAA*, pp. 364, 408.

THE YAKĀN AND RELATED CHĀŪSHLŪ

76. Qarā Pīrī (Beg) (fl. 895/1490–907/1502). This early chief may have been the founder of Khān Muḥammad's lineage group. He commanded part of Ḥaidar Ṣafavī's army at the battle of Kar Rūd in 895/1490. In 906/1501 he was a leader of an expedition against the Shirvān-shāhs for Ismā'īl I. Little else is known about this chief. *Ismā'īl*, pp. 27, 53–54.

77. Mīrzā Beg Khalīfa (d. 906/1500). Father of Khān Muḥammad and perhaps son of Qarā Pīrī. He is scarcely mentioned in the sources, though it is known that he was killed while on campaign against the Shirvan-shāhs. *TM*, p. 194; Sarwar, pp. 36, 53.

78. Khān Muḥammad b. Mīrzā Beg Khalīfa (d. 920/1514). The most famous of Ismā'īl I's generals, he conquered Dīyārbakr from the Mauṣillū and

a large territory that had belonged to the Dhu'l-Qadr Begs of Ma'rash. For this reason, *TJA* mistakenly regards many of the early Dhu'l-Qadr ḥākims of Shīrāz, who had probably owed obeisance to this general after he conquered them, as Ustājlū chieftains. The connection was only a minor one, however, and the Dhu'l-Qadr formed a separate uymāq. Khān Muḥammad was one of the few Safavid generals capable of defeating the Ottoman army when it was accompanied by the Janissaries, a feat he accomplished by attacking the Janissaries before they had time to deploy on suitably even ground. The defeat of the Safavid army at Chaldiran in 920/1514 may be laid to the fact that Ismā'īl I took the advice of qizilbāsh generals who had never fought the Ottomans, and shunned the advice of Khān Muḥammad. When Ismā'īl emerged from exile, Khān Muḥammad was one of the first chiefs to come to his aid. At this time the khān was the leader of a small subsection of a Qarā Bayāt tribe (the Yakān?) consisting of about two hundred families. He must have been closely related to Ilyās Beg Qarā Bayāt, since his yailāq was close to that of Ummat Beg b. Ilyās. In fact, Khān Muḥammad served under Ilyās Beg in the campaign against Baku. Khān Muḥammad was related to the Safavid family by marriage, being the husband of Ismā'īl I's sister. In 907/1501 his career as a top general began with his defeat of Sulṭān Alvand Āq Quyūnlū, the conquest of Persian Iraq from Murād Āq Quyūnlū, and the conquests of Yazd, Kermān, Dīyārbakr, Mauṣil, and other parts of eastern Anatolia. He seems to have been the initiator of the scorched-earth policy that is so touted about as the method the Safavid army employed when dealing with the Ottomans, but which they used only to deprive the enemy of strategic points by depriving them of needed supplies. He was the governor of Kermān, Tabrīz, and then finally Dīyārbakr, which he ruled at his death in 1514 at Chaldiran. The province then passed on to his brother Qarā Khān. *Ismā'īl*, pp. 190, 192, 205, 211-213, 215-223, 225, 226, 227, 230, 231, 234, 235, 237, 238, 240, 245, 535; *AAS*, pp. 81, 110, 115, 121-122, 139-147, 152-153, 155-164, 308, 328, 454-455, 482, 484, 490-491, 493, 514; *TAAA*, pp. 27, 32, 33, 43, 139; *AT*, pp. 19, 26, 41, 68-69; *HS*, 460, 488-490, 532 (which is generally inaccurate about this chief); Sarwar, pp. 35, 36, 37, 38, 45, 46, 53, 54, 76, 78, 79, 80, 81, 82, 83; and *PZP*, p. 11.

79. Qilīch Khān b. Khān Muḥammad. He revolted along with Kūpūk Sulṭān and the other Ustājlū chieftains in 933/1526. *AT*, p. 95; *TAAA*, p. 47, 138; *TJA*, p. 283.

80. Delü (Dalv or Deli) Durāq (fl. 919/1513). He was an officer of Khān Muḥammad. In 919/1513 he defeated the Mamlūk Sulṭān Qansū in battle. His name Delü ("crazy" in Turkish) refers to the berserk

courage that soldiers might obtain in the midst of battle. This officer was noted for his prowess on the battlefield. *AT*, p. 68.

81. Qarā Beg (Khān) b. Mīrzā Beg Khalīfa (d. 922/1516). He accompanied his brother Khān Muḥammad on most of the conquests in Mauṣil, Iraq, and eastern Anatolia. aiding him immensely, and succeeding to the governorate of Dīyārbakr at his death. He also received Khān Muḥammad's widow, Ismā'īl's sister, as his wife, and had 'Abdullāh Khān by her. He took control of his brother's haram and combined it with his own. Selim I sent an army of Kurdish chieftains against Qarā Khān, and they defeated and killed him in 1516. *Ismā'īl*, pp. 214, 216, 219, 220, 222-225, 228, 229, 231, 240-242, 263, 381, 500, 520, 526, 534, 538-546; *AAS*, pp. 122, 139, 140-147, 158-159, 161, 308, 328, 455, 482, 490, 504, 513-526, 536; *AT*, pp. 42, 71, 75-76; *TAAA*, pp. 42, 81, 178, 197; Sarwar, pp. 53, 54, 83, 84, 85.

82. 'Abdullāh Khān b. Qarā Khān (fl. 919/1513 and in the reign of Ṭahmāsp I). This chief may actually be the son of Muḥammad Khān. He was the maternal cousin of Ṭahmasp I. His military experience included campaigns against the Üzbeks and the Ottomans, though much of his career was spent in Georgia and in subjecting Shirvan (up to Darband) for the Safavids. He married Ṭahmāsp I's sister and maintained an extremely close relationship with the shah. Later in life he contracted an illness that his physician attempted to cure with opium. As a result 'Abdullāh Khān became an addict and his health deteriorated steadily. Even the shah tried to get the khan cured of his addiction by sending all over Iran for the best physicians. All this fuss was to no avail: the khan remained an addict to the end of his life. *AT*, pp. 146 (n. 4), 75 (n. 1), 188; *TAAA*, pp. 40, 49, 71, 73, 81-83, 138, 166, 168, 280; *THA*, p. 34; MD, p. 200; *SN*, p. 550.

83. Khāja Dhīyā' al-Dīn Silmānī-yi Iṣfahānī (Tājīk). He was the vazīr of 'Abdullāh Khān. *TAAA*, p. 166.

84. Ḥakīm 'Imād al-Dīn Maḥmūd (Tājīk). He was a physician in the service of 'Abdullāh Khān. He failed to cure the chieftain of his disease, so he was left naked in the snow to freeze to death. *TAAA*, p. 168.

85. Amīr Ḥamza Khān b. 'Abdullāh (fl. 986/1578–early 1580s). He was the ḥākim of Shirvan at Darband in 986/1578, but the Tātārs made his government there untenable, and he was forced to leave Darband. Muḥammad Khudābanda gave him an ūlkā in Khorāsān, and, together with other amīrs who had lost their ūlkās to the Tātārs, sent him to attack the Tātār army. The Ottoman conquests in Azerbaijan put a tremendous burden on the Safavid system, throwing many chiefs out of their ūlkās and contributing immensely to an already aggravated situation. New amīrs, who were becoming more and more dependent upon the royal court or the largesse of greater amīrs, were pushed

even further into the background by the loss of territory to the Ottomans. This created an explosive situation, leading to factional strife and a movement that eventually placed a new shah on the throne through violent means. This chief himself took full part in the disputes between the Mauṣillū and the Ustājlū/Shāmlū. *TAAA*, pp. 237, 238, 252, 253, 257.

86. ʻAlī Qulī Sulṭān b. Amīr Ḥamza b. ʻAbdullāh (d. 1002/1594). He was the governor of the ūlkā at Qā'īn in Khorāsān. During his brief tenure there, he served on an expedition against the Üzbeks under the command of the Afshār governor of Kermān. There was another claimant to his ūlkā, however, by the name of ʻAlī Khalīfa Shāmlū, who attacked the Ustājlū chief and deposed and killed him. *TAAA*, pp. 456, 488.

87. Shāh Qulī Sulṭān b. ʻAbdullāh (d. 988/1580). In 953/1546 Shāh Qulī was the ḥākim of Mashhad, a post he may have held as early as 949/1542. By 958/1551-1552 he was transferred to Chukhur-i Saʻad, being replaced at Mashhad by ʻAlī Sultān Tātī-oğlū. By 984/1576 he had become the governor of a third place–Hirāt, inclusive of Isfizār. His wife was Ṭahmāsp I's sister. Murād Beg Afshār put him to death in 1580, appropriated his properties, and divided them among other Afshār chiefs. *TAAA*, p. 136, 139, 244, 255; *KhT*, p. 41; *TJA*, p. 300; *THA*, p. 31.

88. Shāhvirdī Beg b. Shāh Qulī (fl. reign of Ṭahmāsp I). He was one of the chief advisors of Ṭahmāsp and the uncle of Murshid Qulī Khān. Shāhvirdī Beg was sent on a mission with troops to give aid to the Dhu'l-Qadr beglārbegī of Fārs who was hard pressed by the rebel chief Qalandar, whose army had siezed Kūh-Gīlūya and was attacking Fārs. He died while on campaign, and his death caused great grief to his nephew, Murshid Qulī Khān. *TAAA*, pp. 280, 281, 283.

89. Silmān Khān b. Shāh Qulī (d. 1034/1625). His mother was the sister of Ṭahmāsp I. He himself married another member of the royal family. A very strict pattern of endogamy can be seen in the marriage practices of his family. As far back as the marriage alliance between Khān Muḥammad, who may have been his ancestor, and the house of Ismāʻīl I, his family had contracted marriages with the royal family. Silmān was no exception, marrying Shahra-Bānū Begūm in 988/1580-1581. But so much intermarriage with a particular family had left Silmān Khān, the final product of this continual endogamy, sterile, so that when he died in 1034/1625, he had left no heirs. In 998/1550-1581 he was ḥākim of Shamākhī, and his holdings were threatened by the Ottoman attack of that year. He sent levies of troops to help oppose the Ottomans. Meanwhile, he busied himself with the political machinations that were beginning to plague Iran. The Ustājlū came

into competition with the Turkamān/Takalū faction, and Pīra Muḥammad Khān, then the Ustājlū rīsh sifīd who had been the retainer of Silmān Khān's grandfather, was killed in the fighting. Silmān Khān replaced Pīra Muḥammad as governor of Gīlān and became the leading figure within the Ustājlū of that period. After the Turkamān were defeated and the war with the Tātārs had come to an end, Silmān Khān made assignments of ūlkās to chieftains who had none. These arrangements were made through Silmān's lala and rīsh sifīd, Shāh Qulī Sulṭān Qarāncha. Silmān's rule among the Ustājlū was greeted with dissension, and the government in Gīlān was met with rebellion. He was forced to deal with the spreading revolt of Iranian subchiefs in his province, like Mīrzā Kāmrān, Khān Aḥmad, and others. To stem the tide of rebellion he attempted to conclude marriage alliances with some Iranian chiefly families like that of Jamshīd Khān. Such measures were only partially successful, though, and his efforts were compromised by the revolts of lower-level chiefs of qizilbāsh status (the Ṭālish and Qarāmānlū) as well as by incursions into Gīlān by bands of uprooted Kurds (the Ṣūrla, to name only one group). The expansion of the Ustājlū uymāq into areas outside Gīlān, notably into Khorāsān, was beginning to bear the fruits of intra-uymāq dissension as well. Silmān Khān was appointed ḥākim of Mashhad by Murshid Qulī Khān, an act that signified the lesser status of the Gīlānī chief, who had traditionally been the pillar of the Ustājlū uymāq. This position was simply untenable for Silmān Khān as well as for his supposed patron. Murshid Qulī Khān gathered together his army of Qarā Bayāt tribesmen and drove Silmān Khān out of Mashhad, retaking the governorate for himself. Silmān Khān maintained the decorum of uymāq solidarity after this brief but bitter episode, but when Murshid Qulī Khān placed 'Abbās I on the throne in 995/1587, he remained aloof of the whole affair and ostensibly sent no aid. 'Abbās I favored Silmān with the grant of the ūlkā of Tūn and Ṭabas in 996-997/1588. By 1021/1612–1613 'Abbās I had given him the ḥukūmat of Qazvīn. By 1622 he was serving the shah as *dīvān-bāshī* (head of the royal council). His administration was of the highest quality: in late 1624 an inspection revealed that the revenues of state were in very good order. *KhT*, p. 41; *TAAA*, pp. 136, 260, 261-264, 267-270, 290, 293-296, 403, 853, 966, 1013, 1022, 1091.

90. Ismet Khān (d. ca. 995/1587). Only *DJ* mentions this individual. It states that he was governor of Mashhad and that he was killed during an Üzbek attack. His name is a corruption of a Persian name. It is not possible to identify him further. *DJ*, p. 220.

91. Murshid Qulī Khān b. Shāh Qulī (d. 996/1588). As the lala and vazīr of 'Abbās I before the latter became shah, he became the most powerful

chief in Iran during the mid-1580s. His career evidently began as governor of Sīstān in 1576, while his brother Ibrāhīm served in some capacity in the government of Qazvīn during that same year. These two brothers became the closest of allies and formed a powerful institution that was opposed to the enterprise of Shāh Qulī's other children, who were evidently not of the same mother as they. Murshid Qulī soon received other places to govern in addition to Sīstān, such as Tajīr and other parts of Khorāsān. In the early 1580s he was the ally and junior partner of 'Alī Qulī Khān 'Abdillū, who held a major portion of the northeast portion of the Safavid domain. Together with this Shāmlū governor of Hirāt, Murshid Qulī opposed the presence of the Turkamān (Mauṣillū and Purnāk) in Mashhad. The main problem that brought about the confrontation of these three forces was the ever-growing population of chieftains who could rightfully possess domain but who did not receive any revenue districts. Each uymāq tried to get properties for their own amīrs and to elbow out the chiefs of the other uymāqs. Since Khorāsān was still relatively open and there were more possibilities of carving out new domainal properties, this province became the ground for the opening of hostilities, because legal hold over landed and nonlanded resources was not clearly established here. As a result, when Murshid Qulī Khān took retribution against Murād Beg Afshār for killing his father by seizing Isfizār and then attempting to assign it to an Ustājlū dependent, he confronted the open resistance of Murtizā Qulī Khān Purnāk (governor of Mashhad). The two governors considered the town part of their respective provinces. The consequence was a showdown that reached alarming proportions and embroiled the Safavid Empire in a civil war that did not end until the early seventeenth century. As the dispute grew, the Ottomans invaded Azerbaijan, and while the begs of Khorāsān were wrapped up in their internecine struggle, the Ottomans were establishing a foothold in the northwest. The Shāmlū joined Murshid Qulī, and together they set about eliminating all the Turkamān protégés who held governorships in the beglārbegī of Mashhad. In order to provoke the Shāmlū/Ustājlū even more, Murtizā Qulī Khān appointed his own man to govern in Nishapur, taking a region claimed by the Ustājlū. This led to open hostilities, which ended in the triumph of the Ustājlū/Shāmlū faction. Murshid Qulī placed his half brother, Silmān Khān, into the governorate of Mashhad, but the two were not compatible, and Murshid Qulī ejected Silmān from Mashhad by force, taking over the ḥukūmat and the beglārbegī of the province himself. The strained relations between the two were never patched up. His victory in Mashhad was not complete, however. The coalition between the Shāmlū and the Ustājlū was disrupted by the mutual greed of the parties involved. Murshid Qulī Khān enticed 'Abbās I away from 'Alī Qulī Khān, who had been the future shah's lala. 'Abbās Mīrzā consented to an alliance with Murshid Qulī Khān and made ready to depart for Mashhad. But 'Alī Qulī Khān had heard of these machinations, considered them a breach of his authority in Hirāt, and attempted to assassinate Murshid Qulī Khān. Once Murshid Qulī obtained the backing of 'Abbās Mīrzā, he was no longer the underling in the alliance. He was able to back his new status with the increased resources acquired from the conquest of Mashhad. At this point it is obvious that the authority of the Safavid state had broken down in northeast Iran and that there were two statelike institutions poised on the brink of mutual liquidation. There was no independent authority capable of resolving this dangerous situation peacefully. War broke out between the two camps. 'Alī Qulī Khān's forces were overwhelmingly defeated. This set the stage for the seizure of the Safavid throne in the following year when 'Abbās I became the new shah. The ambitious Murshid Qulī Khān attacked the qizilbāsh chiefs of Persian Iraq, whose affairs were thrown into complete disarray by the purge of the Mauṣillū in their midst and the wars with the Ottomans. Murtizā Qulī Khān Purnāk and the Īnāllū Afshār of Kermān, former enemies, joined Murshid Qulī Khān and overwhelmed the western amīrs. Murshid Qulī's rise was in many ways like the establishment of a totally new dynasty, and in fact Murshid Qulī Khān had been exploiting 'Abbās Mīrzā to gain more power. Once 'Abbās was in power, the Ustājlū grand vazīr, after a brief period spent consolidating his power, attempted to replace the Safavid dynasty with his own. But in other respects, too, the accession of 'Abbās to the throne represented the victory of the forces of the periphery—the Khorāsānī chieftains—over those that had been the bulwark of the old-style central government supported by the chiefs of Persian Iraq and Fārs. Murshid Qulī Khān's success was predicated upon makeshift alliances, though, which were extremely weak, even in his own uymāq. When he attempted to depose 'Abbās I and place himself on the throne, the makings of dynastic authority evaporated immediately, leaving him powerless and laying the qizilbāsh system open to further civil strife and disaffection from within. In this condition of dysfunction, 'Abbās I was able to carry the disruption of the tribal system to an extreme, without, however, destroying it, and increased his own power amidst a thrall of competing and ineffectual tribal authorities. Murshid Qulī Khān was assassinated by his own chieftains. The Ustājlū uymāq reacted against the crass and manipulative tactics that he had employed against them to eliminate him at the first opportunity. *KhT*, pp. 27, 39-40, 42, 48-49; *TAAA*, pp. 172, 206, 216, 227, 245-247,

255, 257, 258, 262, 263, 276, 277, 280-284, 290, 293-295, 302-305, 350, 352, 354, 356, 357, 359, 362-364, 366-372, 380-387, 399, 400-405, 413, 420, 438, 439, 441, 442, 504, 828, 1090, 1103.

92. Shāh Qulī Sulṭān b. Murshid Qulī b. Shāh Qulī. Lala of Ismā'īl Mīrzā in the 1580s. Little else is known of his life and activities. *TAAA*, pp. 283, 1102.

93. Ibrahīm Sulṭān (Khān) b. Shāh Qulī b. 'Abdullāh. Brother of Murshid Qulī Khān. In early 984/1576 Ibrāhīm was the ḥākim of Sarakhs, but later that year he was promoted to the governorate of Qazvīn. With the accession of Muḥammad Khudābanda in 986/1578, Isfarā'īn was handed over to him. During the civil wars with the Mauṣillū, until he was captured, Ibrāhīm served under 'Alī Qulī Khān Shāmlū. He escaped and returned to 'Alī Qulī Khān, remaining with him until civil war broke out between the Ustājlū and Shāmlū. At this time he seems to have been the ḥākim of Varāmīn. He remained there until he was appointed to Mashhad in Murshid Qulī Khān's place as a reward for his services in placing 'Abbās I on the throne. When the Üzbeks attacked and besieged Mashhad in 996/1588, he led the defense of the city. He was deposed from the government of Mashhad when his brother's rebellion was put down. Ummat Beg Ilyās-oğūllarī took his place. Nothing else is mentioned of him in the sources. *TAAA*, pp. 204, 206, 216, 227, 285, 302, 303, 364, 389, 401, 403, 411; *KhT*, pp. 29, 41, 46, 47, 51.

94. Muḥammad Sulṭān (fl. 996/1587). He was the cousin of Murshid Qulī Khān and the governor of Alamut in 996/1588. *KhT*, p. 35.

95. Mīrzā Aḥmad b. 'Atā'ullāh. Tājīk administrator. At the peak of his career he was in the service of Murshid Qulī Khān. *TAAA*, p. 172.

96. Mīrzā Shāh Valī. A Tājīk dependent of Murshid Qulī. He was deposed and fined 8000 tumans when Murshid Qulī rebelled and was deposed and assassinated. *KhT*, p. 49.

97. Kūr Ḥasan (Beg?) (d. 999/1590-1591). This chieftain was the Īshīk-āqāsī-bāshī at the royal court and acted as a liaison officer between the court and various provincial officers. His career began in the service of Murshid Qulī Khān. Through this patron's intercession he entered the service of the royal court. He helped to obtain the support of Būdāq Khān Chignī for 'Abbās I by carrying the message granting this chieftain certain concessions. Būdāq Khān kept him on in his service for a time, ordering him to attack Ḥusain Khān Shāmlū (governor of Qum) and to plunder his properties (in 999/1590). Later he reverted to the service of the shah, and he was sent to fetch Ya'qūb Khān Dhu'l-Qadr from Shīrāz, where he was showing signs of rebellion (in 999/1590). With so much sedition in the air about him, Kūr Ḥasan could not help but be affected himself. When he too showed

signs of rebellion, the shah ordered him to be executed. It is somewhat ironic that the hatchet man was himself killed for lack of loyalty. This demonstrates that the bond between social groups in Safavid society was increasingly based upon intermediate loyalties, such as loyalty to one's intisāb, or upon the payment of service in return for material considerations. Gone was the old spirit of cooperation between different intisāb groupings as inspired by the leadership of the Safavid shah. Even ʻAbbās I was not able to restore the resiliency that had characterized the qizilbāsh system of Ṭahmāsp I's period. While personal loyalty still remained a strong factor, it was released into a morass of intrigue and was often transformed into a fever of rebellion pushed to the fore by the development of lower-level loyalties. *KhT*, pp. 74, 86; *TAAA*, pp. 404, 433, 438.

98. Ḥasan Beg. ? . This individual is known only as the father of Mehdī Qulī Beg. *TAAA*, p. 281.

99. Mehdī Qulī Beg b. Ḥasan. This chieftain was the *qūrchī-yi tīr va kamān* (qūrchī commander whose troops had bows and arrows), and dependent of Shāhvirdī Beg Yakān. *TAAA*, p. 281.

THE QARĀNJA OR QARĀNCHĪ-OĞLŪ CHĀŪSHLŪ, CONSISTING OF THE MĀHĪ-FAQĪYA-LŪĪ (OR LAVĪ) TRIBE–THE DEPENDENTS OF SILMĀN KHĀN

100. Qarānja Beg (fl. mid-1520s). He was the founder of this lineage group or the descendant of a founder bearing the same name. He supported Kūpūk Sulṭān for the vikālat and was opposed to Dīv Sulṭān Rūmlū. Dīv Sulṭān had in fact been his master, but Qarānja Beg had abandoned him for Kūpūk. For this reason Ḥasan Beg Rūmlū called this chieftain a "faithless man" and denounced his action as rebellion. Even though the political inclination of *AT* is clearly in favor of the Rūmlū, it is evident that Qarānja Beg's abandonment of a political commitment was a sign of the direction in which the qizilbāsh system would later go. His political faithlessness was the result of an imbalance in the Iranian tribal system that was shored up temporarily by Ṭahmāsp I after these initial troubles in the mid- to late-1520s. Yet the problems of collective rule remained, and though buried for a time in the new system of Ṭahmāsp I, again revived permanently in the mid-1570s. *AT*, p. 93; *TAAA*, p. 47.

101. Shāh Qulī Sulṭān Qarānchī-oğlū (fl. 984–994/1576–1585). He was the ḥākim of Sadī late in the reign of Ṭahmāsp I, when he gave aid to Dāvūd Khān Gurjī (the Georgian), the governor of Tiflis, against the Ottomans. His service in Azerbaijan was conducted under the command of Muḥammadī Khān "Tukhmāq", the beglārbegī and the ḥākim of Chukhur-i Saʻd. With the Ottoman invasion of the early

1580s, Shāh Qulī lost his ūlkā and was transferred to a new one in Khorāsān by the shāh. He was also active in the civil wars that plagued Khorāsān in the 1580s. An Ustājlū army under his command was defeated by a Turkamān army near Varāmīn-i Rayy so he fled to the royal camp, where new fighting broke out between the two factions. Again, the Ustājlū chiefs in the camp, including Shāh Qulī, were defeated, and the Turkamān/Takalū faction enjoyed a temporary tenure of power in the Safavid state. Shāh Qulī was probably the retainer of Murshid Qulī Khān during this period. Later Shāh Qulī served in expeditions against Khān Aḥmad, whose perennial insurrection was attacked yet another time. In 994/1585 this chief received the government of Jām through the intercession of Murshid Qulī and became the lala of Silmān Khān. His assignment to this position indicates that Murshid Qulī Khān did not trust Silmān while he was governor of Mashhad and that he gave the government of the province to Silmān only in deference to the traditional hegemony of the governor of Gīlān in the Ustājlū organization. Shāh Qulī's assignment as the lala of the individual who was supposedly the superior of Murshid Qulī signified a shift within the power structure of the Ustājlū uymāq. That Ustājlū chieftains were spying on one another and that supposedly lesser chiefs were making assignments of property allocations to supposedly greater chiefs indicates that the Ustājlū power network had reached the full extent of its expansion and that too many coequal powers were causing a dissolution of the uymāq institution. *TAAA*, pp. 139, 204, 252, 255, 257, 263, 264, 267-270, 290, 294.

F. THE QARĀ BAYĀT AND ILYĀS-OĞLŪ

102. Bābā Ilyās Sulṭān (d. 920/1514). The uymāq section under his control and the control of his descendants was known as the (Qarā) Bayāt and was of Chaghatāī origin (*TAAA*, p. 295). His surname Uighūr-oğlū (often miscopied by scribes as Inghūt-oğlu) indicates that his family may have originated somewhere in Chinese Turkestan among the Uighūrs at some point during or after the Mongol expansions of the twelfth century. The fact that he was designated Chaghatāī also indicates that he, or more likely his ancestors, had been in the service of the Chaghatāī khans of Central Asia, descendants of Changīz Khān's son, Chaghatāī. Like many other chiefs who had served the Chaghatāī khāns, they had probably entered the service of the Timurids. Eventually some of Bābā Ilyās's ancestors had moved into Safavid service. Certainly the accounts of Tīmūr-i Lang's grants to the Safavids do not contradict the main outlines of such an occurrence (see chapter 7). Bābā Ilyās first appeared in Safavid service in

899/1494 as a retainer and military chieftain of Shaikh Sulṭān ‘Alī. He maintained his allegiance to Ismā‘īl I, accompanying him in his exile to Lāhijān. In 906/1500 a glimpse of the Qarā Bayāt familial institution in Gīlān is obtained from the sources. Bābā Ilyās raised an army at Sang-i Kul, where his kinsman Ummat Beg Chāūshlū maintained his fortress for the supervision of his subtribes' affairs while in summer quarters. This indicates that Bābā Ilyās's family had been in Safavid service long enough to hold regularized patterns of control over a compact bloc of territory long before 906/1500. Bābā Ilyās was in the service of Khān Muḥammad and engaged in numerous campaigns that helped defeat the Āq Quyūnlū and establish Safavid suzerainty in Azerbaijan. In 909/1503, though nominally in the service of Khān Muḥammad, he captured Rayy in an independent action. As a reward, he was given the governorship of the town. His conquest of Rayy was the first step in an eastward expansion of the Ustājlū and their subtribes. There are differing versions of his death. *HS* (p. 475) and *TJA* (pp. 268-269) state that he was killed in Gīlān, attempting to put down the rebellion of an Iranian amīr named Ḥusain Kīya, but *AT* and *TAAA* state that he was killed at Chaldiran. There can be no doubt that his family was descended from a chiefly family that had served the Chaghatāī khāns and that he and his kinsmen represented a general assimilation of Central Asian elements into the Iranian pastoral systems. *TAAA*, pp. 42, 43, 295, 445, 453; *AT*, p. 234; *HS*, pp. 454, 460, 473, 475; *TJA*, pp. 268, 269; Sarwar, pp. 33, 35, 37, 38; "Une liste", p. 100.

103. Pīra ‘Umar Beg b. Bābā Ilyās (d. 920/1514). He held the office of *shīrachī-bāshī*(?) and was among the many amīrs who died at Chaldiran. *TJA*, p. 277.

104. Bābā Sulaimān b. Bābā Ilyās (d. 920/1514). He was killed at Chaldiran along with his father and brother. There are difficulties in assigning this chief to the Qarā Bayāt. *TJA*, which consistently assigns this chieftain's family to the Dhu'l-Qadr (including Bābā Ilyās) seems to have confused the houses of two chiefs with the same name: Ilyās "Kachal" Beg Dhu'l-Qadr and Bābā Ilyās. But since *TJA* shows these two chiefs with sons of the same name, it is difficult to determine who is who. Perhaps the similarities in name are due to some affinity of blood relationship, to the fact that part of the Qarā Bayāt went into the service of some unknown Dhu'l-Qadr chief, or to a relationship of marriage (A similar problem occurs in identifying the Purnāk and the Afshār house of Manṣūr Beg at this time). Bābā Sulaimān's son was said to be Ummat Beg Dhu'l-Qadr, who became the governor of Shīrāz. *TJA*, pp. 270, 277.

105. Maḥmūd Sulṭān b. Bābā Ilyās (d. 1001/1592-1593). Perhaps a grand-

son of Bābā Ilyās, though the sources imply that he was his son. If he was Bābā Ilyās's son, he must have been well over seventy-five years old at his death. He was the ḥākim of the Qarā Bayāt and appears to have acted independently of the Ustājlū after the death of Murshid Qulī Khān by making alliances with Būdāq Khān Chignī and 'Alī Qulī Khān Shāmlū. He was killed in 1001/1592-1593 in a massacre of the Bayāt chiefs perpetrated by the Üzbeks in revenge for the killing of many Üzbeks. At his death he was probably governor of Isfarā'īn. *TAAA*, pp. 445, 827.

106. Maḥmūd Khān b. ..... Ilyās (fl. 984-998/1576-1589). Probably another name for Maḥmūd Sulṭān, though no certain identification can be made. Perhaps the grandson of Maḥmūd Sulṭan, who was a very old man by the time the name "Maḥmūd Khān" appears in the sources. He was the governor of Turshīz in Khorāsān in 984/1576 at the death of Ṭahmāsp I. Muḥammad Khudābanda reconfirmed him as the possessor of Turshīz in 986/1578. His ūlkā was in the territory of Murtizā Qulī Khān Purnāk. When civil war broke out between the Ustājlū and the Turkamān (including the Purnāk), he was threatened with the loss of his holding. He applied to the royal court for aid in extricating himself from such a distressful situation yet nonetheless gave aid to Murtizā Qulī Khān in order to preserve his material possessions in the province of Mashhad. Materialism greatly loosened the ties of uymāq affiliation. In this case the prerequisites of materialism countered Maḥmūd Khān's loyalty to his uymāq. Even though he may not have attacked the Ustājlū directly, Maḥmūd's position was so untenable that he was attacked by the Shāmlū allies of Murshid Qulī Khān (led by Valī Khalīfa Īnāllū). He defeated and killed the Shāmlū leader. The Shāmlū reciprocated by killing one of Maḥmūd's brothers. This violent exchange was the beginning of a new civil war between the Shāmlū and the Ustājlū. Maḥmūd's role in affairs after this time is not clear from the sources. By 997/1588, after having been involved in the assassination of Murshid Qulī Khān, he had gained control of Nishapur. That city was taken from him in 1588-1589, but his retainer, Shāh Nazar Sulṭān, regained it for him. Shortly afterwards, Shāh Nazar had a dispute with his master, went to the royal court complaining of him, and succeeded in having him removed from power. In 998/1589 he was involved in driving the Üzbeks out of Khorāsān. The individual referred to in number 105 above was probably the same person, since he was killed in revenge for the deaths of Üzbeks in these campaigns. The fact that the two individuals have different titles in *TAAA*, however, argues against this conclusion. *TAAA*, pp. 139, 227, 255-256, 259, 400, 407-408, 411, 414.

107. Shāh Nazar Sulṭān "Kushik-oğlū" (fl. 998/1589). He was the retainer of Maḥmūd Khān (#106), whom he had served a very long time. Maḥmūd had rebelled against 'Abbās I at the instigation of some qūrchīs under his command. 'Abbās I placed Shāh Nazar in the governorship of Nishapur in place of Maḥmūd. When the latter refused to leave Nishapur, the shah deposed and replaced him. *TAAA*, pp. 407, 408.

108. (Mīrzā) Muḥammad Sulṭān (d. 1030/1621). This chieftain was the descendant of Bābā Ilyās since *TAAA* says that he was the son of "Uīghūr Sulṭān." He may even have been a son of Bābā Ilyās, though this does not seem likely. He started his career as governor of Sabzavār in 1588-1589. By 1010/1601-1602 he had become governor of Nishapur and was active in defending Khorāsān against the Üzbeks. He succeeded Maḥmūd Sulṭān as rīsh sifīd of the Qarā Bayāt in Khorāsān, establishing a special relationship with 'Abbās I that he left his tribe separate from the Ustājlū. From 1000-1006/1592-1597 he held Isfarā'īn as part of his ūlkā. Then he lost it to the Üzbeks, and never regained it after the Safavid reconquest. He died as governor of Nishapur. *TAAA*, pp. 408, 445, 453, 470-472, 507-510, 604, 827, 828.

109. Ummat Beg b. Bābā Ilyās (fl. 905/1500). One of the early chiefs to support Ismā'īl I, he was the possessor of the fortress compound at the summer campgrounds of Sang-i Kul belonging to the Ustājlū. He served Ismā'īl as an envoy on at least one occasion. *AT*, p. 234 (note 1); *TJA*, pp. 269-270; Sarwar, p. 34.

110. Ummat Beg b. ? b. Ummat Beg Qarāsārlū Kūshik-oğlū (d. 998/1589). One other chief, Shāh Nazar Sulṭān, possessed the nisba "Kūshik-oğlū" (#107). His career began as a qūrchī in the service of Murtiẓā Qulī Khān Purnāk, but he left the royal service and became the retainer of 'Alī Qulī Sulṭān Ustājlū (Fatḥ-oğlū). After serving 'Alī Qulī for a time, in 995/1587 he was sent into the service of Murshid Qulī in recognition of the latter's supreme position in the uymāq. In reality Ummat Beg was a spy for the Fatḥ-oğlū and in 996/1588 took a leading role in the assassination of Murshid Qulī Khān. After the death of the vakīl, the Ustājlū lost some of their power. This resulted in a struggle for certain holdings, especially in Khorāsān, where in 997/1588-1589 Ummat Beg was engaged in a struggle with Būdāq Khān Chignī for the ḥukūmat of Mashhad. To complicate matters, Ummat Beg was forced to deal with the Üzbek invasion of the province in that year: his power was severely undercut by a massacre of Qarā Bayāt chieftains by the Üzbek army. As a result, he was no longer able to resist Būdāq Khān Chignī and was deposed from the government of Mashhad. *TAAA*, pp. 229-230, 400-403, 407-408, 411-415; *KHT*, pp. 32-33, 49, 51, 61, 63-64.

111. Bairām 'Alī Sulṭān b. ? b. Bābā Ilyās (fl. 1030-1039/1621-1629). He succeeded Mīrzā Muḥammad Sulṭān as governor of Nishapur in about 1030/1621. He was probably the son or near relative of Mīrzā Muḥammad and continued to hold office until 1039/1629. *TAAA*, pp. 828, 1087.

112. Ḥājjī Uvais Beg (Sulṭān) (fl. 983-986/1575-1578). This chief does not seem to have been of Ustājlū status, though he was a Qarā Bayāt. He was ostensibly a relative of Bābā Ilyās (though this is not ascertainable). He served Nazar Beg Āsāyish-oğlū, until the civil war over the succession to Ṭahmāsp I erupted. The specter of revolutionary disruption threatened to release a monsoon of troubles upon the evermore complicated and unwieldy social organization of the Ustājlū uymāq. Ḥajjī Uvais rebelled, took custody of Sulṭān Muṣṭafā Mīrzā (a contender for the Safavid throne whether he wanted to be or not), and broke all ties with his former Ustājlū masters. This episode marked the beginning of the dissolution of the great uymāq. From this time on Ḥājjī Uvais was always referred to as an independent chief, not as an Ustājlū, like his kinsmen. To all appearances of the same blood line as other Ustājlū chiefs, he struck out independently and refused to kowtow to the leading members in the tribal hierarchy. For this reason the qizilbāsh chroniclers like Iskandar Beg and Ḥasan-i Rūmlū begrudge him Ustājlū status in accordance with their own sense of order and propriety, and seek to buttress what was fast becoming a failing world order (the uymāq tribal system). His betrayal was not all-encompassing, and indeed, Ḥājjī Uvais may have been responding to Pīra Muḥammad Khān Ustājlū's political interests and was thus rebelling against his immediate superiors only. Nonetheless, the stultifyingly rigid thinking that came more and more to characterize the social outlook of uymāq leaders in the late sixteenth century began to be noticeable here when this chief was placed in a separate category as an independent (qazāq). *AT*, pp. 202-205; *TAAA*, pp. 134, 196, 201, 205.

113. Badr Sulṭān (fl. 1039/1629). In 1629 he was the ruler of several places in Chukhur-i Sa'd. *TAAA*, p. 1086.

114. Yār 'Alī Sulṭān (fl. 1039/1629). This chief served as the ḥākim of Bāyazid citadel in 1629. *TAAA*, p. 1086.

115. Gidā 'Alī Sulṭān (fl. 1039/1629). He was the governor of Mākū at the end of 'Abbās I's reign. *TAAA*, p. 1086.

116. Muḥammad Khān (fl. 995/1586-1587). Perhaps the same person as Mīrzā Muḥammad Sulṭān (#104), but a definite identification cannot be made. Because he was the governor of Turbat-i Ḥaidarīya in 996/1587, when it fell to an Üzbek assault, he almost lost the favor of the shah, who pardoned him only after the intercession of some "good friends." *DJ*, p. 222.

117. Shāh Qulī Sulṭān (fl. first half of the seventeenth century). He was the brother of Ughurlū Sulṭān (#118) and the governor of the Qarā Bayāt first in Qazvīn and later in Mashhad. When in 1594 his brother was killed by Lurs, he succeeded him in the leading office of the Qarā Bayāt uymāq. Shāh Qulī served as a qūrchī officer and then as a retainer of Nazar Beg Tavakulī Khān. For a time he also ruled in Burūjird. *TAAA*, pp. 472, 568, 735.

118. Ughurlū Sulṭān (d. 1003/1594). He was the vakīl of 'Abbās I's son Muḥammad Bāqir Mīrzā by appointment of the shah in ca. 1001/1592. He was the main rīsh sifīd of the Qarā Bayāt, controlling all the other rīsh sifīds in the uymāq. 'Abbās I tried to unseat him from this position by appointing Shāhvirdī Khān 'Abbāsī-Faylī, a Lur chieftain to govern the Qarā ūlūs. He was eventually attacked and killed by the Lurs, but his brother Shāh Qulī succeeded in regaining control of the tribal institution. *TAAA*, pp. 440, 465, 471, 472, 537.

119. Ṭahmāsp Qulī Sulṭān b. Muḥammad Khān (fl. 1039/1629). He was the governor of Dizfūl and Shūshtar. *TAAA*, p. 1087.

120. Bāyazīd (fl. 949/1542 to 999/1591). He was a Chaghatāī chieftain of the Qarā Bayāt in the service of the Mughal emperor Humāyūn. He established a family at the emperor's court in the service of the Mughals which survived at least until the beginning of the seventeenth century. *THA*, passim.

G. THE KIRĀJĪYĀ USTĀJLŪ, ĪJAK-OĞLŪ OR TUKHMĀQ-OĞLŪ

121. Shāh Qulī Sulṭān Ījak-oğlū (d. 984/1576-1577). In 952/1545-1546 this chief was the governor of Mashhad, where he was active in campaigns against the Üzbeks. After 958/1551-1552 and before 984/1576 he was appointed to the government of Chukhur-i Sa'd, where he was active in campaigns against the Ottomans. By 984/1576 he had returned to Khorāsān as the amīr al-umarā of the region. Here he was assassinated in the reign of Ismā'īl II. *AT*, pp. 141, 158, 207; *TAAA*, pp. 76, 83, 93, 117, 126, 131, 138, 203, 204.

122. Muḥammadī Khān "Tukhmāq" (d. after 999/1591). After 984/1576 he became the governor of Chukhur-i Sa'd, where in 986/1578 he was confirmed as the amīr al-umarā of the province by Muḥammad Khudābanda. His army was large, but this did not prevent the Ottomans from gobbling up Chukhur-i Sa'd early in the 1580s. During Muḥammadī Khān's entire tenure in office he was involved in fighting the Ottomans, but he did not participate in the civil wars with the Mauṣillū. Don Juan, otherwise known as Ūlūgh Beg, was probably one of his distant relatives. *TAAA*, pp. 121, 138, 139, 203-205, 207, 216, 225, 227, 232-235, 293, 306, 311, 317, 324,

326, 331, 332, 438, 442, 444; *KhT*, pp. 87, 89; *AT*, p. 206; *DJ*, pp. 136, 145, 146, 160, 170, 198.

123. Allāh Qulī Sulṭān (fl. 975-984/1568-1576). The son of Shāh Qulī Ījak-oğlū. In 975/1568 Allāh Qulī led one of many expeditions against Khān Aḥmad, who had lodged himself in Gīlān at Lāhijān. After defeating the Khān, Allah Qulī was named governor of Lāhijān, but when the province became appealing to Pīra Muḥammad Khān, he was deposed and appointed to the office of dārūgha of Tabrīz. The accession of Ismā'īl II to the throne had left him in difficult straits, since he had been a supporter of Ḥaidar Mīrzā. His brother interceded in his behalf during these factional struggles and saved his life by having him appointed ambassador to the Ottoman court. Nothing is known of him after this time. *AT*, pp. 191, 195, 197; *TAAA*, pp. 112, 113, 114, 117-119, 139, 193-198.

124. Bektash Beg b. Allāh Qulī (d. 979/1571-1572). His father put him to death for a rebellion in Gīlān in ca. 1572. *AT*, p. 195.

H. THE SHARAFLŪ TRIBE, RULED BY THE CHĀŪSHLŪ

125. Kurd Beg (fl. 916-932/1510-1526). Kurd Beg served as Chāyān Sulṭān's retainer. Chāyān Sulṭān assigned him to defend Bidlīs, 'Ādiljavāz, and Arjish in 916/1510 or 1511. He became governor of Arjish in 932/1526 and fought on the Ustājlū side at Saksanjūk and Kharzavīl. *SN*, p. 285; *AT*, pp. 95, 191, 194.

126. Muṣṭafā Sulṭān (fl. 988/1581). He was one of a number of chiefs in the uymāq who possessed no ūlkā until 988/1581, when he received one in Shirvan from Silmān Khān, his patron. *TAAA*, pp. 261, 267.

127. Ibrāhīm Sulṭān (fl. 993/1585-1586). His patron was Murshid Qulī Khān. He came from a tribe subordinate to the great vazīr. *TAAA*, p. 304.

128. Valī Beg (Khān) (fl. 986-998/1578-1589). He was a lower level military chief who served as commander of the scouts in the Ustājlū army of Khorāsān and as the retainer of Muḥammadī Khān "Tukh-māq". He participated in wars against both the Üzbeks and the Ottomans. He also served under Murshid Qulī Khān. *TAAA*, pp. 139, 227, 233, 255, 573.

129. Pīr Ghaib Khān (d. 995/1588). The brother of Amīr Aṣlān Khān. In 993/1586 he was involved in expeditions against the Ottomans. For his services he was given the ūlkā of Ṭārum near Khalkhāl. While in the service of Muḥammadī Khān "Tukhmāq" he helped to put down the revolts of renegade qizilbāsh chiefs (Takalū, Mauṣillū and Dhu'l-Qadr and became involved in a dispute with the Shāmlū (Īnāllū) over Hamadān. Both the Shāmlū and the Ustājlū had assigned chiefs to the governorate of Hamadān. Pīr Ghaib, the Ustājlū

candidate, was edged out of this position, however, and apparently received little compensation for his losses from the Ustājlū high command. This was reflected later in 994/1587, when he became the leader of some Ustājlū conspirators who made an abortive attempt on the life of Murshid Qulī Khān. For his role, he and his son were killed. *TAAA*, pp. 308-309, 316, 332, 335, 337, 341, 342, 357, 358, 366, 381, 384, 1007; *KhT*, pp. 27, 35, 38, 40.

130. Abu'l-Qāsim Sulṭān b. Pīr Ghaib Khān (fl. 1033/1624). He was promoted to the rank of amīr in 1033/1624 and was given the ūlkā of Javāzir and its dependencies. By 1038/1629 he was listed as the governor of Hala in Arabian Iraq. *TAAA*, pp. 1007, 1085.

131. Amīr Aṣlān Khān (d. 994/1587). He was killed for attempting to assassinate Murshid Qulī Khān. *TAAA*, p. 384; *KhT*, p. 38.

I. THE KUNGURLŪ (OR KANGARLŪ)

132. Aḥmad Sultān Kangarlū (fl. 933/1527). Perhaps the same person as next entry. He ruled Rayy for the Safavid state in 933/1527. *Afzal al-Tavārīkh*, p. 102, N. 1; "Une liste," p. 98.

133. Aḥmad Sulṭān. An Ustājlū dependent chieftain, he governed Shahrīyār and Varāmīn in 933/1526. "Une liste", p. 98. He may be the same Aḥmad Sulṭān who governed Rayy in 933-934/1527.

134. Ṣadr al-Dīn Khān (d. 955/1549). This chief was governor of Astarabad from 943/1536-1537 to 955/1549. He was instrumental in defeating two Üzbek drives into Astarabad after 950/1543. His presence in Astarabad represented another link in the Ustājlū chain of colonies spread throughout the northern sphere of Iran around the Caspian Sea. *TAAA*, pp. 105-107, 138; *AT*, pp. 125-126, 130.

135. Shāhvirdī Beg (fl. 945/1538-1544). He was a young man at this time, serving as a retainer of Ṣadr al-Dīn Khān. He captured the rebel Ṣāliḥ, who had been causing problems in Astarabad. *AT*, p. 130; *TAAA*, pp. 107, 201.

136. Shāh 'Alī Sulṭān (d. 957/1551). His first position was in the qūrchī establishment. Later he went into the service of Pīr Sulṭān Khalīfa Rūmlū. He served in campaigns against the Üzbeks, during one of which he was killed. *AT*, p. 130; *TAAA*, pp. 51, 107, 331.

137. Pīr Qulī Sulṭān. He was the governor of Simnān and Khār in 932/1526 but, according to another chronicler, may also have been the governor of Isfarā'īn. MD, p. 103; *HS*, pp. 579, 591; "Une liste", p. 109.

138. Kachal Shāhvirdī Beg (fl. 957-965). He was the governor of Astarabad in 957/1551, two years after the death of Ṣadr al-Dīn Khān, his kinsman. He ruled there until 965/1559. *TAAA*, p. 107.

139. Muṣṭafā Beg (Sulṭān) b. Kachal Shāhvirdī. (fl. 984-1002/1576 to 1594). He was governor of Ṭabas-i Gīlakī in Khorāsān at the end of

Ṭahmasp I's reign. His career was mainly spent fighting the Üzbeks in the border wars of the 1590s in which victory seesawed between the partners. He lost his life in a campaign waged some time after 1002/1594. *TAAA*, pp. 139, 455, 456, 488, 489, 490; *KhT*, pp. 78, 79, 80, 95.

140. Tīmūr Sulṭān (d. after 1002/1594). He replaced Muṣṭafā Beg as governor of Ṭabas and may have been the deceased governor's brother or close kinsman. Like his predecessor he, too, died fighting the Üzbeks in the same year. *TAAA*, p. 490.

141. Murād Khān (fl. 983/1575-1576). Nothing is known of this chief except that he was a supporter of Ismā'īl II. *TAAA*, p. 201.

142. Maqṣūd Sulṭān. He was the governor of Nakhchavān from 1013/1605 to after 1039/1629 and was active in waging war against the Ottomans. *TAAA*, pp. 656, 668, 670-671, 677, 901, 902, 908, 1085.

143. Farrukhzād Beg. Nothing is known of this chief except that in 984/1576 he was a supporter of Ismā'īl II. *AT*, pp. 202-205.

144. Ja'far Beg (Sulṭān) (fl. 968/1561-1562). He was the commander of a troop of soldiers designated for envoy service and hence probably belonged to the qūrchīs. It is possible that his office as the head of a unit specially designated for envoy service was a survival of the Mongol īlchī system. *TAAA*, p. 342; *AT*, p. 181.

145. Paikar Lurdī Khalīfa b. Ja'far Beg. He was a Ṭālish chieftain with an ūlkā in Gīlān where he was active in suppressing revolts. *TAAA*, pp. 267-268.

146. Allāh Qulī Sulṭān b. Ja'far. See appendix A, Ṭālish chieftains.

J. THE FATḤ-OǦLŪ (AND VARIANT SPELLINGS)

147. 'Alī Beg Qizillū (d. 1034/1624-1625). He was the yüz-bāshī of the Qizillū (Fatḥ-oǧlū) qūrchīs. *TAAA*, p. 1042.

148. Muḥammad Beg وو لطحى ? (fl. 984/1576). This chief served at the royal court as the head of the royal stables. He was probably a close relative of Pīrī Beg (# 149). *TAAA*, p. 119.

149. Pīrī Beg Qūchilū (d. 984/1576). Varāmīn-i Rayy was his ūlkā. The Bayāt tribes around Rayy provided him with retainers and other forms of support. In the civil wars of 984/1576 Pīrī Beg attached himself to the faction of Ḥaidar Mīrzā. He was attacked by the forces supporting Ismā'īl II, captured, and killed together with his officers. *TAAA*, pp. 119, 121, 139, 196, 198; *AT*, pp. 202-205.

150. 'Alī Qulī Sulṭān Fatḥ-oǧlū (d. 995/1587). One of the most influential Ustājlū chieftains in the 1580s, he was named governor of Tabrīz after the defeat of Amīr Khān Mauṣillū. Thereafter he also involved himself in conflicts with the Ottomans, and with the Īnāllū (with Shāmlū backing) for the control of Hamadān, a governorate that

Pīr Ghaib Khān Sharaflū (#129) had claimed but lost. At a very early date he had also been involved in a dispute between his sub-tribe and that of the Sharaflū which involved the capital, Qazvīn, in a ferocious series of street fights that lasted fourteen days. *TAAA*, pp. 132, 296, 298, 299, 301, 306, 315-317, 320, 324-329, 331, 335, 337, 338, 341-342, 345-349, 352-353, 356-362, 365, 371, 372, 400, 425.

151. Muḥammadī Khān "Sārū Sūlāgh" Fatḥ-oğlū/Qich-oğlū. This chief was the vakīl of Ḥusain Qulī Khān Shāmlū at one point in his career, but afterwards he mainly served 'Alī Qulī Sulṭān Fatḥ-oğlū. Like 'Alī Qulī, he was able to work his way into the confidence of Muḥammad Khudābanda. He was active as a general in the civil wars with the Mauṣillū. *TAAA*, pp. 267, 298, 299, 301, 320, 322, 325, 327-329, 349, 357, 359, 362, 370, 372; *KhT*, pp. 31, 34.

152. Ḥusain Qulī Sulṭān Fatḥ-oğlū (fl. 996/1587). The brother of 'Alī Qulī (#150). He opposed his brother and threw his support to 'Abbās I in 996/1587. Thus he escaped massacre at the hands of 'Abbās's compatriots while his brother was put to death for continuing to support Muḥammad Khudābanda. As a result he remained the *kutvāl* (warden, castellan) of the fortress at Rayy, which his brother had granted him earlier. *TAAA*, p. 365; *KhT*, p. 31.

153. Bairām Qulī Beg Qipchilū (fl. 1017/1608-1609). He was the governor of Alamut and an envoy at the court of the Crimean Tātār Khān. *TAAA*, p. 778.

154. Ḥasan Beg Fatḥ-oğlū (fl. 965/1555). He served in an expedition led by Badr Khān Ustājlū against the Yaḳa Türkmen in Astarabad. *TJA*, p. 303.

K. THE KIRĀMPĀ

155. Aḥmad Āqā. See Appendix C, #70.

156. Chirāgh Sulṭān b. Aḥmad Āqā (fl. 941/1534-1535 to 999/1591). He was governor of Varāmīn between 941/1534 and 999/1591, and served in campaigns against the Ottomans and the Üzbeks. *AT*, p. 117; *KhT*, pp. 72, 87; *TAAA*, p. 572.

157. 'Alī Beg b. Aḥmad Āqā. He was the dārūgha of Isfahān in 998/1590 and was active on a campaign against the Üzbeks. *KhT*, p. 72; *TAAA*, p. 572.

158. Aḥmad Beg b. Chirāgh Sulṭān (fl. 996/1587-1588). This chief had been the commander of the fortress of Tabarak. As kutvāl of this fort, he controlled the approaches to the city of Isfahān. He took over the fortress of Varāmīn at Rayy for a brief period in 996/1587, holding several members of the Safavid family prisoner there. It was his

ambition to use these royal prisoners to increase his own power. When the fort was recaptured by 'Abbās I's forces, he was killed. *KhT*, p. 72; *TAAA*, pp. 386, 487.

159. Chirāgh Sulṭān b. ? b. Chirāgh (fl. 1011-1016/1603-1608). He was the retainer of Dhu'l-Fiqār Khān Qarāmānlū and held the ūlkā of Darband. He was active in wars and negotiations with the Ottomans. *TAAA*, pp. 643, 644, 752, 906, 908.

Bibliography

A. Pre-Safavid Primary Sources

Āşıkpāşāzade

1970 *Tārīhī*, 'Ālī Bey, ed. England: Gregg International Publishers Ltd.

Beveridge, A. S.

1969 *The Bāburnāma in English*. London: Luzac and Co., Ltd.

Ḥamdullāh Mustawfī

1915-1919 *The Geographical Part of the Nuzhat al-Qulūb*. G. LeStrange, ed. and trans. 2 vols. E. J. W. Gibb Memorial Series, no. 23. London/Leiden: Luzac and Co., Ltd.

Ḥudūd al-'Ālam

1937 *Ḥudūd al-'Alam*, V. Minorsky, trans. E. J. W. Gibb Memorial Series, n.s. vol. 11. London: Luzac and Co., Ltd. (*HA*)

Juvainī, 'Atā-Malik

1958 *The History of the World Conqueror*. J. A. Boyle, trans. 2 vols. Manchester: Manchester University Press. (*TJG*)

Kāshghārī, Maḥmūd al-

1939-1943 *Dīvān ül-Lüghāt it-Türk*. Besim Atalay, ed. 3 vols. Ankara: Türk Dil Kurumu. (*DLT*)

Nizām al-Mulk

1343/1964 *Sīyāsat-Nāma*, Tehran: Tahuri. (*SīNā*)

Raschid-Eldin (Rashīd al-Dīn Faḍlullāh)

1836 *Histoire des Mongols de la Perse*. Paris. Repr. Amsterdam: Oriental Press. 1968.

Rashīd al-Dīn Faḍlullāh.

1338/1959 *Jāma' al-Tavārīkh*. Tehran: Iqbal. (*JT*)

1940 *Tārīkh-i Mubārak-i Ghāzānī*. K. Jahn, ed. E. J. W. Gibb Memorial Series, n.s. vol. 16. London: Luzac and Co., Ltd., (*TMG*)

B. SAFAVID PRIMARY SOURCES

Afshār, Ṣādiqī Beg. *See* Ṣādiqī Beg Afshār

Aḥmed Feridūn
1264-1265/1847-1848 *Münşe'āt üs-Selātīn*. 2 vols. Istanbul.

'Ālam Ārā-yi Ṣafavī
1350/1972 *'Ālam Ārā-yi Ṣafavī*. Tehran: Intishārat-i Farhang-i Iran. (*AAS*)

'Ālam Ārā-yi Shāh Ismā'īl
1349/1971 *'Ālam Ārā-yi Shāh Ismā'īl*. A. Muntazir Ṣāḥib, ed. no. 43, Persian Texts Series, Tehran: Bungāh-i Tarjūma va Nushr-i Kitāb. (*Ismā'īl*)

Bayāt, Bāyazid.
1360/1941 *Tadhkira-yi Humāyun va Akbar*. Calcutta: Royal Asiatic Society of Bengal. (*THA*)

Bidlīsī. *See* Sharaf Khān Bidlīsī.

Busse, H.
1959 *Untersuchungen zum Islamischen Kanzleiwesen*. Cairo: Sirović Bookshop. (Busse, *Untersuchungen*)

Chardin, Jean, Chevalier de
1711 *Voyages en Perse*, vol. 2, *Description de la Perse*. Amsterdam: DeLorme. (*VP* 2)

Dede Korkut Kitābı
1975 *The Book of Dede Korkut*. G. Lewis, trans. Baltimore: Penguin Books, Ltd. (*DK*)

Don Juan of Persia (Ūrūch Beg Bayāt)
1926 *Don Juan of Persia: A Shi'ah Catholic, 1560-1604*. G. LeStrange, ed. and trans. London: Broadway Travellors. (*DJ*)

Fūmenī, Abdullāh
1349/1970 *Tārīkh-i Gīlān*, Manūchihr Sutūda, ed., Tehran: Intishārāt-i Bunyād-i Farhang-i Iran. (*TG*)

Ghaffārī-yi Qazvīnī, Qāḍī Aḥmad
1964 *Tārīkh-i Jahān Ārā*. Tehran: Hafez. (*TJA*)

Ḥasan-i Rūmlū
1931-1934 *Aḥsan al-Tavārikh: A Chronicle of the Early Safawis*. Baroda: Oriental Institute. (*AT*)

Iskandar Beg-i Munshī (Turkamān)
1350/1971 *Tārīkh-i 'Ālam Ārā-yi 'Abbāsī*. 2 vols. Tehran: Amīr Kabīr. (*TAAA*)
1317/1938 *Dhail-i Tārīkh-ī 'Ālam Ārā-yi 'Abbāsī*. Suhailī Khānsārī, ed. Tehran. (*Dhail-i TAAA*)

Khāndamīr, Ghīyāth al-Dīn b. Hamām al-Dīn al-Ḥusainī
1333/ 1955 *Ḥabīb al-Siyār*. 4 vols. Tehran: Kitāb-hā-yi Khayyām. (*HS*)

Khūnjī, Faḍlullāh B. Rūzbihān
1957 *Tārīkh-i 'Ālam Ārā-yi Amīnī: Persia in A.D. 1478–1490*. V. Minorsky, trans. London: Royal Asiatic Society of Great Britain and Ireland, Luzac and Co., Ltd. (*Amīnī*)

Martin, B. G.
1965 "Seven Safawid Documents from Azarbayjan." *Documents in Islamic Chanceries*, S. M. Stern, ed. Oxford: Bruno Cassirer. Pp. 171-206. (Martin, "Seven Safawid Documents")

Minorsky, V. (ed.)
1942 "The Poetry of Shāh Ismā'īl I." *Bulletin of the School of Oriental and African Studies*, 10:1007*a*-1053*a*. ("PSI")

Rūmlū. *See* Ḥasan-i Rūmlū.

Qazvīnī, Muḥammad Ṭāhir Vahīd
1329 *'Abbās-Nāma*. Tehran: Kitāb-furūshī Davūdī-Arak. (*'Abbās-Nāma*)

Qumī, Qaḍī Aḥmad
1964 *Khulāsat al-Tavārīkh*. Hans Muller, ed. *Die Chronik Khulāsat al-Tavārīkh: Der Abschnitt über Schah 'Abbās I*. Wiesbaden: Franz Steiner Verlag. (*KhT*)

Ṣādiqī Beg Afshār
1949 *Majma' al-Khavāṣṣ*. Tabriz: Akhtar-i Shumāl. (*MK*)

Sharaf Khān Bidlīsī
1860-1862 *Sharaf-Nāma*. V. Véliaminoff-Zernof, ed. 2 vols. St. Petersburg: Imperial Academy. (*SN*)

Tadhkirat al-Mulūk
1943 *Tadhkirat al-Mulūk: A Manual of Safavid Administration*. V. Minorsky, ed. and trans. E. J. W. Gibb Memorial Series, n.s. vol. 16. London: W. Heffer and Sons. (*TM*)

Ṭahmāsp, Shah
1912 *Tezkire*. Calcutta: Bibliotheca Indica. (*T*)

C. Modern Sources

Adīb al-Shu'ara, Mīrzā Rashīd
1345-1346/1967-1968 *Tārīkh-i Afshār*. Tabriz: Shafaq. (*TA*)

Avrich, P.
1972 *Russian Rebels: 1600–1800*. New York: Norton. (*RR*)

Bacon, E.
1958 *Obok: A Study of Social Structure in Eurasia*. New York: Wenner-Gren.

Bacqué-Grammont, J.
1976 "Une liste d'émirs ostağlus révoltés en 1526." *Studia Iranica*, 5:91-114. ("Une liste")

Banani, A.
1978 "The Socio-economic Structure of the Persian Empire at Its Zenith." *State and Society in Iran*, A. Banani, ed. *Iranian Studies*, 11:83-116.

Bartold, W.
1938 *Herat unter Ḥusain Baiqarā*. W. Hinz, trans. Leipzig.

Bergel, E.
1962 *Social Stratification*. New York: McGraw-Hill Book Co., Inc. (*SS*)

Birge, J. K.
1965 *The Bektashi Order of Dervishes*. London: Luzac and Co., Ltd. (*BOD*)

Bloch, Marc
1968 *Feudal Society*. Chicago: Chicago University Press. (*FS*)

Bosworth, C. E.
1968 "The Political and Dynastic History of the Iranian World (1000-1217)." *CHI*, V:1-202. (*CHI*)

Braudel, Fernand
1966 *The Mediterranean and the Mediterranean World in the Age of Philip II*. New York: Harper and Row.

Browne, E. G.
1968 *A Literary History of Persia*. London: Cambridge University Press. Volume IV. (*LHP*)

Cahen, Claude
1949 "Le Malik-Nameh et l'histoire des origines seljukides." *Oriens*, 2:31-65.

Cambridge History of Iran
1968 *Cambridge History of Iran*, J. A. Boyle, ed. Vol.V. *The Saljūq and Mongol Periods*. Cambridge: Cambridge University Press. (*CHI*)

Chadwick, Nora, and Victor Zhirmunsky
1968 *The Oral Epics of Central Asia*. London: Oxford University Press. (*OECA*)

Cuisenier, Jean
1976 "Kinship and Social Organization in the Turko-Mongolian Cultural Area." In E. Forster and O. Ranum, trans. and eds., *Family and Society: Selections from Annales, Economies, Société, Civilisations*. Baltimore: John Hopkins University Press. ("KSOTM")

Dickson, Martin B.

1958 "Shāh Ṭahmāsp and the Üzbeks: The Duel for Khurāsān with 'Ubayd Khan, 930-940/1524-1540." Ph.D. diss., Princeton University. (MD).

Encyclopedia of Islam

1960- *Encyclopedia of Islam*. 2nd ed. Leiden: E. J. Brill. (*EI*²)

Esin, E.

1970 "The Turkish Bakši and the Painter Muḥammad Sīyāh Kalam." *Proceedings of the 11th meeting of the International Altaistic Conference*. In *Acta Orientalia*, 33:100-114.

Fasā'ī, Ḥasan-i

1972 *History of Qajar Rule in Persia*. New York: Columbia University Press. (Fasā'ī)

Finley, M. I.

1968 *The Ancient Economy*. Berkeley and Los Angeles: University of California Press.

Garthwaite, G. R.

1969 "The Bakhtīyārī Khāns: Tribal Disunity in Iran, 1880-1915." Ph.D. diss., University of California, Los Angeles. (*BK*)

Gölpinları, A.

1955 "Kızılbaş." *İslam Ansıklopedisi*, 6:789-795.

Hobsbawm, E. J.

1959 *Primitive Rebels*. New York: W. W. Norton and Co., Inc. (*PR*)

Hodgson, M. G. S.

1974 *The Venture of Islam*. Chicago: University of Chicago Press.

Johnson, Chalmers

1962 *Revolutionary Change*. Boston: Little, Browne and Co. (*RC*)

Kasravī, Aḥmad

1339 *Tārīkh-i Pānsad Sālaḥ-i Khūzistān*. Tehran: Intishārāt-ị Bungāh-i Matbū'ātī Gutenberg. (Kasravī)

Kazemi, Farhad, and Ervand Abrahamian

1978 "The Non-Revolutionary Peasantry of Modern Iran." In *State and Society in Iran*, A. Banani, ed., *Iranian Studies*, 11:259-304. ("NRPMI")

Lambton, A. K. S.

1970 "Islamic Society in Persia." In Louise Sweet, ed., *Peoples and Cultures of the Middle East*, Garden City, New York: Natural History Press. ("ISP")

1953 *Landlord and Peasant in Persia*. London: Oxford University Press. (*LP*)

Nikitine, B.

1929 "Les Afshars d'Urummiyah." *Journal Asiatique*, n.v.: 67-129. (Nikitine)

Perry, John
1975 "Forced Migration in Iran in the Seventeenth and Eighteenth Centuries." *Iranian Studies*, 8:199-217. (Perry)

Petrushevsky, I. P.
1968 "The Socio-economic Condition of Iran under the Ilkhans." *CHI*, V:483-537. ("SECII")

Plessner, M.
1928 *Der Oikonomikos des Neupythagoräers Bryson und Sein Einfluss auf die islamische Wissenschaft*. Heidelberg.

Röhrborn, Klaus M.
1966 *Provinzen und Zentralgewalt Persiens im 16. und 17. Jahrhundert*. Berlin: Walter de Gruyter and Co. (*PZP*)

Rypka, Jan
1968 *History of Iranian Literature*. K. Jahn, ed. Dordrecht: D. Reidel.

Sarwar, Ghulām
1939 *History of Shah Isma'īl Safawī*, Aligarh: Muslim University. (Sarwar)

Savory, R. M.
1980 *Iran under the Safavids*. Cambridge: Cambridge University Press.
1960 "The Principle Offices of the Safavid State during the Reign of Ismā'īl I." *Bulletin of the School of Oriental and African Studies*, 23:91-105. ("PO" [1])
1961 "The Principle Offices of the Safavid State during the Reign of Ṭahmāsp I." *Bulletin of the School of Oriental and African Studies*, 24:65-85. ("PO" [2])

Shaw, S. J.
1976 *History of the Ottoman Empire and Modern Turkey*. Vol. I, *Empire of the Gazis*. London: Cambridge University Press.

South African Wool Board
1970 *An Illustrated History of the Sheep and Wool Industry*. Pretoria: South African Wool Board. (SAWB)

Stone, Lawrence
1967 *The Crisis of the Aristocracy, 1558-1641*. London: Oxford University Press. (*CA*)

Sümer, F.
1967 *Oğuzlar: Türkmenler*. Ankara: Ankara Üniversitesi Basımevi.

Tabrīzī, Sayyid Aḥmad Āqā
1928 "Īl-i Afshār." *Āyanda*, 8-9:597 ff. (*Āyanda*)

Tapper, Richard
1974 "The Shahsevan in the Safavid Era." *Bulletin of the School of Oriental and African Studies*, 37:321-340. ("SSE")

1966 "Black Sheep, White Sheep and Red-Heads, A Historical Sketch of the Shāhsavan of Āzarbāijān." *Iran*, 4:61-84.

Trimingham, J. S.
1973 *The Sufi Orders in Islam*. London: Oxford University Press.

Vazīrī-Kermānī, Aḥmad ʻAlī Khān
1340/1960 *Tārīkh-i Kermān*. Tehran: Persian Book Company. (*TK*)

Vryonis, Speros, Jr.
1971 *The Decline of Medieval Hellenism in Asia Minor*. Berkeley and Los Angeles: University of California Press.

Welch, Anthony
1976 *Artists for the Shah*. New Haven, Conn: Yale University Press. (*ASh*)
1973 *Shah ʻAbbas and the Arts of Isfahan*. New York: The Asia Society, Inc. (*SAAI*)

Woods, J. E.
1976 *The Aq Quyunlu: Clan, Confederation, Empire*. Minneapolis: Bibliotheca Islamica. (*AQ*)

Index

References in parentheses are to the Appendixes.

TRIBALISM AND SOCIETY IN ISLAMIC IRAN 1500-1629

JAMES J. REID

Studies in Near Eastern Culture and Society 4

Issued under the auspices of the G. E. von Grunebaum Center for Near Eastern Studies, University of California, Los Angeles

Iranian society came under the domination of tribal elites during the first part of the Safavid era. While other elites also played a role in controlling the Iranian empire, the tribal ruling clans were the most important at first. In order to analyze this period, materials concerning the socioeconomic organization of tribalism in the Iranian plateau are presented, and a prototypical model of tribal state structure is constructed based entirely on contemporary accounts. Three tribal organizations, each representing a separate tradition, are then examined in detail; the lives and careers of their chieftains are traced in a biographical dictionary containing nearly 240 entries. The theory that initial support for the Safavid movement came from Anatolian or North Syrian tribes is demonstrated to be false, and to be either the product of nationalist historiography or due to the misunderstanding of certain tribal names. The book seeks to show how Iranian elites differed from other contemporary elites, to assess the place of the Iranian system in the world pattern of the sixteenth and seventeenth centuries, and to contribute toward the understanding of a non-European society on its own terms and according to its own realities.

UNDENA PUBLICATIONS
P.O. Box 97, Malibu, California 90265

ISBN: 0-89003-125-8/cloth; 0-89003-124-x/paper